BUENOS AIRES, ARGENTINA, 1976-1983:

The Exile of Editor Robert J. Cox

DIRTY

SECRETS,

DIRTY

WAR

WRITTEN BY DAVID COX

FOREWORD BY ROBERT J. COX

Published by
**Evening Post
Publishing Company**
Charleston, S.C.,
in cooperation with Joggling Board Press

Published by
**Evening Post
Publishing Company
Charleston, South Carolina,**
in cooperation with Joggling Board Press

Edited by: John Burbage/Susan Kammeraad-Campbell
Designed by: Courtney Gunter Rowson

First printing 2008
Printed in Hong Kong.

A CIP catalog record for this book has been applied for from the Library of Congress.

ISBN 978-0-9818735-0-3

For Julia, Agustin, Tomas,
Sofia and James.

Tomorrow's rain will wash the stains away,
But something in our minds will always stay.

GORDON MATTHEW THOMAS SUMNER (Sting)

There is always a moment in childhood when
the door opens and lets the future in.

GRAHAM GREENE

TABLE OF CONTENTS

Foreword by Robert Cox   9

Author's Preface by David Cox   15

Chapter 1 A Latin American Adventure (1959)   21

Chapter 2 A Bride, a Newspaper and a Walrus (1959-1968)   26

Chapter 3 The Huguenot Spirit (1968-1969)   38

Chapter 4 A Deadly Virus (1970-1973)   49

Chapter 5 An Englishman's Conscience (1973-1975)   55

Chapter 6 A Sunny Day for a Coup (1572; 1976)   69

Chapter 7 Families Saved (1974-1977)   79

Chapter 8 Danger at the Family Door (1977-1978)   95

Chapter 9 Knowing the Terrible Secret (1977)   105

Photographs   113

Chapter 10 The Kiss of Judas (1978)   126

Chapter 11 An Interlude in Charleston (1978)   132

Chapter 12 A World Cup, a Plot, a Royal Visit (1978)   142

Chapter 13 Living with Fear (1979)   160

Chapter 14 Searching for the Missing (1979)   171

Chapter 15 A Family under Attack (1979)   180

Chapter 16 Fleeing for Safety (1979)   189

Chapter 17 End of a Journey (1979-1983)   204

Epilogue December 2007   218

Author's Note   220

Index   223

FOREWORD
By Robert Cox

This is the book that I could not write. Nearly a quarter of a century has passed since the end of the aptly named "Dirty War" in Argentina, yet I still find it too painful to relive those malevolent times by writing about them. So, I am deeply indebted to my son David for telling the story of a small English-language daily newspaper, the Buenos Aires Herald, which saved lives by refusing to be silenced by terrorism.

It is a story that should be told, but not by me. I have always believed in impersonal journalism, the reporter in a shabby raincoat that nobody notices who writes his stories without a byline. I was, trite as it may sound, just doing my job as editor of the newspaper, and the Herald was continuing a tradition of reporting in English what the Argentine press covered up in Spanish.

It wasn't easy to "just do your job" in Argentina in the 1970s. During the first half of the decade, Argentina was under attack from terrorists who may be loosely described as "left-wing," although in the early 1970s, I counted more than 30 armed groups that covered the political spectrum from strutting Nazis to mad Maoists. The second half of the 1970s was characterized by state terrorism. I personally went from being seen as a right-wing imperialist by the left for denouncing their acts of terror to finding myself transformed into a subversive Communist by the right for opposing state terrorism. I didn't change. The political climate changed. I was just doing my job.

At first I didn't understand why the other media didn't do their jobs by simply reporting what was happening in Argentina. It was true that television was a government monopoly, and most of the radio stations were state owned. But the newspapers were another matter. They could have made a difference, as the Herald did. Perhaps years of adaptation to dictatorship prior to the military takeover of

March 24, 1976, explained why the owners and editors of the major newspapers instinctively looked the other way when counter-terrorism took on a terrifying new dimension, through what are now known as "forced disappearances."

The military junta abducted people they suspected of "subversion" – which took in a swathe of humanity from armed militants to radicalized high school kids and almost everyone in between. They were rounded up and hauled off to clandestine jails where they were tortured, the easiest but most treacherous way to secure information. The routine use of torture explains why so many innocent people died in the maw of the military's killing machine.

If you have nothing to tell your interrogators when you are under torture, the torment is increased to the point where the victim expires. The other sinister consequence of using torture as a counter-terrorism method is that once someone has been taken into the netherworld of the torture center, he or she has to be silenced so that the general public will not know that illegal methods are being used by the state. The easiest solution is to murder the innocent person who might testify against you. Thus it was that Catholic nuns and priests and an unknowable number of innocent people were killed so that they would not tell what they had suffered and seen in their passage through hell.

The Argentine military found themselves in the same area of transcendent evil as the Nazi SS. They could never admit what they did because their crimes were so terrible. To this day, only one military officer, Navy Capt. Adolfo Scilingo, has disclosed how thousands of people were tortured and killed. His trial was held in Spain, not Argentina. On a cold day in February 2005, I gave evidence at Scilingo's trial in Madrid. He cut a pathetic figure because he originally went public, describing how he threw prisoners to their deaths from a Navy plane into the Atlantic, because he was aggrieved that he had not been promoted.

Eighteen years later in 1995, he admitted to taking part in two "death flights" from a Navy school in the heart of Buenos Aires that was used as a clandestine torture center and concentration camp. Prisoners were drugged under the pretense that they were being vaccinated before being transferred to a legal prison. Navy officers pushed them from the planes into the Atlantic Ocean. It's estimated that some 3,000 of the 5,000 people held at the now notorious ESMA (Navy Mechanics School) were liquidated in this way.

Scilingo, neatly dressed in a light-gray suit and tie, was in court because in 1997 he voluntarily traveled to Spain to repeat his confession made earlier in Argentina to a journalist who subsequently wrote a best-selling book about it. He told the investigating judge, Baltasar Garzon, that he wanted to see justice done and that was not possible in Argentina. He told the judge everything he knew about ESMA in two long tape-recorded declarations that were played at the trial a few days before I gave testimony for the prosecution.

He described the methods of torture, the cremation of bodies in what were called *"asados"* (barbecues), and the "humanitarian" treatment of pregnant women. "For humanitarian reasons, the pregnant women could not be transferred ... I mean, eliminated," Scilingo explained. "We had to wait until they gave birth." Then the mothers were killed, and their babies, complete with false papers, were given to childless military officers.

There was not anything new in what Scilingo recounted. Argentina in the 1970s was like Germany under Hitler. Everyone knew what was going on but refused to see or react, either because they were acquiescent or fearful, to the systematic mass murder of suspected enemies of the regime. What was new was that Scilingo was the first and still is the only military officer to break the pact of silence protecting the dictatorship's torturers and executioners.

"I was not a monster," Scilingo told the judge, but "without coercion and of our own free will, we were changed into monsters."

Judge Garzon then asked Scilingo if he ratified his statement that he threw live people from the planes on two flights that carried 30 victims to their deaths. When he did so, to Scilingo's surprise and anger, the judge ordered his arrest. He has been in jail since, sentenced in April 2005 to 640 years for crimes against humanity. On appeal, the Spanish Supreme Court increased his sentence to 1,084 years, finding him guilty of murder and unlawful detention. Under Spanish law, he will serve a maximum of 25 years. When brought to trial, Scilingo recanted his testimony and claimed that he made up the story of his own participation in the "death flights" to draw attention to the crimes committed by the military. At ESMA, he said, "I was just the electrician."

The ultimate objective of the trial was to end impunity for those accused of crimes against humanity. Spanish justice, perhaps psychologically impelled to compensate for Francisco Franco's long dictatorship, intends to pursue cases in which the crimes of institutionalized murder and torture would go unpunished in the countries in which they were committed.

When I agreed to testify about the military regime at Scilingo's trial, I did so because I felt it was my duty. As a newspaper editor in Buenos Aires, I was mortified as successive Argentine governments denied Israeli requests to extradite Nazi war criminals who had been welcomed by the government of Juan Domingo Peron. Nazi influence over Argentina was never eradicated.

Indeed, Nazi methods were imitated when the military took power in 1976. The Argentine version of the Einsatzgruppen, SS squads who hunted down Jews in Europe, was known as *"grupos de tarea"* (task groups). People were dragged from their homes in the early hours, routinely tortured and killed in the thousands. I myself saw the symbol of the regime, a huge swastika and the sign *"Nazinacionalismo"* painted at the entrance to one underground prison and torture center.

I also had another reason for testifying: unfinished business. Following the return to democracy in Argentina in 1983, I was asked by the government to take the stand in a trial that was unprecedented in Latin America. For the first time, a dictatorship was on trial.

Nine generals and admirals – who served on the military juntas that imposed a rule of terror on Argentina from the March 1976 coup until the military's departure after the humiliating defeat in the war over the Falkland Islands – were brought to justice. Five were convicted and sentences ranging from life imprisonment for Gen. Rafael Videla, the first de facto president, as well as for Adm. Emilio Massera, to much shorter terms for the other three commanders. But after only a few years spent at military prisons that were more like country clubs, all were pardoned.

It was not until 2005 that the Argentine Supreme Court declared the "impunity laws" unconstitutional, and trials have resumed with life sentences imposed on a police officer and a police chaplain for their complicity in torture and murders in clandestine prisons.

Justice in Argentina is long overdue. The statement of the special commission appointed in 1983 to investigate the disappearances is still valid today: "We can state categorically – contrary to what the executors of this sinister plan maintain – that they did not pursue only the members of political organizations who carried out acts of terrorism. Among the victims are thousands who never had any links with such activity but were nevertheless subjected to horrific torture because they opposed the military dictatorship, took part in union or student activities, were well-known intellectuals who questioned state terrorism, or simply because they were relatives, friends or names included in the address book of someone."

The commission's report was titled *"Nunca Mas"* (Never Again). The paradoxical role of Adolfo Scilingo, the man who said he wanted justice, confessed and then recanted but was finally found guilty of crimes against humanity in Spain, shamed the Argentine judiciary into action.

I spent 20 years as a journalist in Argentina, the last 10 of them as the editor-in-chief of the Buenos Aires Herald. The most important thing that I learned from those tumultuous years was the answer to a question that puzzled me deeply. How was it possible for the Nazis to exterminate millions of people without significant protest from ordinary, decent Germans? To put it more bluntly: How could decent people, especially those who lived next door to a concentration camp, deny what was obvious.

The "Dirty War" in Argentina answered that question for me. Human beings flinch from reality and deny the obvious, particularly when they feel threatened by acts of terror. In Argentina people didn't want to know their government's dirty secrets, and the press obliged by not reporting what was going on.

I was often asked in Argentina how it was that the Buenos Aires Herald, a small foreign-language newspaper, was able to report in English and comment in Spanish on topics that were never mentioned in the Argentine press. Argentine journalists had two theories: That we were supported by the U.S. Embassy and that, as a foreign-language newspaper, we had immunity.

Neither was true. What we did have was respect for the Herald's traditional independence and unqualified support from Peter Manigault, president and publisher of the Charleston, S.C.-based Evening Post Publishing Company, which owned the newspaper. He simply wanted us to do our job and report the truth. That was the difference between the Herald and the mainline Argentine press. They were accomplices of the dictatorship. The Herald was not.

Argentina's "Dirty War" also made me realize more forcefully than ever before that a free press is indispensable in upholding democracy in times of terror. Faced with a terrorist threat, the Argentine military commanders responded with their own brand of terrorism. They stole, they raped and they murdered, and they were not held accountable. The country's institutions broke down, including the ordinary citizen's safeguard and last resort – the media. Citing the threat of terrorism, the armed forces and police justified torture and murder. Their enemies were demonized and the "subversive" citizens they saw everywhere were considered dispensable "non-persons." The military, as Scilingo acknowledged, "changed into monsters."

The last time I saw Cardinal Pio Laghi, whom I knew when he was the Apostolic Nuncio in Buenos Aires during the dictatorship, was in Washington in 1980 after he became the Vatican's top diplomat in the United States. He used the same words to describe the military commanders he knew so well when he was the Apostolic Nuncio in Buenos Aires: "They were monsters," he told me.

He hadn't wanted to see me again, and I had to insist that he receive me in his office at the Nunciature on Massachusetts Avenue. I understood he didn't want to be reminded of his days in Buenos Aires when Adm. Massera, the most murderous member of the junta, was his tennis partner. He doesn't want to think about those monsters, as I have never wanted to write about them.

A reviewer of *En Honor de la Verdad (In Honor of the Truth)*, a memoir of my exile from Argentina written by my son David, said that a father could not hope for a greater honor than a son's appreciation of his work. I am doubly grateful to him for writing the book I could never write.

AUTHOR'S PREFACE
By David Cox

More than 30 years ago my father routinely worked until the first rays of sunlight filtered through the curtains of the kitchen window of our apartment in Buenos Aires. A curious blend of newspaper ink, sweat and black coffee permeated the room. I remember the movement of his hands over the keys of his Olivetti typewriter. I remember the sounds his fingers made and the slam of metal on ribbon, paper and carriage. Over and over again the word *desaparecido*, Spanish for "the missing," erupted from the machine and ricocheted off the kitchen walls like an echo from the darkness of an endless cave.

The windows were shut tight, always. Asthma, a curse since his birth in 1933, hammered his chest, assaulted his lungs, stole his breath. He did not complain. Our dog Spotty – a mixed-breed shepherd, mostly German, always vigilant – barked each night. It was as if she, too, heard that awful word – *desaparecido* – reverberate throughout the apartment. She, too, sensed the danger always waiting just outside.

Argentine citizens disappeared daily during the 1970s and 1980s. Everyone wondered who would be next. Someone would leave for work or to run an errand or to visit friends and never be heard from again. My father was editor of the Buenos Aires Herald, the only English-language newspaper in the nation's bustling capital. He wrote about the missing people – who they were, where they lived, when they were last seen, why this was happening. He listed their names in the newspaper, spelled them out for all to see. He understood the personal risks. He did it anyway. The more his readers knew about those who had disappeared, the better chance each *desaparecido* had of coming home alive.

I remember that dreadful day, April 22, 1977, when he was arrested by Argentine authorities for reporting information the government censored in its "Dirty War" against left-wing terrorists. I remember the agony of not knowing if I would ever see him again and the relief I felt upon his release. But he would not be deterred. With dogged determination, he resumed reporting the truth despite the threats against his life. I will never forget the suffocating fear that smothered my childhood innocence when I was told that all of us – a family of seven – were marked for death. There were many threats – in writing, over the phone, relayed to us by friends and by people whom we thought were friends. It was impossible to keep up with them all.

Argentine military generals ordered surveillance of our apartment in the city and our weekend retreat in the country. They posted armed guards to watch us at night. It was for our own protection, we were told. Perhaps they did protect us for a while. Sometimes, late at night in the darkness of my bedroom, I heard explosions rumbling like the thunder of a passing storm. I was only 10 years old. But I remember the sounds of Argentina's war on terrorism.

I recall frantic rides at night in our tattered blue Peugeot with a headlight that refused to stay fixed, the dread of being stopped by police because the beam was out again and what might happen to us if they did. *Desaparecido!*

Then came the letter that we could not ignore. It was no ordinary death threat. Someone close to our family was watching us. The letter included information from someone who knew everything about our daily routine. It referenced information secured through electronic surveillance of our homes and contained specific details that only an insider would know. That letter led directly to our exile.

Leaving Argentina in the summer of 1979 was like stepping from a thick fog of fear into pitch-black despair. Bidding farewell to the nation of my birth was like attending my own funeral. I did not know what would happen to me or to my family. I remember closed suitcases, changes of address, and calls for help to relatives, to friends, to journalists, to embassies in London and in Washington, D.C. I remember leaving, wondering if I would ever feel safe and at home again.

That terror is a distant yet persistent memory. It consumes like no other evil. It lodged like an incurable disease inside me. I yearn for the peace that comes with naiveté. I cannot find it. But we still have the comfort of each other – my mother, my father, my two brothers, my two sisters and me. We have memories of good times we shared before the darkness came. We have hopes and dreams and wives and husbands and children of our own now.

In 1969, we lived in an apartment on Alvear Avenue in the heart of Buenos Aires. It was a comfortable place with a balcony, very European in many ways. We were contented there at first. We relished the stories that our father read to us about

Willy Wonka and his chocolate factory and cherished walks in a pumpkin garden our father took us to explore. The biggest, brightest pumpkins would grow into orange-colored mansions, he said.

We had at that time just such a retreat of our own, not far from the capital. Almost every Friday before dawn, we left our apartment in the city to spend the weekend at our spacious house in the country. My father gathered up his children from our beds, carried each of us still sleeping down to the garage and placed us into our cozy niches inside the Peugeot where we slept until the first light of day. Our bright, pumpkin-esque mansion was at Highland Park, a gated community forty miles outside Buenos Aires. By the time breakfast was served, we were wide-awake, sitting and laughing at the dining-room table in the front room of the house my parents had named "Victoria" in honor of my older sister.

I have only to close my eyes to see "VICTORIA" neatly painted in black letters on the white, wobbly, wooden gate of the fence that hugged our yard. My father pushes open the gate; it scrapes across the pavement. The grass is dense and green. The swallows sweep low among the eucalyptus trees that buffer the corners of the house.

We were happy in that house, away from the city, away from the phantoms whose whispers became the screams of a living nightmare. *"Desaparecido! Desaparecido!"* they said again and again, louder and louder. As the innocence of our childhood was looted – slowly at first, then completely – "Victoria" became our only shelter from the hideous sound.

In the autumn of 1975, before we understood that everything dies a little each day, we satisfied our wishes with leaves. Trees are different in South America from those in the United States. The soil and the seasons are not the same as those in coastal South Carolina, where I live with my wife, daughter and son today. In Argentina, my grandfather, whom we called Papito, helped us collect leaves so we could create our own special worlds. My sister Ruthie, the youngest of the family, was content to submerge herself in enormous piles of leaves while I made a colorful mat of them – a magic carpet, I would pretend – on which I could fly.

In those days, we looked forward to Carnival, Argentina's annual celebration of Shrove Tuesday and the start of Lent. We filled five-gallon plastic buckets with water balloons, which we threw at each other and anyone else who happened to pass within range. At Christmas, we gathered around Mother's piano and sang as she played so beautifully. Our tree, carefully adorned with lights and ornaments, was always a huge, locally grown pine – not the store-bought kind.

I often climbed onto the red-tile roof of our country house to contemplate. One's perspective changes when considering things in such lofty fashion, especially when one is a lad. The gable provided a perfect perch from which to observe the world anew. I could gaze straight down through the ripples of crystal-clear water in our swimming pool and admire its sparkling blue-tiled bottom. In the summer, my father lined us up early every Saturday, handed each of us a bucket and a brush, and ordered us to clean. Obedient, the five of us worked as efficiently as possible. The sooner the pool was spotless, the sooner uninterrupted hours of fun would begin. We were his ungainly army, faithful and true.

Many years later, at our home in South Carolina, I asked my father to fulfill his promise to write about those days of my youth. I hoped his words would heal the incessant sense of distrust that infected me to my core. It was in the summer of 1990 when I made the request. I was 28; he was 57. He sat down at his personal computer and his fingers moved slowly and quietly from key to key:

A huge yellow wicker basket arrived in Charleston, South Carolina, a year or two after I left Argentina. It was some time before I could finally bring myself to swing back the iron hoops and open the lid. Inside were all the papers that I had dumped hastily into the basket in my office in the Buenos Aires Herald, the last day before taking the Aerolineas Argentinas flight to London.

Sorting through the basket tentatively with the fear that touching objects from that time still gives me, I was transported back over the years. I came across papers I had been handling that day still tucked inside my office diary.

I remembered the appalling emptiness in my mind as I had tried to write my last article for the Herald. I had sat at the typewriter mentally stunned by the difficulty of expressing what I thought needed to be said and could be said.

Now as I struggled to come up with a sentence that would break the seals clamped on my mind, I see my colleague James Neilson, who was bringing out the paper that day, frowning and tensing up as the deadline drew near. I can't do it, I thought. Neilson never had this difficulty and I sensed his disdain as I battled with another impossible-to-write piece.

My father wrote three pages of his memoirs. They have yet to be completed. As I sifted through stacks of documents he collected through the years, I found a handwritten quotation by Argentine journalist Jacobo Timerman. My father scribbled down the quote after reading Timerman's account of his captivity and torture in a prison in Buenos Aires 30 years earlier. He copied Timerman's words soon after we arrived in the United States:

> Each time I write or utter words of hope, words of confidence in the definitive triumph of man, I'm fearful – fearful of losing sight of one of those gazes (of prisoners who know they are about to be executed). At night I recount them, recall them, re-see them, cleanse them, illumine them.

> Those gazes, which I encountered in the clandestine prisons of Argentina, and which I've retained one by one, were the culminating point, the purest moment of my tragedy. They are here with me today. And although I might wish to do so, I could not and would not know how to share them.

He knew Timerman well. As editor of the Buenos Aires Herald, my father helped save Timerman's life by alerting readers that his jailed colleague might become another *desaparecido*. The great man was freed eventually, thanks largely to public outcry. Like Timerman, my father had seen the horror and could not forget the faces of imprisoned people whose lives he could not help save.

Before we left Argentina abruptly in December 1979, my father reached a crucial moment in his life as he struggled to write his final piece as editor of the newspaper. He started and restarted the article. It was as though he had to distill in a few column inches the sum and substance of everything that had happened since coming to his adopted country two decades earlier. The words did not flow. He wondered if he was capable of delivering the goods. Suddenly, my father's friend Harry Ingham thundered into the newspaper office and demanded that my father join him for supper. With his customary infectious energy, basso-voiced Harry noted that the newspaper deadline was a distant two hours away and that all harried editors must eat. They must drink, too.

"A good bottle of red wine with our meal will do the trick," Harry said. And it did.

My father's farewell commentary was titled "Au Revoir" and it ran in the Buenos

Aires Herald on Dec. 16, 1979. A heartfelt piece about his life and his family in Argentina, it was an adieu to the people of a nation he had grown to love over a period of more than twenty years. Harry Ingham surprised me years later when I returned to Argentina to reclaim what I could of my hijacked childhood. He placed into my hands a box containing letters written to him from my father through the years. "Here. These are yours," he said.

The letters offer a perspective on life in Argentina during the worst of times, containing insights from two men who lived it. Those letters, which Harry entrusted to me, are at the core of this book, which I write from the sanctuary of my home in the Lowcountry of South Carolina. It is here in Charleston, a diverse Southern city whose people have endured so much adversity, that we found refuge. It is here that my narrative begins. It's a drama and a tragedy and a love story about Argentina's "war on terrorism" three decades ago. An estimated 30,000 people disappeared in the 1970s and early-1980s. Left-wing groups, right-wing groups, the military and the government terrorized an entire nation. It is a story that is relevant today.

The hero is Robert J. Cox, a journalist who knew that a free press is crucial in a civil society and a potent weapon against terrorism. He maintained his commitment to telling the truth and to reporting what the other newspapers ignored at terrible risk to his safety, his health and ultimately the safety and health of his family. Terrorism is not just a word to me. I grew up afraid for my father, never knowing if or when he might become a *desaparecido*. Terrorism is the worst form of fear; a kind of insanity where no place is sacred and no one is safe. It never ends.

As I begin to fill my own pages, I close my eyes to remember those happy times before the terror thoroughly disrupted our lives, to summon those stashed-away memories of special things that made us happy: the gathering up of autumn leaves with my grandfather and the view of life from atop a red-tiled roof, Mother's piano, the Christmas tree, the swimming pool and our motley bucket-and-brush brigade. I share these things with you along with the story of a newspaperman who did his job expecting little in return. His voice appears in italics in the pages that follow.

CHAPTER 1
A LATIN AMERICAN ADVENTURE
(1 9 5 9)

On an overcast day in March, Robert John Cox stood anxiously on a wharf in the port of Tilbury, outside London. Next to him were his sister Norma and her young sons Iain and Neil. A few steps behind them stretched the gangway to the ocean liner *Highland Monarch* of the Royal Mail Lines. At the age of 26, Bob Cox sought adventure about which he could write. A towering ship waited to take him to a new job half a world away.

He was born into a middle class English family on December 4, 1933, the year Adolf Hitler became Germany's charismatic new chancellor. In far off Argentina, a similar infatuation with deft proponents of extreme nationalism flourished. Argentine Gen. Agustin Pedro Justo was in power, launching what would become known as the "Infamous Decade," named so for the extreme measures he undertook to halt democracy.

In 1933, as Gen. Justo ruled through what has been described as "patriotic fraud," Cox took his first breath in London. The Cox family lived at 47 Grosvenor Road, a quiet street in the western sector of the capital. It was the same year the man who would become his favorite author, George Orwell, published "Down and Out in Paris and London," an autobiography about living in poverty in the two cities.

Although the United States was in the grip of the Great Depression, construction of the Golden Gate Bridge was under way in San Francisco, and Franklin D. Roosevelt inaugurated his presidency with a speech that defined the spirit of the times: "So, first of all, let me assert my firm belief that the only thing we have to fear is fear itself – nameless, unreasoning, unjustified terror which paralyzes needed efforts to convert retreat into advance." It was as if President Roosevelt had whispered words of counsel into young Cox's ear.

It was also the year Albert Einstein arrived on his third visit to the United States, where he would become a citizen and spend the rest of his life. Newsweek was published for the first time. The ice cream cone was invented in Brooklyn and Ruth Wakefield baked her first batch of chocolate chip cookies. But everything dimmed in the ominous shadow of Nazi Germany. In 1933, the first concentration camp, Dachau, was built 10 miles northwest of Munich to stoke the fires of murderous Nazism. Across the Atlantic, a similar belief in the inherent superiority of a supposed Aryan race burned in the hearts of many Argentines.

Cox's father, Edward John Cox, was a World War I veteran. He joined the British Army at age 13 and later served as a cavalryman with the 14th Hussars in India. He wore a uniform most of his life. After the army, he became a radio officer in the merchant marine and one of the first "Marconi Men" in charge of communications aboard the great ships of the Pacific and Orient Line. But his merchant marine career ended with the stock market crash. To support his family, he invested what was left of his savings in a grocery store with an upstairs apartment on Grosvenor Road. It was a family affair. Bob, pedaling his bicycle through the streets of London, delivered groceries to the homes of customers.

Cox's proudest possession was a photograph of his father wearing a dashing cavalry uniform while astride a large white horse. Edward John Cox was a mounted messenger during the early days of the First World War before the British and German armies became bogged down in the trenches. When World War II began Sept. 1, 1939, his father tried to rejoin the army for a second crack at the Germans, but his age prevented it. So his father volunteered as an air raid warden. Five-year-old Bob Cox listened in awe to the stories his father told about heroic London firemen and Civilian Defense Force workers. He created an imaginary army to fight the Nazis, pretending he was a boy soldier like his father. All the while, real bombs rained down upon London at a time when patriotism ran high and England was united in the fight against Fascism.

Young Cox set up a "command post" in a nearby railroad yard in preparation for a German invasion. It was inside this child's hideout that he and the neighborhood boys kept *candle stubs, filched from our homes and tins of potato soup that were never eaten, never even tasted, but kept for emergencies.* He and his friends had other secret bases in attics and cellars, and among the thick rhododendrons in Ealing Park.

They combed the streets of London after air raids and collected shrapnel and shell casings while keeping a "watchful eye" for unexploded ordnance. The Blitz taught Cox some enduring life lessons: stick by your principles; strive to be decent and kind; never lose your sense of humor. His shy Aunt Mildred helped him to form such a view when one day at the dining-room table she picked up a carving knife and vowed that if a German paratrooper landed in her garden she would cut him into "little bits." Later, when a German pilot did parachute near her house in Derbyshire, she treated the terrified man kindly, offered him a cup of hot tea.

Cox's childhood ended when his father's heart stopped suddenly soon after the war. His mother could not run the store on her own, so the family moved to Frinton-on-Sea to live with Aunt Gladys. The sale of the grocery store and the combined retirement incomes of the two sisters were enough to buy a house not far from a greensward on the cliffs above a mile-long stretch of beach.

At age 14, Cox took up a newspaper route to supplement the family's income. Realizing early in life that his ambition was to write, he convinced the local editor to let him work without pay at the East Essex Gazette during school holidays. The bicycle ride from Frinton-on-Sea to the Gazette office at Clacton-on-Sea was an eleven-mile roundtrip. Soon afterward, he was put on the Gazette's payroll writing obituaries for two pounds a week, which allowed him to join the Café Society of Frinton-on-Sea where he talked among friends about life, poetry and girls.

Before he could get his hands on a bigger story, he was drafted into the Royal Navy to serve during the Korean Conflict. He was assigned as a cryptographer to HMS Mounts Bay and traveled by troopship to join the frigate in Sasebo, Japan. His anti-aircraft frigate patrolled the west coast of the Korean peninsula. The frigate and its crew survived a friendly fire incident, when, inexplicably, a U.S. plane dropped two bombs that narrowly missed the vessel. After two years of naval service, for which he received two combat medals, Cox returned to England and resumed with passion his life's work. He joined the East Anglian Daily Times as a reporter in Ipswich. Later, at the Hull Daily Mail, he himself made headlines for being trapped on the top floor of a blazing tannery while covering the fire.

Cox enjoyed his work but wanted more. He longed not only to write but also to travel, so he answered a classified advertisement in the World Press News that sought a young British journalist for a newspaper job in Buenos Aires. It was at an English-language newspaper in the Argentine capital, and it offered a second-class ticket and a three-year contract, at the conclusion of which he would get a three-months' paid vacation in England.

He applied for the job and was shocked when contacted by the newspaper's London agent. The managing editor of the Buenos Aires Herald, Basil Thomson, came to Hull and met with Cox. They discussed the job over dinner at the best restaurant in town. He waited for months before receiving notification that he was hired. *England was very drab in 1959... Latin America seemed more promising,* Cox noted in his diary.

Edward John Cox often told his son about his trips to Argentina when he was a radio officer on ships that called at the port of Buenos Aires. "That great, wonderful country has such a fine capital city," he said, adding that his family should immigrate to Argentina some day.

Young Bob Cox was fascinated by Argentina. He read everything he could find about the vast and mysterious South American nation. Its history read like a novel; its natural allure was irresistible. He remembered reading one story about storms so strong over the Rio de la Plate (Silver River) estuary that birds would fall dead from the sky on the streets of Buenos Aires.

The first European to lay claim to Argentina was Spanish conquistador Juan Diaz de Solis, who sailed into the la Plata estuary in 1516 and found a body of brown water he called Mar Dulce. While sailing past the island of Martin Garcia, he spotted natives signaling him from the shore. They offered him gifts, including gold. Solis and some of his men were lured away from his ship to the mainland, where they were ambushed, dismembered and perhaps eaten by cannibals. The only survivor was a cabin boy, who was taken prisoner by the natives.

Alejo Garcia, who sailed with Solis, spread the news that Argentina possessed great riches, including an abundance of silver. "Argentina," in fact, is derived from the Latin word for silver, *"argentum."* Argentina was a Spanish colony until it won independence in 1816.

When Cox's father visited Buenos Aires in the early 1900s, Argentina was a thriving nation whose citizens looked toward Europe and the United States for ideas and support. His father saw Argentina at a time when exports were growing and foreign investment was strong. Buenos Aires was a bustling port city.

Argentina's fertile Pampas region was divided into vast ranches owned by a handful of wealthy families. Hipolito Yrigoyen, a charismatic and popular leader of the newly formed Radical Party, was president of Argentina in 1929 when the stock market crashed. Soon afterward, he was overthrown in a military coup backed by the wealthy elite. Fascist and nationalistic political movements followed, allowing Gen. Juan Domingo Peron to rise to power in the 1940s before he too was deposed in 1955.

Peron had been in exile for nearly four years when Robert J. Cox accepted the newspaper job in Buenos Aires. Cox went to his mother's house in Frinton-on-Sea and packed his few belongings in a steamer trunk. He took care to include his tennis racket, a dinner jacket and the anthology of English poetry given to him by his sister. Cox, his sister and his nephews soon stood anxiously at the docks of Tilbury. Norma and her children followed him up the gangway to the ship's main deck and lingered until the horn blasted and a crewman yelled: "All ashore that's going ashore!"

From the deck, Cox waved goodbye as the 14,216-ton *Highland Monarch* eased through the port's archway into the River Thames, crossed the English Channel and steamed out to sea. Four weeks later, after stops in Spain, Portugal, the Canary Islands, Rio de Janeiro, Santos and Montevideo, he reached Buenos Aires.

In Argentina, Arturo Frondizi, a progressive with a Mona Lisa smile, rose to power after Peron was overthrown in 1955. He became president in 1958 with the support of Peronistas. However, ultra-conservative forces in the military arrested Frondizi, annulled the elections and placed Jose Guido in the presidency. Not long afterward in Cuba, troops led by Che Guevara of Argentina and Fidel Castro captured Havana.

CHAPTER 2
A BRIDE, A NEWSPAPER AND A WALRUS
(1959-1968)

It wasn't a particularly pleasant time, Cox scribbled in his diary about his inauspicious arrival in Argentina in 1959. Darsena Norte, the transatlantic arrival point in the port of Buenos Aires, appeared grim as he stepped onto the docks. The streets were unlighted. Argentina did not have an efficient electrical system.

Everyone there seemed to be bad tempered and ill mannered. Two muscular men, on instructions from a customs officer, shouldered Cox aside, nearly knocking him to the ground. They demanded that he empty the contents of his trunk, then scattered his belongings on newspapers spread out on the floor of the dingy shed.

Also present was handsome and soft-spoken Basil Thomson, the Buenos Aires Herald publisher who was hard of hearing, having been shell-shocked during World War II while fighting in France. Born in Argentina, Thomson volunteered to serve in the British Army and was commissioned as an officer. He wore a hearing aid that, at his convenience, he turned off to shut out the world.

Thomson, who witnessed the treatment Cox received from the authorities, was apologetic about the coarse reception and offered to make up for it by taking him to dinner for thick slabs of Argentine beef. Cox moved into an early 20th-century apartment building on Libertador Street, one of the main avenues of the city not far from the docks. On the first floor was a restaurant, and just above it, his room, which overlooked rail lines that led to the nearby train station built by the English in the style of a London terminus. Cox rented the room from Lily Attwood, an elderly woman who took in lodgers. She was not a typical Argentine. She was a Christian Scientist highly critical of her countrymen; considered them narrow-minded and elitist.

Cox roamed the city that first night to acclimate himself. Buenos Aires boasted the most commanding edifices in the country, but he quickly noticed that the massive European-style government buildings with imposing columns were covered with soot. Located along the Río de la Plata, the city was at once full of activity as well as decay. Cox wandered down wide boulevards and explored the narrow streets. He looked forward to getting to know the industrious *porteños* (people of the port).

The next day, Cox walked more than twenty blocks to the Herald to begin his new job. He described the offices as *one floor with heavy wooden doors that connected with each other. You had to climb up marble stairs to reach the newsroom. The Herald was in a beautiful old building that was crumbling.*

William Cathcart, of Scotland, who spent 50 years in Argentina, started the Herald in 1876 as a single sheet about shipping news. By the time Cox arrived 83 years later, it was a reputable daily newspaper with six writers and 10 office staff.

Cox's editor was Norman Ingrey, a quiet, unassuming, very English man. Ingrey had traveled the world as a reporter, living many years in China before settling in Buenos Aires. He helped transform the Herald into an international newspaper. Once, during World War II, he was held captive in the Congress for a day, accused of violating Argentina's neutrality when the newspaper's coverage upset the pro-Axis government. Cox noted in his diary that the newspaper was praised for printing in English what others hushed up in Spanish.

Ingrey, *whose outlook on the world stemmed from his experience as a neocolonialist*, reminded Cox of his own father and soon became his mentor. Ingrey often took Cox to dinner at a small restaurant half a block from the office, a luxury for someone with little money. Cox got to know the restaurants in Buenos Aires where he could eat cheaply – places with stand-up tables that served savory vegetable soup along with thick cuts of meat and slices of crusty bread, exotic fare for an Englishman accustomed to post-war austerity in Britain.

Within a few months of his arrival, Cox purchased a train ticket to Mendoza, an Argentine province in the central western part of the country where in 1817 national hero Jose San Martin led his army across the Andes and liberated Chile from the Spanish.

Cox especially enjoyed the rich taste of Mendoza wines. He also visited Villavicencio, an area famous for its mineral springs. On his return trip to Buenos Aires, Cox talked to passengers about their country, its politics and Juan Peron, the former president who gave Argentine workers a degree of dignity for the first time. Cox soon began working as a stringer for international newspapers and magazines with bureaus in Buenos Aires to gain experience, supplement his income and meet veteran journalists who covered Argentina and neighboring countries. At the bureau of Time magazine, he met Count Piero Saporiti, a writer who had lived in Italy during the dictatorship of Benito Mussolini. Saporiti wrote "Empty Balcony," a book about Mussolini's downfall. Saporiti was a Time correspondent in Spain and Portugal before being assigned to Buenos Aires. Cox described him:

He was a true count who carried a cane with a silver knob. He said to me that, under Juan Peron, the press didn't cover some stories because they were scared of the government. In time the press became lazy and didn't report anything that might be considered unfavorable.

While many Argentines considered Peron and his wife Eva champions of the poor, Cox came to view Peronism as another brand of Fascism. He concluded that their efforts to bring dignity to the poor by providing them with basic needs were mere theatrics paid for with money Peron claimed the upper classes had stolen from the country. Nor was Cox's landlady Lily Attwood sympathetic to the Perons. "When he was in power you could not walk the street without some lout knocking your hat off," she said.

Juan Peron was born in 1895 about 60 miles south of Buenos Aires. His father's family came from Sardinia. Peron also had Scottish, French Basque and possibly Indian ancestors. He began his formal education at age 10 while living with an uncle in Buenos Aires and entered the national military academy six years later. A German military mission started the academy decades earlier.

Peron's early military career was relatively uneventful, but it gave him time to marry (though his first wife would die of cancer within a decade), write five books, and develop skills in boxing, archery, horsemanship and skiing. He was six feet tall, handsome, muscular and confident.

Peron was a member of an army delegation sent to study in Germany and Italy in the late-1930s. He became captivated by Mussolini's oratorical skills and worked hard to emulate him. Upon his return to South America, Peron began his rise to power with the help of Argentine nationalist and pro-Axis military officers. By 1943, Peron had accumulated enormous power in Argentine government, leading an effort to provide significant benefits to rank-and-file workers.

Peron's nationalist rhetoric condemned British foreign investment in Argentina. Increasingly, he was at odds with the traditional ruling class of landowners, big ranchers, the aristocracy and others who worked with the British. His mounting popularity was undeniable, as was his obvious ambition. Senior officers took heed. When anti-Peron elements led by Gen. Eduardo Avalos took control of the government, Peron was forced to resign.

Though defeated, Peron was still a formidable force. The new government allowed Peron to make a radio address to his followers before he was taken to Martin Garcia, a prison island used to sequester Argentina's most significant political prisoners. The actions of those who were against Peron only served to further mobilize and seal the commitment of the masses to him. Peron, they believed, was their only defender.

Peron's mistress Eva "Evita" Duarte, a former movie actress, gave impassioned radio addresses, mobilizing support of union leaders and masses of laborers. A week after Peron's exile, in the most massive demonstration in Argentine history, thousands flocked to the main square, forcing the military government finally to free Peron.

Instead of resuming his position as vice president, Peron seized the opportunity to set in motion his campaign for the 1946 presidential election. He and Eva married. As husband and wife, the Perons were a force with which to be reckoned. On Feb. 24, 1946, Peron won the presidency after receiving 54 percent of the vote.

Eva enchanted the working-class masses, systematically positioning herself to be their voice and defender by forming the Eva Peron Foundation. The organization built schools, hospitals, orphanages and housing for the elderly.

While Juan Peron made his way to power democratically, once in office the system began to change. Modeling Mussolini, Peron used gangs of thugs to silence opposition. His secret service force numbered 30,000. They followed the Fascist model and wore brown suits. Argentina became a refuge for Nazi war criminals.

Peron undermined the power of the unions, seized property and nationalized the railroads and banks. He systemically dismantled and reconstituted the judicial system. Officials could be dismissed or imprisoned for speaking out against Peronists. Commissions were established to investigate un-Argentine activities. Informants were everywhere.

Peron also moved against the newspapers. By controlling the information that flowed to the public, he could better control the nation. The purchase of newsprint was nationalized, and Peronists ran most newspapers and the radio stations. Opposition leaders were prevented from publishing; and rallies were often broken up violently. The Communist presidential candidate was jailed. Upon his release, he was killed when a mob of Peronists opened fire during a meeting.

Few of the repressive actions of Peron's government mattered to the masses of laborers. What mattered were the reforms that brought them improved working conditions, paid sick leave, paid annual holidays, pension programs, workman's compensation for dismissal or injury on the job and Christmas bonuses.

Six years into Peron's presidency, Eva became sick with cervical cancer and died. Her death elevated her to a mythic figure – the "Saint of the Poor." People appealed to the pope to canonize her. Her death devastated Peron, and marked the beginning of his fall from power. His intolerance increased. In a now-famous speech, Peron declared that, "anyone, in any place, who tries to change the system against the constituted authorities, or against the laws or the Constitution, may be killed by any Argentine."

Peron's campaign against the church included the expulsion of two Catholic priests and attacks on church property. In response, Pius XII excommunicated Peron and all government officials who acted against the faith. Further destabilizing were Peron's efforts to make Argentina an economic force in the international arena. High-priced agricultural exports during the world wars had helped finance rapid industrialization of the country. But that ended in the aftermath. Rejecting the Soviet model, Peron invited U.S. investment as a way to break free of English influence. However, the United States was not interested in aiding an upstart country at the risk of alienating its primary ally.

Peron tried to redistribute income and reduce the wage difference between skilled and unskilled workers. The result was a shifting of the labor force into the least productive sectors of the economy, thus further weakening the economy. Peron's agendas for social justice and economic independence were contradictory. His rule became increasingly repressive and divisive. At a public rally on April 15, 1953, a terrorist group detonated two bombs, killing seven bystanders and injuring nearly 100 hundred others. Two years later, anti-Peronist pilots used navy aircraft to bomb a rally at Plaza de Mayo in the heart of Buenos Aires, killing more than 360 people.

Military officers became increasingly hostile toward Peron. His measures to reduce military budgets while infusing Peronism in military schools raised tensions, as did his favoritism of pro-Peronists and his punishment of others. It was not surprising when in September 1955 the armed forces moved to overthrow him. In response, Peron declared a state of siege and demanded all traitors to his government jailed. Navy and air force officers threatened to attack Buenos Aires if Peron stayed. Sixteen days later, the coup was successful and Gen. Pedro Eugenio Aramburu became de facto president.

Peron lived in exile for 18 years, first in several Latin American countries before settling in Madrid, Spain. While in exile, huge numbers of Argentine citizens demanded that Peron be allowed to return. His policies benefited the poor and underprivileged, most of whom were denied opportunities afforded to other social classes. Peron's presence abroad was a constant worry to those who overthrew him, and several assassination attempts failed.

Gen. Aramburu eventually shut down the Peronist Party, even though it represented the majority of Argentine citizens. He even banned use of the words "Peron" and "Peronism" in public. Peronists were imprisoned and murdered during the dictator's regime. It wasn't until after the election of President Arturo Frondizi in 1958 that Peronists were allowed to run for office again, although under a different party name.

By 1961, two years after he had arrived in Buenos Aires, Bob Cox, now 28, had adapted reasonably well to his new home. He had been promoted to Herald news editor and engaged in an active social life. One night during a massive public transportation strike, he was invited to a dinner party but didn't show up until 11:30 p.m. Uncharacteristically, he was there without his dinner jacket because, rather than walk home after work to get it, he opted to go directly to the party.

As he was arriving, Maud Daverio, 24, was preparing to leave. From across the room, she noticed a young, disheveled man in shirtsleeves. He saw a thin, beautifully attired Latin woman. She was curious. He was in love.

Acutely aware of his rumpled shirt and lack of jacket, Cox hesitated to introduce himself to the young woman, who was almost out the door when he finally did.

"What's your telephone number? I would like to meet you," Cox whispered.

"It's 609-716," she said hurriedly and waved goodbye.

The next day, Cox invited Miss Daverio to join him for tea at the Richmond Café, a *confiteria* in downtown Buenos Aires. The Richmond opened in 1917 on Florida Street. It was posh, with wood-paneled walls, prodigious brass and red leather chairs. Tea was served with toasted ham-and-cheese sandwiches. Bob and Maud talked for hours about political and social issues. He confided that he intended to leave Argentina soon, but not before he could see her again.

For their second date, he took Maud to lunch at the Lancaster Hotel, a 1940s redbrick building in the English style where novelist Graham Greene stayed while researching in preparation for writing "The Honorary Consul." Bob leaned forward from his chair and said to Maud, "I like you very much. I might even be staying here. Perhaps we can meet more often ...."

Within a week, Cox proposed to Maud and called the next day to say he was in earnest. "Would you like to marry me?" he asked again.

"Yes," she said.

"When?"

Maud came from a prosperous Argentine family with conservative leanings. Her father, Agustin Daverio, was born in Argentina to Italian parents who had immigrated to Buenos Aires from Milan and prospered. A heated debate ensued within her family about the nature of this foreigner who expected to marry into a traditional Argentine family on such short notice. Maud's aunts wanted to hire a detective to investigate Cox, but Maud would have none of that. She held her ground and finally, with the blessing of her parents, married "the English pirate."

By this time, the impulsive Englishman was calling her "Toopsy," which he had learned was her nickname from childhood. Her mother and her two aunts were nicknamed "Googoo," "Gigi" and "Gaga" – the first words they were heard to utter as infants. "Toopsy," though not likely anyone's first word, was an endearment that appealed to her fiancé.

They married on April 4, 1961, inside the 19th-century church of Nuestra Senora de las Victorias in downtown Buenos Aires. A black-and-white photograph shows the smiling bride wearing a white silk dress and walking out of the church alongside a lanky groom with a well-trimmed beard and dressed in black tails with a white handkerchief in the top pocket of his jacket. They honeymooned at the Inca ruins of Machu Picchu in Peru before traveling to Paris and London, then returning to Buenos Aires. Victoria, their first child, arrived a year later.

Yet while Papito – what the Cox children would call their maternal grandfather – was prosperous, it was Maud's grandmother Kathleen who provided a touch of class.

Born in Dublin, Ireland, in 1869, Kathleen Milton Jones came from a well-educated Anglican family. She studied literature at the University of Cambridge and in 1889 left with her family for Latin America. They moved first to Brazil, where she taught English, music and the arts. Following an outbreak of yellow fever, she moved south to Buenos Aires. Kathleen Jones became a role model for English teachers in Latin America. She opened her own school, San Patricio's, which welcomed anyone who wanted an English-style education.

"Miss Catalina," as she was called, encouraged modern teaching techniques in Argentina. She was noted for championing women's rights and helping the underprivileged. She often distributed food and clothes to the poor and visited prison inmates. A woman of enormous rectitude, she married late in life to an

Englishman, Major Andrew Thomas Swift Boyle, who was educated at Tonbridge and at Sandhurst Military College. In 1888, he served in the Connaught Rangers' 88th Regiment, which soon fought in India. He received eight combat wounds and carried his scars proudly. After retiring from the army, he traveled to Argentina to work as an engineer for British-owned Argentine Railways, where he met and married Miss Catalina.

Bob Cox was not overly impressed by the aristocratic lineage of Maud's family, whose crest bears the motto, "God's Providence is My Inheritance." He joked that his only link to bluebloods was unveiled when *some crazy uncle, convinced there was aristocracy in the family, discovered to his great disappointment that the closest a Cox came to nobility was an ancestor who was second cook to King Henry VIII.*

Young Maud relished stories about her grandfather, a descendent of Richard Boyle, the Earl of Cork, whose son, Robert Boyle, was known as the "Father of Chemistry." Maud learned from her mother and her English cousins about her grandfather's accomplishments, and that he waited patiently to receive a share of the Boyle inheritance. Her grandfather died still waiting.

As a girl, Maud often visited the school founded by her grandmother and pretended that she, too, was a teacher. Maud remembers when the town of San Martin on the outskirts of Buenos Aires unveiled a beautiful sculpture of Miss Catalina in April 1944 to honor her 48 years of service in public education. Miss Catalina's sculpted face was often mistaken for that of Argentine First Lady Eva Peron. Sometimes Eva's admirers adorned it with flowers; at other times, people who hated Eva defaced the work by throwing stones.

After her grandmother died, Maud attended another English-speaking school run by Americans in a mansion seven blocks from where she lived. Maud usually walked to school while holding her mother's hand and accompanied by her sister Ruth, who was four years older. Maud was shy. Ruth was not. Maud was dark and plain, while Ruth was blonde with dazzling blue eyes. However, Maud was not easily intimidated – there was no sister rivalry. They complemented each other and shared a passion for music.

During summer nights, after dinner, the Daverio family often sat on the patio, listened to records, and danced to waltzes, tangos and foxtrots. Ruth had a beautiful voice and was a popular local entertainer who sang mostly American songs. Maud played piano. She began taking lessons at age six, first with an Italian pianist who slapped her fingers with a ruler when she missed notes. Later she studied under exiled European pianist Joseph Berggrun, a friend of composer Arthur Rubinstein.

U.S. President Franklin D. Roosevelt visited Argentina for the Inter-American Conference for the Maintenance of Peace in December 1936 prior to the outbreak of World War II. More than a million people lined the streets of Buenos Aires to see him. As the most outstanding student of the American school, Ruth was chosen to greet the U.S. president. The next day, newspapers published a photograph of her at the U.S. Embassy handing President Roosevelt a bouquet of flowers as he patted her on the head.

Three years after Roosevelt's visit to Argentina, World War II began. Maud remembers sitting with her family around the radio and listening to the news. Her father was particularly worried about growing Fascism in Italy as well as Argentina. Maud and Ruth often performed in the English clubs in Buenos Aires to raise funds to build Spitfire aircraft for Allied forces. Ruth sang while Maud played the piano or danced the Highland fling with other girls.

In 1946, Ruth, 18, was accepted to Duke University in Durham, North Carolina. Earlier that year, as valedictorian of American High School in Buenos Aires, she cited promising new testing for a cure of tuberculosis. A few months later, preparing to leave for the United States, she was diagnosed with the disease. Two days before she died in 1946, she asked her father to send a telegram to U.S. President Harry S. Truman. It stated in perfect English that she was a college-age girl who was dying and that she had personally met President Roosevelt in Argentina. She asked Truman to stop building atomic bombs because they made the world an even more dangerous place.

The death of her sister hit 15-year-old Maud hard, forcing her to live up to her birth name, Matilda, which means "strength in battle."

Nine years after Ruth's death Maud married Bob Cox, and their first child was born a year later. Bob became assistant editor of the Buenos Aires Herald and had covered 33 coup attempts against Argentine President Arturo Frondizi. Covering coups was a regular assignment for the young journalist. When the military ousted President Arturo Umberto Illia in 1963, Cox was on his beat inside Government House when ejected on orders of a general who helped organize the takeover. A photograph of Cox being forced out of the presidential palace appeared in one local newspaper. He was misidentified as a government official.

It was a sad day for Cox on the day Illia was ousted. Cox considered Illia a gentle man with outdated ideas. A country doctor, he proved incapable of righting either the ship of state or the economy. He had been overthrown by the military with the help of an overwhelmingly hostile press. Illia had defied the threats of military officers to the last minute and was literally pushed out of his presidential office by generals who staged the event. Once on the street, Illia hailed a cab and went home. Cox recalled a conversation he had with him shortly before the coup:

"President Illia. They are planning to overthrow you," Cox warned.

"No. That's ridiculous."

"But Mr. President, as we speak, I have it on reliable sources that the tanks are rolling."

By the time Illia acknowledged he faced resistance from the military and that most of the press was out to get him, it was too late. He was out; the military was in. More coups followed, yet Bob and Maud Cox were optimistic that democracy would soon return to Argentina.

At the same time, the murder of Norma Penjerik, a Jewish girl whose body was found on a garbage heap, underscored deep-seated anti-Semitism within the nation. Most of the newspapers published stories about the murder that included rumors of orgies and blood-sucking vampires written by reporters who were paid by the line. But the Herald sought out the truth and found it.

A cobbler was arrested on the basis of stories in the general press and charged with abusing and murdering the girl. Cox and Herald reporter Barry James covered the trial. "I had to arrest him," the judge admitted during an interview by Cox. "I know he is innocent, but if I let him go, a mob will surely lynch me." The cobbler was later released without charges.

After Illia was overthrown, Gen. Juan Carlos Ongania assumed dictatorial powers. His first major act was to dissolve the National Congress and the provincial legislatures and outlaw political parties. He replaced five Supreme Court justices, giving no indication of when the government would be returned to civilian control. He also embarked on a campaign to purge the nation of immorality.

Cox wrote an article for the Washington Post on July 29, 1966, describing Ongania as an extremist committed to purging Argentina of sin:

> The morality campaign, allied with the need to maintain dignity, has at least revealed the philosophy of the government that replaced ousted President Arturo Illia. The police are patrolling the parks to keep out kissing couples. The age of admission to adult films is to be raised to 22. It is exactly the same policy that Franco adopted to cover up the tourists' bikinis on Costa Brava. Only Argentina has no tourists to speak of, and Franco lost the battle.

Ongania articulated his doctrine of "ideological borders." The military was to complement its obligation to protect Argentina's geopolitical borders with a robust commitment to erase from public consciousness "exotic ideologies." He believed that college students were especially susceptible.

On the day the article appeared, the world awoke to the news that the Argentine president had ordered a violent crackdown on the university students. Cox wrote that Argentina was experiencing the "Era of the Walrus," in reference to the dictator who grew a thick moustache to cover his malformed lip. The violence of those months had a ripple effect on Argentina and caused the exodus of many of the country's brightest citizens.

It was also the year that the Washington Post asked Cox to write about terrorism in Argentina and Uruguay. "The Post's New York Bureau is planning a major story on the growth of urban terrorism in Brazil, Argentina and Uruguay in particular, with contributions from Venezuela and Colombia," the telex to Cox said. "Would appreciate your filing up to 1,500 words on Argentina and, if possible, about 500 words on Uruguay." Cox responded immediately:

> There is so far no evidence to suggest any central organization. The bombings could be the work of one group and it might be extremely small. Intelligence officers believe that no single organization is responsible. Terrorism is not new in Argentina. Extremist Peronists have been carrying out acts of sabotage and labor agitation ever since Peron's downfall. Both guerrilla movements pledge allegiance to Peron, and it is believed that several Peronist groups, occasionally linking up with extremist nationalists, are responsible.

The Era of the Walrus was difficult for Argentina; for Cox, a journalist, it was charged with excitement. It was as though he were back in London during the days of his youth, stumbling upon one unexploded bomb after another. There was so much to write about in Argentina.

In September 1968, Cox was promoted to editor of the Buenos Aires Herald. Less than a month later, he learned that the majority shares of the Herald were sold to Peter Manigault, an American newspaper publisher. The only thing he knew about Manigault was that he was from Charleston, South Carolina.

"I believe I have lost my job," Cox told his wife after returning home from work that night.

Her face turned pale.

CHAPTER 3
THE HUGUENOT SPIRIT
(1 9 6 8 - 1 9 6 9)

Peter Manigault, 41, returned to Buenos Aires on Oct. 14, 1968. It had been two years since his last visit. He lodged in the best room at the elegant Plaza Hotel and hurried to get downstairs. The Inter-American Press Association meeting was about to begin, and he did not want to be late. Manigault took the elevator down to the lobby of the hotel in the heart of the city. He slipped through the crowd of guests and service personnel. As he entered the conference room full of newspaper executives – some of whom he knew personally – he was reminded of Argentina's troubled past.

He remembered how Juan Peron seized the presidency and shut down the public press. He knew both the father and son of the wealthy Paz family, owners of Buenos Aires' largest daily, La Prensa. They fled Argentina in 1951 to Uruguay after Peron confiscated their newspaper. Manigault and his wife had been guests at the Paz's huge *estancia* (ranch). As Peter Manigault sat in the grand conference room of the lavish hotel surrounded by hundreds of representatives of the Inter-American Press Association, he was fully aware that change came slowly in Argentina.

He recalled the two-week, 12-hours-per-day crash course in Spanish he had taken in 1966 before setting out to write a series of newspaper articles about Central and South America. He still had trouble adapting his Charleston accent to pronounce Spanish words with double-consonants such as *desarrollo* (economic development). But he was proud of himself for being able to talk to people of Colombia, Argentina, Uruguay, Chile, Peru, Ecuador and Cuba whom he had met during his travels. He was convinced that *desarrollo* would succeed in Latin America. His passion for Latin America – its politics, cultures and people – was ignited.

Within days after taking the intensive Spanish course, Manigault sat strapped and spellbound in a helicopter flying over the Andes as a huge condor soared effortlessly alongside. Few things could match the colossal bird which, he noted in his journal, was twice the size of a Carolina turkey buzzard. Nothing, he added, compared to a sunset flight across South America's great, snow-peaked mountain chain as the sky – streaked in shades of purple, red, magenta, and blue – faded into night. "I feel as if I have flown into a huge oil-painting by Bierstadt," Manigault wrote.

He considered Latin America as an extension of himself, as if the Old South of the United States in which his family roots were deeply planted had no southern border. Yet he was appalled to find that so many injustices and inequalities remained in Latin America.

Manigault visited rugged Peru and walked among the carefully fitted stones of the stunning architectural legacy of the Incas. He later interviewed the president of Ecuador, the flamboyant Otto Arosemena, who was dressed in a white linen suit reminiscent of those that bankers and lawyers wore to work on Charleston's Broad Street. He rode hard on horseback across the Argentine Pampas and thought about the flatness of a coastal Carolina salt marsh. He befriended a local gaucho, a "swarthy, stocky and mustachioed" South American cowboy.

Manigault was fascinated by Latin America, but Argentina in particular staked a claim on his heart. He wrote about his love for Argentina's rough-and-tumble culture and his concern about the nation's future. His article was published November 14, 1966, in the News and Courier, his family-owned daily newspaper in Charleston.

The 1960s were not the best of times for Argentina. Manigault noted that the country was vast and variegated, little known and greatly misunderstood. Of all the Latin American nations that he had visited, Manigault was convinced that Argentina had the best economic prospects. He also recognized warning signs: "One does not have to be there long to realize that much of this apparent prosperity is a misleading shell. And within a few days, one encounters signs small and large of what ails and threatens this potentially great nation: political extremism and economic chaos."

This was so true, Manigault thought two years later as he sat in the Plaza Hotel conference hall during the Inter-American Press meeting. Not much had changed since he had first visited Argentina other than the fact that the gnarly grip of authoritarianism squeezed Latin America even tighter, and the conferees agreed that something must be done to ease it.

As president of the Evening Post Publishing Company – which owned the News and Courier, the Charleston Evening Post, and two small South Carolina newspapers in Aiken and Beaufort at that time – Peter Manigault voted in support of the Inter-American Press Association's resolution asking leaders of all American nations to apply pressure on Panama's military junta to restore freedom of the press in that troubled nation.

As Manigault cast his vote, he recalled a visit to Panama and the favorable climate for negotiations between U.S. and Panamanian authorities about nationalization of the Panama Canal. He met with the Panamanian president, and they talked about promising new economic opportunities. Manigault had also befriended Panamanian ranchers who reminded him of ranchers he knew during the many summers he spent at cattle ranches in Wyoming when he was growing up.

As the Inter-American Press Association discussed sending a fact-finding mission to Peru, where a new military government had clamped down on the press, Manigault noted that democracy, freedom of speech and capitalism were essential in Latin America no matter who was in power – the new left, the old right, or a hybrid government. He wrote about how Latin Americans needed to mine their natural resources conscientiously and modernize their communication systems, which would require foreign investment. He had interviewed numerous Latin Americans leaders – in government, academia, the military, agriculture and business – and most agreed that enlightened capitalism was the best way to spark economic development.

As he left the conference room, Manigault glanced out of a window overlooking San Martin Park and saw a young Argentine couple enjoying a stroll in the fresh spring air as they walked past an old man resting on a bench in the shade of an ancient gomero tree. Later, from his room on the top floor of the hotel, Manigault looked out over the city at its crowded streets, bustling sidewalks and tall buildings. One of those buildings was a 10-story structure at 25 de Mayo St. in the old red-light district near the port. It was the offices of the Buenos Aires Herald, which would soon join the Charleston, S.C.-based Evening Post Publishing Co.

Manigault knew investing in Latin America was risky. But he was fascinated by the possibilities that ownership of an independent and defiant paper in the heart of a huge South American port city offered. Buenos Aires was so different from Charleston and yet much the same. Both places are hot and humid in summer, comfortable in spring and fall, mild in winter. Both are bustling Atlantic seaports, historic, cosmopolitan and surrounded by natural beauty. He appreciated the Argentines and wanted to invest in their future.

On his return to Charleston, Manigault discussed with his closest advisers the idea of buying the Herald as part of the Evening Post Publishing Co.'s plans to diversify. Company executives boarded a plane Dec. 19, 1968, and left chilly Charleston for sunny Buenos Aires. Among the executives was Manigault's brother-in-law Frank B. Gilbreth, who wrote the best-selling novel "Cheaper by the Dozen" in collaboration with his sister Ernestine Gilbreth Carey. That book and another by Gilbreth and Carey ("Belles on Their Toes") became popular movies. It was 80 degrees, humid and summertime when they landed. The group stayed on the top floor of the Plaza Hotel.

The men spent 14 hours the next day meeting with Argentine bankers and lawyers to complete the sale. That night, as the temperature dipped to 65 degrees, they walked to a restaurant and dined on wine and thick Argentine steaks as they discussed the purchase.

Any acquisition must first be a good investment, or a company is either spinning its wheels or going backward, Gilbreth later wrote in his popular column in the News and Courier about their decision to buy the Herald. "Charleston and Buenos Aires are sister seaports and each can learn a lot about the other as a result of the purchase. Latin American trade had been vital in the development of Charleston's maritime industry," he wrote, adding prophetically that the future of the Americas hinged on well-conceived, mutual trade agreements among the nations. He said a communications venture involving newspaper ownership in Charleston and Buenos Aires had great potential.

Manigault had quickly recognized that the Buenos Aires Herald had a distinct compassionate quality that reflected the hopes of a succession of his ancestors' lives starting five centuries earlier in France and expanding into the New World. The Manigaults were shrewd businessmen and businesswomen who deeply cared about their employees, neighbors and qualities of life.

The Manigault family odyssey began in the late-1500s with the persecution of French Protestants by the Roman Catholic Church. The St. Bartholomew's Day massacre in 1572 was disastrous for these Protestants called Huguenots. Thousands were killed in the streets before relative calm ensued for the next 87 years following the issuance of the Edict of Nantes that ended the initial purge. However, French King Louis XIV revoked the edict in 1689, legalizing government-sponsored terrorism against citizens who refused to renounce their Protestant beliefs. The King's dragoons were instructed to do whatever necessary to intimidate them into returning to the Roman Catholic faith.

Judith Giton, a widow, was one of a multitude of Huguenots who fled France.

She escaped in the middle of the night from her home in La Voulte after soldiers forcibly quartered in her house. In the morning, they searched for her, but Judith and her family had left for England. They later immigrated to the Carolina colony at Charleston, where she met and married another Huguenot immigrant, Pierre Manigault, of La Rochelle, France, an Atlantic seaport city founded in the tenth century. La Rochelle was home to many Huguenots persecuted by Cardinal Richelieu in the late-1600s.

When Pierre Manigault left LaRochelle in about 1695, he settled on the Santee River working as a barrel maker and victualer, and, eventually, a distiller of brandy and rum. Soon he amassed enough money to purchase a small house in Charleston where he took in lodgers. The Manigaults invested in other businesses and prospered.

The Evening Post was published by his eldest son Robert following Arthur Manigault's death in 1924. Two years later, the Manigaults bought Charleston's morning daily, the News and Courier. Robert Manigault died in 1945 and younger brother Edward became president of the company. Edward's son Peter took over in 1959, the same year that Robert Cox began working for the Buenos Aires Herald. By 1968, when Peter spearheaded the purchase of the Herald, the Evening Post Publishing Co. was an established family-owned newspaper chain that continues to grow to this day.

Cox had little knowledge of the Manigault family's history when he met his new employer. He only knew the majority of the Herald's stock had been sold to a South Carolina-based newspaper owner. Cox was sure Manigault would bring in his own editor. Throughout the night in the bedroom of their Buenos Aires apartment, Bob and Maud talked quietly about their future. He could work at another paper in Buenos Aires and continue to write as a correspondent for international newspapers, or they could start a new life elsewhere.

"I was told he's from Charleston. That's all I know about him," he explained to Maud as the sounds of the awakening city filtered through the French doors of the balcony of their apartment. Cox also told his wife he was worried about a recent story he had written about former U.S. first lady Jacqueline Kennedy's marriage to Greek multimillionaire Aristotle Onassis, who years earlier immigrated to Buenos Aires, took a job with a shipping company and became rich. Onassis was well known in Argentina, and the breaking story of his marriage to the glamorous widow of assassinated U.S. President John F. Kennedy was front-page news everywhere.

The night before the story broke, Cox was chaperoning Katharine Graham, owner of both the Washington Post and Newsweek magazine. He worked part time as a correspondent for Mrs. Graham's publications. She reminded him of the Queen of England. She mentioned to Cox that news of the Kennedy-Onassis marriage would break soon. The next day, Mrs. Graham told Cox she was shocked and disappointed to learn the Boston Globe had scooped the Washington Post. Cox reported in the Herald how upset Mrs. Graham was about missing the exclusive. Afterward, Cox heard he would lose his correspondent's job for writing about her. The rumor was false.

A few days later, Peter Manigault arrived at the Herald offices. He was slim, handsome and had a certain European reserve about him. Cox met Manigault in the newspaper's boardroom, overlooking 25 de Mayo St., and they shook hands for the first time.

"I would like to reassure you that the newspaper will benefit from the purchase," Manigault said. "Our newspapers are among the best edited in the United States," adding he planned no changes in the Herald's management. Thus an understanding was reached between the two men that went beyond formalities. They were alike in many ways. Both were quiet and humble. Both enjoyed writing. Both served in their respective navies during the Korean War and received combat decorations.

Cox knew that, from 1940 to 1944, Huguenots in the village of Chambon-sur-Lignon, France, risked everything by sheltering 5,000 Jews from occupying Nazi forces during World War II. He recognized that Manigault inherited that same compassion for his fellow man, no matter what the circumstances. It was just such a spirit that would guide the Herald under the ownership of the Manigault family and editorship of Robert J. Cox.

Argentina's ongoing economic and political problems kept Cox busy editing the Herald and as an international correspondent for the Washington Post, Newsweek and other publications. He worked hard during the week but made time to be with his family on most weekends at their country home in Highland Park where his children usually awoke to the smell of freshly cut grass and an English breakfast of newly gathered mushrooms, fried eggs and pancetta.

Cox would come home from work on Fridays at about midnight, carry each of his five sleeping children to the garage and place them like heirloom china inside his Peugeot 403. In Highland Park, the children loved seeing Daisy and Pergamino, two horses the neighbors asked them to look after. Daisy, the white one, often poked her head through a window of the house in search of lumps of sugar. Maud often played on piano "Daisy Bell" while the children delighted in singing the chorus:

"Daisy, Daisy give me your answer do. I am half crazy all for the love of you."

In February 1969, the News and Courier in Charleston published an article by Cox titled, "Guest Editorial: Argentina Needs a New Image (from the Buenos Aires Herald)," which, ironically, was positioned on the page below a political cartoon lampooning the recent election of Richard M. Nixon as 38th president of the United States. Cox wrote about the crackdown in light of Argentina's reputation for harboring Nazi war criminals:

> *The more deeply an inquiring reporter probes, the more convinced he becomes that Argentines know very little about themselves. No wonder extremism seems to loom so large here. The smear of fascism is unfair. But it is not realistic to ignore it … Argentina really does suffer from a bad image abroad.*

Peter Manigault wrote to Cox from Charleston that he would soon return to Buenos Aires. He attached an article written by Washington Post staff writer John M. Goshko that included complimentary references about the Herald and its editor. Titled "The Anglos Accent the 'Si'," it was a story about how British immigrants and their descendents living in Argentina attended English schools and met in clubs, restaurants, bars and shops that were in many ways more "British than the original model."

Goshko also wrote that Herald Editor Robert Cox brought to the newspaper a more urbane view of the world. For the newspaper to cover stories and become more involved in Argentine politics, Cox had typed on Herald notepaper the newspaper's new general policy and distributed it to the staff. It stated that the "Herald has long ceased to be a community organ" and "in all writing it should be remembered that we are catering to an international community, for the greater part composed of men and women of intelligence..." It stressed that Argentine stories and local reporting had wide appeal, and the nation should take advantage of economic opportunities sure to come from foreign investment.

"The Herald is being published in an era when economic investment and expansion constitute a main line of news," according to point No. 5 of the new general policy.

Cox's observation about extremism playing a sinister role in Argentina was also a major concern of Manigault, who had identified just such a threat in the 1960s during his visit to Latin America. Indeed, as both men would soon know, political extremism was about to terrorize the nation.

The clash between the labor unions and the state hit a fevered pitch in the industrial city of Cordoba in the spring of 1969. Cordoba had grown rapidly, primarily because of the booming automobile industry. Fiats, Fords and Renaults were assembled in Cordoba, though work was being shifted to the province of Buenos Aires, forcing layoffs locally. Autoworkers staged an insurrection that was met with bloody military force.

Known as the first *cordobazo*, workers rampaged for a week, destroying public buildings. Approximately 5,000 special army troops and 4,000 police crushed the uprising in a manner that invoked the memory of the "Tragic Week" of 1919 and the Patagonian Rebellion of 1917-1921. Disdain for the Ongania regime mounted as Peron's influence in exile grew, with unions fighting among themselves for control of the labor movement. The economy was in crisis. Debt, inflation and cost of living were out of control.

This led to the end of the "Era of the Walrus." Chronic economic woes accounted for much of Argentina's instability, but ultimately the nation's problems were due to poor management and bad government. Meanwhile, Marxist guerrilla warfare spread in Latin America.

In 1959, before he left for Buenos Aires from England, Cox's view of the Argentine-born revolutionary Che Guevara was that of many young idealists who hoped Cuba's revolution would herald widespread democracy in Latin America. But when the political executions began, Cox realized that Guevara's ideology was flawed. Che was a fascinating man, and Cox understood why many people admired him, but the myth masked the man's ruthless streak.

Guevara was well known in Argentina, so when he was suddenly no longer in the news, Cox set out to find out what had happened to him. Everyone assumed Guevara returned to Cuba after his failed military adventure to establish communism in Africa. But he had not been seen or heard from in months.

"Where is Che Guevara?" people everywhere asked. Some speculated that he had been arrested and imprisoned by Cuba's new dictator Fidel Castro. One man might know, Cox thought after seeing a photograph of Marxist guerrillas on the news wires. The photo was purportedly taken in a jungle camp in Bolivia. Was one of the bearded men the legendary rebel leader? Before moving to Cuba, Guevara's father, Ernesto Guevara Lynch, lived in a rundown house in Buenos Aires. Cox and Herald News Editor Andrew Graham-Yooll, whose wife was a friend of Che's sister Celia, paid Ernesto Guevara a visit.

> The old man talked about everything – Che as a rugby player overcoming asthma, as a child playing in the house the family had in the hills of Cordoba – but he wouldn't tell us if Che was in Bolivia. He said he did not know, and that was probably true. He spoke with enormous love and affection about his son, and with humor. He made it sound as if Che was on vacation, not as was the case, attempting to start a revolution in Bolivia. Che's father was friendly and humorous, not at all a revolutionary. He said that Che got his revolutionary fervor from his mother.

The father described his stormy relationship with his wife. "She had such a strong character, and we had such tremendous arguments. I used to place a loaded revolver at the dining table when we argued," he quipped. He said their famous son possessed many of her characteristics.

After the story appeared in the Herald, Cox and his colleagues worried about the safety of the family, fearing they might pay with their lives for having the Guevara name. Che's younger brothers came to see Cox for advice on what they should do to remain safely in Argentina. They did not want to be driven out.

DAVID COX JOURNAL: MAY 2007

As fate would have it, some 30 years later, I met Che's brother, Juan Martin, when I worked for the Kuwaiti Ambassador in Argentina. Juan Martin's eyes were the same as Che's, intelligent and caring. He was the youngest son and he admired Che. We talked about Argentina, his family and his father. He remembered my father with great respect. We also talked about how difficult it was in Argentina to acknowledge Che's place in the nation's history.

In Argentina, no left-wing guerrilla groups had leaders like Che Guevara – only poor imitations. At first, their tactics were idealistic. For instance, they hijacked trucks loaded with soft drinks and drove them to shantytowns for distribution to the poor. But once their senseless killings began, most Argentines rejected their image as gun-carrying Robin Hoods.

While the violent tactics of Marxist and nationalist groups intensified, new terrorist organizations were formed. The Revolutionary Worker's Party (ERP), was an especially active organization. It merged with a military group called the People's Revolutionary Army (PTR). Another powerful terrorist organization was the Montoneros – influenced by Marxism, Che Guevara, Fidel Castro, Juan Peron and the Third World Priest Movement.

One of the Montoneros' first actions was to target the military leader who had overthrown Peron and ordered the massacre of Peronists who tried to launch a rebellion. On May 29, 1970, former Argentine President Aramburu was kidnapped by the Montoneros. The organization acknowledged responsibility for the kidnapping, saying he was one of the military commanders who removed the embalmed body of Eva Peron and secretly buried it in the Maggiore cemetery in Milan, Italy. Eva's body was a powerful symbol of Peronism and inspiration for supporters. The military government believed that by hiding her body, her influence would fade.

Escorted from his home at 1:30 p.m. by uniformed men he assumed were his own army officers, President Aramburu was whisked to a guerrilla hideout and given a mock trial. After being read charges that he ordered the execution of Peronists who had tried to stage a counter-coup, Aramburu was found guilty and shot dead. A communiqué issued by the Montoneros announced that the president was executed in the name of the people.

On the same day, Cox wrote an editorial condemning the execution. Aramburu was ruthless when dealing with those he considered enemies, and everyone knew it. But his murder by a shadowy terrorist group spread a new kind of fear across the nation. Violence quickly spiraled out of control. Wealthy citizens hired personal bodyguards out of fear of being kidnapped and held for ransom. The Herald reported a new kind of terrorism was growing.

Union bosses became targets of assassinations. Many had amassed huge personal wealth, stealing overtly from their organizations. The assassinations were frequently the work of the military or opposing union forces but often were attributed to the Montoneros. The ERP guerrillas, whose cadre had been trained in Cuba, kidnapped

170 businessmen in 1973 alone, securing multi-million dollar ransoms. From time to time, they still played at Robin Hood, once requiring that $1 million in protection money received from Ford Motor Company be spent on medical equipment for the poor.

Cox later wrote Manigault about out-of-control rightist elements as well as the kidnapping of several U.S. executives by left-wing terrorists who demanded ransoms to finance operations. Cox also told him that the newspaper had a crucial role to play in Argentina's future.

The letter provoked an immediate response from Manigault:

"With the future so unpredictable in so many ways, we certainly agree that the thing we ought to do is go ahead and put the newspaper itself on the securest and most independent footing possible. Certainly it is the purest and most satisfying way to proceed as conscientious journalists, and of course continuation of the Herald as the best newspaper of its kind is our number one goal."

The two men could not have been more in agreement, and there would be challenges and terrible dangers ahead that would test their resolve.

CHAPTER 4
A DEADLY VIRUS
(1 9 7 0 - 1 9 7 3)

"It's going to be 12 bags," Maud Cox said as her husband was leaving for work.

"How many?" he asked.

"Twelve. So as soon as you are finished at the paper, hurry home. We have to be at the airport at 8 p.m."

With four children to get ready, planning for a vacation in Italy in the summer of 1970 required careful organization. Maud had been packing for weeks and arranged with friends to take the Cox entourage in three cars to the airport. Cox came home, the family made it to the airport on time, and all were safely off to Rome.

They rented several rooms at the Pensione Sitea in the heart of the ancient city. Aunt Norma and Uncle Donald crossed the English Channel to meet them. Once the wooden shutters of their hotel room were opened, the window offered an angled view of a quiet plaza paved with stone across which an old woman shuffled en route to the bakery, just below. A tantalizing aroma of fresh-baked bread rose to fill the hotel room.

Early each morning, the Coxes planned their day together and proceeded to walk the ruins of Rome. They traversed the hallways and exhibition rooms of museums and rested often from the exhaustion that results from attempting to absorb too much art and too much history in so little time. Each afternoon, as the boys soaked their aching feet in the Fontana di Trevi, Robert, 7, practiced his Italian with anyone who would listen.

DAVID COX JOUNRNAL: MAY 2007
One day at lunch in a small café, the waiter asked Mother, as

he pointed toward me, *"Signora, il bambino vuole mangiare il spaghetti al burro?"*

"No! Please, I don't want to eat a donkey," I shouted.

She explained that "burro," which in Spanish means "donkey," is "butter" in Italian, and that was very good news.

Later, I stared at the Leaning Tower of Pisa, thinking it surely would fall. At the coliseum, it was as if I were sitting upon that magic carpet of leaves as I rested after the long climb up what seemed to be a thousand stone stairs. I imagined gladiators fighting each other and lions in the center of the arena, filled by a cheering crowd.

The vacation was a perfect respite from the troubles back home. It was as though Argentina itself were suffering from a deadly disease. The sickness was pervasive, the cure elusive. Cox had spent 11 years in Buenos Aires covering coup after coup, upheaval and violence. His need to get away, if only briefly, became overpowering at times. The family's side trip to the Baths of Carcalla, built in 212 A.D. for public use, was more than a vacation. Immersing themselves in the imaginary waters of the ancient baths was a spiritual cleansing, especially for Bob Cox. It was rejuvenating.

Not long after the Coxes returned to Buenos Aires, their daughter Ruth was born on April 2, 1970. She was the fifth and final child. The contradictory rhythms of their lives persisted: great joy in the context of great heartache. At the time of Ruth's birth, another junta took power in Argentina and again the generals promised peace and prosperity. As usual, they delivered bloodshed instead.

A Fiat auto executive was abducted by terrorists in Buenos Aires and died in a shootout with police who were trying to rescue him. Kidnappings were common, and heavy ransoms were used to finance terrorist operations. Bodies riddled with bullets were dumped on the streets, and the Herald dutifully reported the carnage. News Editor Andrew Graham-Yooll kept a book of the names of victims who had been identified. Cox kept his own handwritten list of the victims as well as a brief accounting of each man, woman and child.

The military was overwhelmed by the violence, and the clamor for Peron's return from exile increased. The generals decided to hold elections and withdraw from politics. The Peronists were victorious, and a new Argentine head of state,

Hector Campora, was sworn in on May 25, 1973. *He was the president that never was.*

Though Peron was allowed to return to Argentina after 18 years in exile, he was barred from running for the presidency. Campora was his proxy. The slogan that Peronists chanted during the election campaign described the situation perfectly: "Campora in government; Peron in power."

Unlike inaugural ceremonies of the past, this one was remarkably informal. Relations with Cuba were restored, and Castro's vice president attended along with other Latin American left-wing leaders. Jacobo Timerman, a prominent Argentine journalist and owner of Buenos Aires' daily newspaper La Opinion, was in attendance, along with Bob and Maud Cox of the Herald. As he passed the Coxes, who were already seated, Timerman said: "News Flash. They are going to release all the prisoners tonight," before hurrying to his designated seat among the honored guests.

Indeed, President Campora issued a blanket amnesty to all political prisoners, including convicted murderers. Cox wrote an editorial condemning the releases, describing the action as an opening of the gates of Hell. He warned his readers to expect more violence.

The English scientist Sir Isaac Newton said in 1687 when he published *Philosophiae Naturalis Principia Mathematica*: "For every action, there is an equal and opposite reaction." He developed his theory in physics. But, in essence, Newton's dictum became Juan Peron's mantra: *"La violencia de arriba engendra la violencia de abajo* (Violence from above will create violence from below)." As obvious as this is today, it wasn't so clear in Argentina in the 1970s. In the midst of the political fog that engulfed the country, the Herald's editorial staff warned in 1974 of the dangers ahead. The editorial "Lament for Three Policemen" noted:

> *Three policemen were slaughtered in cold blood by terrorists on a single day this week. And how right those who argue that only atrocities against the left seem to prompt condemnation and protest were proved! None of the human rights groups expressed outrage. None of the lawyers or politicians who have made their names as defenders of the people spoke out.*
>
> *Of course, we all know that the people who point out those organizations, which set themselves up as guardians of liberty, do not care that policemen or prison wardens are killed... They usually want to justify some particularly nasty piece of brutality that they*

themselves secretly approve. But they are more honest: They don't form organizations to defend human liberties and they don't go around denouncing atrocities. If you want a really honest reaction, you have to ask ordinary people what they think. Then you find people who care about the loss of life and all that it means in human terms.

It is the ordinary person who immediately thinks of the policeman's widow and his children and wonders how the family will get by. It is the ordinary person, who relates to those who have lost someone they love. The ordinary person does not ask himself or herself what side the victim was on. The ordinary person wonders vaguely if there is a way to help and if there is a way to put a stop to politically motivated murder before it is accepted as part of the Argentine way of politics.

It is not so long ago that local commentators were wondering whether the country was heading toward a Guatemala-like institution of violence. Nobody seems to mention Guatemala any more, probably because we are too close to that scale of violence for comfort. There is also sad evidence in the conversation of the young people that they now accept without question the use of criminal methods for political purposes. The posters that went up on the Berkeley campus with the words, "We love you Patty" and showing the Hearst heiress with a machinegun are echoed here among the young people who see nothing wrong with killing and kidnapping for a cause they approve. Although they probably won't admit it, their attitude is exactly the same as that of a government which condones torture.

Criminal action is not a legitimate form of political protest any more than brutal repression of dissident opinion is acceptable as a means of maintaining public order. If only the quiet voice of the civilized conscience of the ordinary person could make itself heard, we might see an end to the violence. That conscience needs arousing, for there is a drift toward acceptance of violence. This time, not only didn't the civil rights' groups condemn the murder of the three policemen – no voices were raised to condemn them for not condemning it … .

Cox realized at that time that these words placed his own security and that of his staff at tremendous risk. He looked around the cluttered newsroom. In one corner near the constantly clacking waist-high Associated Press wire machine sat News Editor Andrew Graham-Yooll and next to him was Assistant Editor James Neilson. The Herald's chief reporter Toby Rowland was buried behind stacks of books and notes at his desk in another corner by the window. Dear old Toby, Cox thought. Here was a man in his late 70s who worked now as he did his first day on the job at the Herald more than 25 years previously. Toby was the incarnation of Mr. Banks, the good-natured character in the "Mary Poppins" musical who was ready to fly a kite with anyone, any time. Cox was surrounded by bright-eyed decent souls, and Toby was the best of them.

A former Herald reporter was husky Bill Montalbano, a big-bearded man who became a well-known American correspondent, having covered wars on three continents. He often visited the Cox homes bearing Fisher-Price gifts for the children, always paying special attention to David, his godson. Their playmates in the neighborhood were envious of these *juguetes Americanos* (American toys).

Walter Klein, a slightly built academic in composure and style, was another family friend. He was a young lawyer who met Cox in the 1960s after Klein earned a master's degree from Harvard and returned to Buenos Aires. He was full of ideas about how Argentina could become a great nation. He wrote for the Herald occasionally before becoming a prominent government official. His son joined the Cox boys at St. Andrew's Scots School, a preppy British academy founded in Argentina in 1838 by Scottish settlers.

All three of the Cox boys attended the academy and grudgingly wore their uniforms – grey woolen pants, a tie and a blazer that had on the upper left an embroidered shield with a Saint Andrew's cross over a representation of a thistle. Legend has it that the Scots were alerted that an army of Norsemen was nearby thanks to a thistle. It was in the middle of the night and one of the attackers stepped on the prickly plant and cried out loudly in pain.

Bob Cox's best friend, Harry Ingham, had two sons who attended St. Andrew's Scots School. They too were raised in Scottish-British tradition. Ingham came into the Coxes' lives unexpectedly through Juan Peron.

Upon his return to Argentina in November 1972, Peron moved into a mansion next door to the Inghams in Buenos Aires. Peron's huge dwelling on Gaspar Campos Street soon became the center of Argentine political power. Cox wrote an editorial about Peron's return and noted that masses of people gathered regularly in and around the general's house. Soon afterward, Ingham called the newspaper office.

"Hello. Mr. Cox. This is Harry Ingham speaking. I am calling you about an editorial you wrote concerning Peron. I want to thank you for your comments. I am a neighbor of Peron."

A few days later, Ingham appeared at the newspaper office, introduced himself to Cox and took the editor to lunch at the Alexander restaurant. They were an odd couple – Cox, tall, lean and disheveled looking; Ingham, big-boned and clean-shaven with slicked-down hair. One was soft-spoken, reticent; the other was loud, loquacious.

Inside the Alexander, a quaint Anglo-Argentine restaurant, the men found a seat at a table near a wall on which hung a large portrait of Queen Elizabeth. Ingham thanked Cox for expressing concern for the feelings of Peron's neighbors. He said tumultuous crowds gathered at the mansion, which was purchased for Peron by supporters. All day long they chanted, "Viva Peron! Peron! Peron! How great you are!"

Within short order, the new friends also established that Harry and Maud had attended the American school in Buenos Aires together as children.

The circumstances that brought the Inghams to Argentina were ominous. Ingham, born Jewish in 1932 in Berlin, was 8 years old when his family left England for Argentina on June 21, 1940, from Tilbury, the same port from which Cox departed 19 years later. A year earlier, Harry's father, who was the manager of the Berlin office of a private telephone company, received an unexpected knock on his door.

Standing at the door was another company employee who wore a swastika armband. He said from that moment on, each decision Harry's father made must first be approved by the *Schutzstaffeln*, Hitler's elite guard unit. Mr. Ingham understood what that meant and soon fled with his wife and children first to England and then to Argentina where, through family connections, they were allowed entry.

Although Harry Ingham was aware of the Peron's Nazi sympathies, this did not bother him as much as the noisy admirers. Ingham became an excellent source for Cox with news about the aging Juan Peron, whose post-exile resumption of power led first to an enthusiastic hero's welcome and then to an unprecedented explosion of violence. Peron was dying. Against his doctor's sound advice, he returned to Argentina because he yearned to relive his glory days.

CHAPTER 5
AN ENGLISHMAN'S CONSCIENCE
(1973-1975)

The country was in tumult on June 20, 1973. Juan Peron was back, and legions of his admirers believed everything was possible. Pan Am Flight 201 landed at Ezeiza International Airport near Buenos Aires. Climbing down from the plane was a man who represented all that was good in the world. He was not, however, Argentina's legendary leader back from exile. This man who was greeted from the tarmac enthusiastically by loving fans was the legendary *el Zorro*, "the Fox!"

Actor Guy Williams carried in his suitcase the accouterments of his fame – the sword and black mask, hat and cape. Children and adults cheered wildly. It was Williams' second visit to Argentina, and the people held a special place in their hearts for Zorro and the character's alter ego, nobleman Diego de la Vega.

All five of the Cox children knew Zorro was coming to town. In preparation, they planted themselves in front of the family's black-and-white television set on which they watched reruns of their hero. They beamed when the moonlight broke through the dark clouds and shone into the eyes behind the mask. A shock of energy ran through each of them as he swished the tip of his sword and carved a "Z" across the chest of the military uniform that represented corrupt authority.

Cox also knew the story of Don Diego de la Vega's fight against injustice. He wrote that there was a great need in Argentina at that time for Zorro himself to step down from a huge jet plane and put an end to the violence. His column was titled, "Zorro for President," and he signed it with his own initials, "RJC."

> ... *if the vote were extended to 4-year-olds and over, there would be no doubt about the outcome. Zorro would lead the nation ... Zorro, the character whose "Z" you may see on the walls of Buenos Aires alongside other political graffiti, turns out to be a relaxed Sicilian-American called Guy Williams (that's an Americanization*

of Armando Catalano), who is still a little bemused by the discovery that jet lag comes with fame.

Guy Williams met with Cox at the Florida Garden café, near the city's tourist district. Williams told him he was overwhelmed by his reception. Everywhere he went hundreds of admirers, young and old, stopped to say hello and get his autograph.

"Why are you so popular here?" Cox asked.

"I don't know," Williams said between sips of *cortado*, an espresso coffee topped with skimmed milk. "It's as if I have stepped through the looking glass when I come here."

The character who wore the mask represented for Argentina something larger than life. Zorro righted the wrongs that tyrants had forced on the citizens. "The character has touched a chord in this society," Williams noted. Cox was intrigued. The presence of this swashbuckling hero in their midst was a form of magical realism. The country embraced him for the hope he represented.

"What is it like to play the role of a chivalrous young nobleman, a lover of music and poetry, a wealthy don who owns thousands of acres of ranch land in California, a masked fighter for justice?" Cox asked.

"When I walk into restaurants here, a ripple of polite applause usually fills the room," Williams responded. "It's as if I'm living out the fantasy."

He shared Cox's understanding of the on-going Argentine tragedy. He worried about politically motivated crimes plaguing the nation, he said, adding that he had noticed some of Peron's burly secret service agents following him around.

"Are you concerned for your own safety here?" Cox asked.

"Before I arrived this time, my friends solicited pledges to pay a ransom, if necessary," Williams quipped. "Once we reached $15, I said, 'What the hell, I'll go because if I am kidnapped it will be by kids whose demands will be: No more spinach, no more homework, no having to go to bed at night!' "

The Cox family bonded with Guy Williams, a connection that was as deep in real life as the children's love for his fictional character.

DAVID COX JOURNAL: JUNE 2007

One afternoon as I was returning home from school, the attendant at the desk in the lobby of our apartment building blurted out, *"el Zorro esta arriba con tus padres!* (the Fox is upstairs with your parents!)." Imagine the look on the face of a 7-year-old boy when he learned that Zorro was waiting upstairs in his living room! Every child on our block came to our apartment that day.

I have a photograph of Zorro, unmasked, alongside me at Christmas in our house in Highland Park. He stands erect and smiling with his left arm around a skinny, shivering, bare-chested boy who has just leapt out of the swimming pool.

"OK, everyone to the tree, Zorro is here!" Mother yelled.

Our Christmas tree was a huge, freshly cut pine, so tall that nobody was able to put lights at the top because we didn't have a ladder that could reach its crown. We stood there, Zorro and me, as the camera flashed again. Guy Williams often visited with us after that. His love for Argentina was so great that he lived in Buenos Aires for the rest of his life. He died in 1989 in his apartment in the city, only a few blocks away from ours.

Argentines enjoyed the escape from reality that the adventures of Zorro provided. Argentina's dirty war intensified, and Cox was one of only a few writers who explained what was happening in the most prosperous country in Latin America at that time.

V.S. Naipaul was another, and when Cox heard that the renowned author had arrived in Argentina to write a series of articles, he sought him out for an interview. Naipaul was an expert on post-colonial societies and a scathing social critic. They first met in 1972 and again when he returned in 1974.

For Naipaul, who would receive the Nobel Prize for Literature in 2001, there was little to like about Argentina. His criticism of Argentine racism was acute. He wrote that not even Jorge Luis Borges, the nation's greatest writer, could invent a story as incredible as what actually was happening to the nation.

Naipaul, a Brahmin from an Indian family who settled in Trinidad, was educated at Oxford University after winning a scholarship in Trinidad. He had exquisite manners and could easily pass as an English nobleman were it not for his dark complexion. He simply did not look like a famous English author. It did not take long for him to become acutely aware of Argentine racism.

Maud Cox remembers the morning she met Naipaul. It was 2 a.m. and she was in bed, awakened by the mellifluous English accent of someone talking to her husband in the living room. Bob brought the author home for coffee. She discovered that Naipaul did love one thing about her nation – a lovely Argentine woman named Margaret, who happened to be one of Maud's friends. Margaret revitalized Naipaul's writing at a critical time in his life.

Cox first got to know Naipaul by reading "A House for Mr. Biswas," which is based on the author's experiences as a child. He met Naipaul on his first visit to Argentina, and was captivated. He also made arrangements with the New York Review of Books to reprint Naipaul's essays about Argentina in the Buenos Aires Herald.

Soon afterward, Cox was told that Naipaul's observations about Eva Peron, calling her death the "public passion play of the dictatorship," had upset the left-leaning Montoneros organization. The Montoneros called together a council of war to consider whether or not they should blow up the Herald's newspaper plant for publishing the stories.

Cox was not intimidated. When Naipaul returned to Buenos Aires in 1974, he introduced him to Catholic priest Carlos Mugica, an active member of the Third World Priests' Movement, which was devoted to helping the poor. Mugica supported Peron and his policies and believed that socialism was the only solution.

Cox and Naipaul listened as Mugica described his Utopian vision for Argentina and the world. The innocence of Father Mugica, a handsome man with startling blue eyes, clashed with Naipaul's dark worldliness. The passionate young priest spoke glowingly of Mao Tse-tung and Communist China. He told them that cars should be banned and that people should ride bicycles instead. Argentina should provide free health care and education to all children, he said, and he believed that the goal could be reached through non-violent means.

On May 11, 1974, Mugica was murdered after celebrating Mass; shot five times at close range. The last round was in his back. Bob and Maud Cox attended his funeral. She wrote in her diary:

> Bob and I arrived at the Recoleta cemetery and found a huge throng of mourners from the slums who looked completely out of place in the elegant surroundings. They tried to hush their sobbing but could not hold back their tears. Two middle-aged women from the slum where Father Mugica had built his simple church came to me and, in our shared sorrow, we embraced. 'Señora what's going to become of us now?' one of them asked.

We no longer have Evita, and now they've taken our beloved young priest.'"

Mugica's murder was the work of a covert, government-supported death squad. Jose Lopez Rega, a former policemen and Peron confidant, organized the hit. Lopez Rega, also known as *el Brujo* (the Sorcerer), was essentially a household servant of Peron who took advantage of the aging president. Claiming that he was God's messenger Gabriel, Lopez Rega became Argentina's Angel of Death whose mission was to cleanse the country of leftists.

El Brujo's first victim was Argentine Sen. Hipolito Solari Yrigoyen, a human-rights activist and close friend of the Coxes. The senator, a great-nephew of former President Hipolito Yrigoyen, got into his car one day and inserted the key into the ignition, which detonated a bomb that had been placed under the driver's seat. He was severely wounded but survived.

Subsequent hits ordered by Lopez Rega were more effective. The murders decimated the intellectual left. *El Brujo's* assassins were members of an anticommunist alliance known as Triple A. Its victims included legislators, writers, artists and musicians who were warned beforehand to leave the country or risk death. Insanity reigned in Argentina under the influence of Lopez Rega. UFOs were often sighted. A "Martian" was interviewed on national television.

"What is your mission? Where do you work?" a reporter asked.

"I work for the police. My true age is 1,000 years old, but my documents here on earth state that I am 48 years old," the "Martian" responded.

People believed such rubbish yet they didn't want to openly admit the fact that innocent citizens were being murdered in the streets when caught in the crossfire between terrorist gangs or kidnapped through mistaken identity. Left-wing terrorists targeted the middle and upper classes, and the Peronist government did nothing to protect them. School administrators asked parents to volunteer to help safeguard their children.

"I frankly don't know what we are doing walking in circles around the school," Cox told his wife one day after dutifully serving his shift on the campus. "One lady brought her pastry rolling pin, convinced that she could use it to scare away the terrorists."

But others seemed indifferent about the killings. Some were convinced that they would be safer as a result. Maud Cox, who was raised in a family of Argentine traditionalists, noted in her diary that many people happily went about their daily routines as if nothing unusual was happening. "These images clashed with my reasoning ... they short-circuited my brain and ... the structures within me were breaking apart."

The Cox's teenage daughter Victoria was told at school that it was safer if she and her classmates did not congregate. She was to do her work alone. The irony was that Victoria was never one to work in groups before; she had been previously reprimanded for being a loner.

Every morning before school, the family sat down together for breakfast and prayed for strength. It was a daily renewal of vows for unity in the midst of a fractured world. Breakfast became a ritual, a way to prepare them for the fears and challenges they would surely face throughout the day. Cox never failed to participate in this family rite that began at 6 a.m. Most nights, he worked at his office or in the kitchen early into the morning, hammering away at his manual typewriter. Sometimes he got less than two hours of sleep.

DAVID COX JOURNAL: JULY 2007

On most days, Mother filled our lives with the sounds of classical music as her fingers moved gently across the piano's keys, bringing an uneasy sense of peace within the walls of our home. On Saturdays when my father could spend some time with us, he sang in his English accent, "I'd like to be under the sea in an octopus' garden in the shade." The Beatles' songs coexisted with the Chopin sonata of Mother's piano playing while the world around us brought new dangers.

The children stayed close despite all the distractions, and this was especially true of Peter and David. They were like twins, each knowing what the other was thinking and feeling. Defiantly, Peter held his older brother's hand as they left for school each day, and fear always followed. They were seldom free of anxiety. One day, a neighbor offered them a gift. A puppy was theirs if they wanted her, so the boys ran home to get permission.

"Ask your mother," Cox said with a twinkle in his eyes, and the boys knew Spotty was theirs. Aunt Norma later sent a photograph from England of Cox when he was a child. He sat proudly in that picture next to his dog Marcus. Spotty and

Marcus looked as if they came from the same litter.

The Coxes were preparing to take another vacation in July 1974 when Juan Peron died at the age of 78. The nation came to a sudden stop to mourn his death. Even Peron's enemies paid him tribute. It was the end of an era. Cox rushed to the Herald to put out a special edition. An argument between Cox and the pressmen's union ensued over what would be printed relating to the president's death. The union leaders said that they would not print the newspaper unless it was devoted entirely to praising the life of Peron.

Cox compromised. On the front page he ran a photograph of Juan Peron sitting in his presidential chair while being sworn into office the second time. His face showed great fatigue. "President Peron dies," the headline says. The special edition consisted of eight pages and few photos. Cox was convinced that Peron should have listened to the advice of his doctors to decline the offer to return to the presidency. It was impossible for the old man to fulfill his promise to end the violence between the left and right and bring peace to Argentina. Naipaul summed up the situation under Juan Peron perfectly: "He wanted to make his country great. But he wasn't himself a great man. Perhaps the country could not be made great."

It rained on the streets of Buenos Aires the day Peron was buried. The steady drizzle matched the tear-stained faces of tens of thousands of Argentines as they watched the funeral cortege. It marked a pivotal point in the troubled history of Argentina, and Cox knew it. Peron's return only brought more violence and disillusion. But the editor of the Herald would deal with the fallout later. On the day Peron was buried, the Cox family was on an airliner to France.

They landed and soon boarded a train that glistened in the night as it sped across the French countryside toward Festelemps, in the Dordogne. Dinner was served as the Coxes sat side-by-side in the restaurant car. Upon arrival, they were lodged in a lovely brick house on a hill overlooking the village. Later, they enjoyed a picnic with Aunt Norma and Uncle Donald, and the conversation was upbeat. When only breadcrumbs and an empty bottle of wine were left on the checkered tablecloth, coffee was served on a tray, and the children resumed their play. Young Robert grabbed his sister Ruthie, who was dressed as an American Indian, and "tied" her to a tree. Peter and David crossed swords and pretended to duel. David was dressed as a Musketeer and Peter as D'Artagnan. David won the contest. Peter disagreed. David rescued Ruthie and cherished every moment as a make-believe hero.

The next day during a visit to the caves of Lascaux, the Cox children were asked not to touch the primitive artwork of bison and men painted in a place utterly devoid of natural light thousands of years ago. The ancient drawings are symbols that were shown by elders to boys undergoing a solemn all-male ritual. When the boys returned to the light, they would no longer be children; they would be recognized as men.

The Cox siblings were fascinated by symbols painted more than 16,000 years ago as a way to enlighten young people about what to expect in life. They saw the drawings in the Great Hall of Bulls and were especially impressed by the unicorn.

That afternoon, the Coxes climbed a nearby rocky hill. The adults rested while the children rolled in a bright patch of soft green grass. In Perigord, they visited a 12th-century cathedral and scaled the narrow stairs of the bell tower.

Bob Cox was energized. His asthma was gone. But for the children, the view from the parapet was frightening – the gargoyles seemed to move slowly as the bell chimed. Rose petals covered the streets of the village below in celebration of a wedding as residents had done for more than 800 years. The groom walked to the church and was followed by practically everybody in the village.

The Coxes' return to Argentina was like going from the light of day to the darkness of the caves. They landed at Ezeiza Airport on Sept. 7, 1974. Peron was gone, and the country seemed orphaned. His widow Isabel, the vice president, assumed the presidency. She and her powerful inner circle issued decrees in 1975 that called on the armed forces to "annihilate" those people deemed to be subversives.

Peron had been in exile when he met Isabel in 1955 in a Panama nightclub. She was a dancer touring South America with seven other women when they met. She was 35 years younger than the general and only 43 years old when she became Argentina's first female head of state. Extremists on the left vowed to seize power as soon as her husband died. Her own military commanders moved to do the same. Meanwhile, street violence increased daily. Whatever respect the people had for Isabel disappeared as quickly as the blood of Argentine citizens flowed through the streets and into the drains.

At the Herald, Cox alerted his readers that more violence was coming. He met often with foreign diplomats. It was essential that he see them face to face and tell them what was happening because Argentina's national newspapers were not reporting all the news. A catastrophe was unfolding.

> *It is an inconvenient fact that all disobedience to promulgated law,*
> *whether civil or criminal, is from a strictly legal point of view, illegal*
> *and can be used to justify mobilizing the police power of the state. So*

it was in Argentina with the laws promulgated by successive juntas.

If the country had looked inward and paid attention to itself, tragedy might have been averted. But by May 8, 1975, hundreds of people were casualties of Argentina's "Dirty War."

> *There are, believe it or not, people in Argentina who, while claiming to be law-abiding citizens, approve of the political killings that are staining Argentina's international reputation with blood. They approve of murder, that is, as long as the victims are on the "other side." For some law-abiding citizens violence is acceptable – even welcome, for those who have stopped thinking – as long as the victims are 'leftist.' Who hasn't heard a respectable person say that the situation in Argentina cannot be so bad 'as long as they're wiping out leftists.'*

> *There is one enemy in Argentina today. It is an enemy that threatens to destroy this generous country and decimate its people. Unless we all unite – leftists, rightists and centrists – with those who are completely apolitical in opposing lawless, criminal violence (and this means rejecting the use of force against one's own political enemies), the prospect is too terrible to describe.*

Seven days later, Jorge Money, a writer for La Opinion, was slain. He wasn't the first, and he would not be the last. But in Cox's mind, this murder was symbolic. In the previous four months, 475 people had been eliminated. The execution of the 29-year-old economic journalist struck at the core of Cox's call for a free press.

> *Do we think so little of the power of the pen that we do not use it when we ourselves are threatened? Do we think that by not reporting the news we will have more impact than by publishing it?*

Argentines had not had enough time to bury all the dead when the violence escalated following the murder of army Col. Argentino del Valle Larrabure. He had been kidnapped in 1974 when the ERP terrorist organization attacked an explosives factory. He was tortured for a year before being executed. Cox wrote that no matter who dies in such a senseless political struggle, all humanity suffers the consequences:

Argentina's way of life is not the path of terrorism or what it might bring, and therefore terrorism must be defeated. But for the sake of human dignity, for the memory of Col. Larrabure and for many who are so easily forgotten, there must be a firm and clean finish to terrorism.

A month later, artist Menchi Sabat, a close friend of the Cox family and a Herald employee, disappeared. Sabat was an excellent illustrator and had impressed Cox with his drawings. His illustrations included characters from Jorge Luis Borges' "Book of Imaginary Beings" depicting 120 mythical beasts in folklore and literature. The magazine he worked for in Argentina was shut down by the military.

Maud Cox received the call that Sabat was one of two men kidnapped by armed men in civilian clothes who bundled them into an unmarked Ford Falcon car without license tags. Bob Cox wrote an editorial about the disappearance. In the case of Sabat, as in so many other abductions, police used unmarked cars to take people away. Many of those people never returned. *Is there any possible situation that would justify the use by police of unmarked cars without number plates?*

Sabat was lucky. He was released unharmed.

A few days after Cox asked his readers about the unmarked cars, he received a call from the press supervisor of the Argentinisches Tageblatt, a small daily that served the German community. The Tageblatt printed the Herald until a recent move to a new building at 455 Azopardo Ave. "You are about to get some unpleasant visitors," the caller warned. "They say they are police, and they are coming for you."

"Do they know where we are?" Cox asked.

"We gave them your new address. They're on their way."

Cox was waiting at the top of the stairs when 11 heavily armed men arrived. On the way to the Herald, they had picked up a heavy-set uniformed policeman to make the raid appear more legitimate.

"What's the matter?" Cox asked.

"Where is Andrew Graham-Yooll?" one of the men barked.

"It's his day off. If there are any questions, I can answer them. I will be glad to call him. He will come immediately."

"Nobody calls anyone," said another man who looked like a prototypical Scotland Yard detective. He wore a stylish tweed coat and smoked a pipe in marked contrast to the gun-toting men in dark leather jackets in the entourage.

One of the men turned to Fred Marey, the Herald's music critic, who was sitting at his typewriter. Waving his gun and aggravated because Marey was ignoring him, the officer shouted, "What are you doing?"

"I am writing about music," Marey said and continued typing.

The men fanned out through the editorial department. Cox did his best to calm the staff. He called Andrew Graham-Yooll by phone and asked him to come in immediately. When the Herald's news editor arrived, the well-dressed detective demanded that Graham-Yooll accompany him to the police station.

"He is a terrorist suspect," the detective said.

Cox insisted on accompanying them, and all left in unmarked Ford Falcons that were waiting outside. They entered Federal Police Headquarters via an underground garage. Cox and Graham-Yooll were escorted to the third floor. A radio blared, drowning out the screams of people being tortured in the basement.

"Lindo programa hoy, eh? (Nice program we have today, huh?)," a guard asked with a smirk.

The police held Andrew Graham-Yooll because he had covered press conferences held by terrorist groups. They suspected he was connected to them. Cox stayed with Graham-Yooll until 4 a.m., when he received assurances that the news editor would be released unharmed.

When Cox returned to the newspaper, he discussed the events of the evening with Basil Thomson, the soft-spoken journalist who had traveled halfway across the world to hire him. Thomson wrote a popular humor column for the Herald and later, in telling the story of the newspaper raid, produced one of his most satirical pieces. It was titled, "Wot, No Tanks?" in an obvious reference to the Gestapo-style raid on the newspaper office.

Soon afterward Peter Manigault and Frank B. Gilbreth Jr. met in the Post-Courier's executive boardroom at 134 Columbus St. in Charleston, S.C. The topic was the raid on the Buenos Aires Herald and the way that Cox and the others had handled it.

"You are a couple of cool cats," Gilbreth later wrote to Cox. Despite the light-hearted tone, the raid was a major concern for Manigault and Gilbreth. The Herald's independence had been challenged, and the safety and financial risks were enormous. But they stood firm in their support of the Herald, and each sent a letter to Cox saying so.

Gilbreth wrote on Oct. 29, 1975:

Mr. Thomson and Mr. Cox: We read with fascination your

accounts of the raid – "Wot, No Tanks?" If there's anything about the story that you can't print, please pass it along, as we are interested and sympathetic. With the track record of other trips in the unmarked Falcons, the trip to the station of Bob and G-Y must have been an exercise in (trying to purge my vocabulary of vulgarisms) fingernail biting. When the joking and bravado are forgotten, it still must be terribly difficult for you and your families. We feel for you. Give them Hell. Best, Frank.

Peter Manigault's letter arrived a day later:

Dear Bob: Having been brought up on the mythical-seeming tales of how perilous it was for us journalists during (post-U.S. Civil War) Reconstruction and some of the wild elections thereafter, it seems unreal that a friend and colleague has been literally under the gun in his own office in this supposedly more enlightened day and age.

You certainly handled it with courage and sang-froid and with complete and uncompromising journalistic integrity from the first-cycle news story to the excellent editorial to the human and humorous column.

I trust that the 'authorities' now realize what they are dealing with in you and Andrew. It seems incredible that Argentina, Lebanon and Portugal, of all places (I guess none of us are surprised by what happens in Ireland and Africa), are undergoing what they are.

It sounds a bit inadequate under the circumstances to say 'best wishes,' but needless to say we send them to all. Sincerely, Peter.

Shaken by the raid, the killings and kidnappings in Argentina that had now become what Cox described as an "orgy of blood," the editor feared there was no end to the slaughter. He called for urgent and tough measures within the law to deter terrorists. Twenty-four hours later, the Montoneros responded that indeed they would implement tough measures. They announced that Cox himself was marked for death.

With the economy in tatters and increasing political turmoil daily, Argentina was on the brink of civil war. Isabel Peron sent her henchman Lopez Rega out of the country to serve abroad as "ambassador extraordinaire." This, however, failed to improve her ratings. Unlike Eva, Isabel Peron could not capture the people's hearts.

As the end of 1975 drew near, Cox reported that more than 800 people had died from violence over the previous 12 months. The country was numb. The leaves of the trees outside his window office scraped ominously against the glass as he wrote an editorial titled, "Climate of Horror":

> *For a day or so, it is possible to contend, perhaps, that the violence is abating on the grounds that the latest victims are not publicly known. And then a general and his wife are slain. It is the attitude of not really caring, as long as personal interests are not affected, that created the climate in which the murderers operate with impunity. This is the attitude that helped begin the bloodshed. How many guilty people are there among us who supported murders because they thought they shared the same political beliefs? Unless the attitude is changed – and murder is seen as murder, whatever the supposed cause – the political violence will continue to destroy those values that make life worth living.*

Cox still held out hope for a solution to end the nation's bloodbath. But the word *desaparecido* haunted the Herald's news pages time and time again. He had heard the word prior to 1975 but did not grasp its dimensions initially. He knew that people sometimes went missing. It happened often in large cities such as Buenos Aires. But the idea that government agents were authorized to whisk large numbers of citizens away to secret prisons where they were tortured and killed was incredible.

While the national press continued to ignore the reality of *desaparecidos*, the Herald published story after story about the disappeared. The Herald was often quoted by Jacobo Timerman's newspaper La Opinion. A man as complex as Argentina itself, Timerman admired the "English gentlemen" at the Herald who refused to withhold the truth, who reported regularly that Isabel Peron's government was on the verge of collapse.

In a nationally televised address on Christmas Eve 1975, Gen. Jorge Rafael Videla, a man so thin that he resembled a stick-figure caricature, made it official. The newly appointed commander of the Argentine Army told the nation that order and security must overcome chaos in the nation. "Faced with darkness, the time of the awakening of the Argentine people has arrived," he said.

Gen. Videla – who had a reputation of being a brilliant career officer, a practicing Roman Catholic, a middle class family man and non-political – appeared to represent a new Argentina. He offered a glimmer of *esperanza* (hope) that the violence would end. Two months later, clips of a helicopter rising from the roof of the Presidential Palace appeared on television. Isabel Peron was taken away after being deposed and would be kept under house arrest.

"If only the quiet voice of the civilized conscience of the ordinary person could make itself heard, we might see an end to the violence," Cox wrote in an editorial.

CHAPTER 6
A SUNNY DAY FOR A COUP
(1 5 7 2 ; 1 9 7 6)

In the middle of the night in Paris on Aug. 24, 1572, soldiers surrounded the house where the prominent Huguenot leader Adm. Gaspard de Coligny was lodging. Forcing their way into the house, soldiers ran up the stairs to his room. The admiral was praying, after telling his servants to flee for their lives.

The soldiers broke down the door, and the first to enter Adm. Coligny's chamber was Besme, a servant of the Duke of Guise, with a sword in his hand.

"Are you Coligny?"

"Yes, I am," the admiral answered. "And you, young man, respect these white hairs."

As Coligny spoke, Besme thrust his sword through the French Protestant's heart, and then threw the body out the window. They seized his personal papers and left.

On March 24, 1976 – 404 years later – as the Coxes slept in their home in downtown Buenos Aires, a convoy of 14 army trucks stopped nearby at 2 a.m. on Avenida Libertador. Soldiers jumped out of the vehicles and ran into a nearby apartment building. They had come for Bernardo Alberte, a retired lieutenant colonel and prominent Peronist. The intruders kicked open the door and threw Alberte's wife and daughter to the floor. The women's heads were held down by the soldiers' boots as Alberte watched helplessly.

"*Te venimos a matar, Alberte!* (We've come to kill you, Alberte!)," they shouted before opening fire. The killers seized the dead man's papers and threw his bloodied body out the window. The women were spared.

Adm. Gaspard de Coligny was honored posthumously when a monument was erected in his memory on a street in Paris. Col. Bernardo Alberte was also given posthumous honors, and a plaza was named after him in Buenos Aires. Both were martyred, the Frenchman by Catholics, the Argentine by the military. Coligny was the first victim of the St. Bartholomew's Night Massacre. Tens of thousands of others followed. Alberte was the first of approximately 30,000 victims of Argentina's newest military dictatorship.

Alberte's assassination was not reported in the press initially; the coup was bloodless, according to a spokesman for Argentina's new ruling junta. The day after the tyrants took over *Casa Rosada*, (the pink-painted Government House), Buenos Aires' skies were sunny, and all seemed quiet in the nation's capitol. The tanks trundled back from the Government House, the scene of so many previous coups that most Argentines didn't bother to tally them anymore. It was just another holiday when the roar of traffic stopped and children thronged the streets. The Cox children spent the day at home.

The new president was the army's commander-in-chief, Gen. Jorge Rafael Videla, 50, generally viewed as a humble man who could save the country. The Buenos Aires Herald and other newspapers described him as a political moderate whose objectives were to halt the scourge of terrorism, end official corruption and restore democracy to Argentina. He became known as *la Pantera Rosa* (the Pink Panther).

Cox had praised Videla editorially when he was promoted as the army's commander-in-chief prior to the coup. He cited Videla's reputation as a dove among hawks that would purge the military of ruthless hardliners. Few Argentines knew at that moment that officers under the command of *la Pantera Rosa* had already exterminated many of their countrymen.

Following the coup, the appointment of Walter Klein as Argentina's new finance director in the Ministry of the Economy gave Cox reason for optimism. Klein had written for the Buenos Aires Herald in the 1960s after earning an economics degree from Harvard University. Klein's worldview coincided with that of Cox. Both believed in a U.S.-style free market economy. Klein was convinced that a resolution to Argentina's problems would be through economic reform.

"Once we get the economy right, the rest will follow," he told Cox repeatedly.

But Cox's optimism was soon shaken. Returning from the newspaper in the early hours of the morning less than a week after the military takeover, he sat down on the edge of the bed and gently awakened his wife:

"I'm very worried. Things are not going as we hoped. It looks as if our worst fears are coming true."

"Why? What makes you say that? Things can't get any worse than what we've already been through."

"Toopsy, the killing hasn't stopped. People are still disappearing."

The phone rang soon afterward. She picked up the receiver and a man who identified himself as a senator asked to speak to Robert Cox. "He is not here. May I take a message?"

"*Se temen cosas terribles* (Terrible things are expected)," the senator told her. Years later, Maud Cox recalled this event and recorded her thoughts in her diary:

> I could not understand why he should have these mixed feelings. The takeover was nonviolent. Not one shot was fired. I kept stressing that nothing could be worse than the anarchy that existed before the coup. I believed the new government would straighten out the country and call for elections in two years time. Gen. Videla, an army man, seemed to be a very caring person and the navy had always been democratically minded, so I did not foresee any problem there."

> The reality was very different from the general perception. In 1975, when Videla became army commander-in-chief, he led a campaign against the People's Revolutionary Army in Tucuman Province using counterrevolutionary methods to annihilate the guerrillas. He believed that radical measures were necessary against terrorists to bring peace. In October 1975 at the 11th Conference of American Armies in Montevideo, he declared that "as many people will die in Argentina as necessary to achieve order."

Harry Ingham and Bill Montalbano were skeptical about the new government all along, but the general view was that the country was in safe hands; moderates were in control of the military and would not allow harsh repression.

The Herald continued reporting killings and disappearances. Six days after the government was officially sworn in, the regime censored the media. Most newspapers and broadcast stations accepted censorship even though it was forbidden according to the Argentine Constitution. Most editors quietly cooperated in accordance with a "list of principles and procedures" issued by the junta. The editor of the Buenos Aires Herald did not. To Cox, it was obvious that someone in the military had ordered the killings and disappearances, and he sought to draw attention to continued acts of official terrorism. Less than a week after the coup, the Herald reported that 26 bodies were found burned, blown up and riddled with bullets in and around Buenos Aires.

As the Washington Post reported at the time, the Herald's news coverage and editorials were designed to prod members of the junta into action against far-right factions within the government. The post-coup murders had all the hallmarks of the same death squads the government was supposed to have dismantled. But Lopez Rega's killing machine never stopped. It had been perfected with the knowledge of those who were running the country.

Cox knew the death squads were back in business. His wife confirmed it based on what she was told in May 1976 by Newsweek correspondent James Pringle, a resourceful Scot who took over the magazine's Buenos Aires bureau after distinguishing himself as a war correspondent in Vietnam. Pringle lunched at the Cox home and later, as coffee was served, spoke of a conversation he had with an Argentine Army officer.

Pringle had been to a cocktail party the night before. Several military officers were among the guests, and he congratulated one of them on the government's pledge to restore democracy. He emphasized that it was important to operate within the law to eliminate the excesses in repression that characterized the previous administration. He told the officer he was relieved that the violence would soon be under control. He said he had been shocked to discover while investigating previous killings and disappearances that armed right-wing groups of men operated with impunity.

"They wore stockings over their heads to disguise their features," Pringle said.

The officer laughed heartily, saying, "That was us!"

After having lunch with Pringle, Maud wrote in her diary:

"I thought the story was crazy. No one with any sense would come out in the open and admit it. So I asked Pringle, 'That can't be true, can it?' His face took on a pensive look and he said 'Maud, I myself find it hard to believe, but he seemed to be telling me the truth. He was very convincing.'"

On April 11, 1976, the Herald reported that 101 people had died in political violence since the March 24 coup. Two days later, six more victims were noted. The government's response was to shut down newspapers that did not censor themselves. The military issued a communiqué dated April 22 specifically about press restrictions:

As from today it is forbidden to report, comment on or make reference to subversive incidents, the appearance of bodies and the deaths of subversive elements and/or members of the security forces unless they are first announced by a responsible official source. This includes kidnappings and disappearances.

Junta practices increasingly mimicked those used by Hitler in Germany. So-called "criminals" were picked up by authorities and never seen again. Their arrests were never acknowledged, and trials were never held. The suspects simply disappeared, never seen or heard again. The goal was to paralyze anti-government forces with fear.

Cox wrote a prophetic editorial about Argentina at that time. He cited the German philosopher Nietzsche: "If you look into the eyes of the dragon, you run the risk of becoming the dragon yourself."

Herald News Editor Andrew Graham-Yooll learned soon afterward that acclaimed Argentine writer Haroldo Conti was abducted on May 5, 1976. Before he disappeared, Conti sent a letter to fellow writer Gabriel Garcia Marquez (later awarded a Nobel prize) that he, Conti, was in mortal danger because of his left-wing views.

"Martha and I live practically like bandits," Conti wrote, hiding for fear of being picked up by government security forces. "Below is my address, if I am still alive."

Garcia Marquez said later that Conti had been advised by friends early on to leave Argentina because his name was on a right-wing hit list. But Conti refused. "I will stay as long as I can, and after that, God only knows."

Graham-Yooll wrote the story of Conti's disappearance and handed it to Cox, who published it despite the government's prohibitions. Conti's life was at risk and by reporting that he was missing, the military might be pressured into either announcing his arrest and giving him a trial, or setting him free. To give reports of abductions an official source, Graham-Yooll suggested that relatives of the missing come to the Herald to secure writs of *habeas corpus* and file them with the authorities.

Cox suggested to Graham-Yooll that one problem was that lawyers willing to sign the writs for their clients were also disappearing. Besides, there was no time to waste in searching for a courageous attorney. The story was published on the front page, and the Herald stood alone in reporting the abduction.

But Conti's fate had been sealed. Men with machine guns entered his hiding place, separated him from his wife and tortured him. His wife, blindfolded and kept in another room, was told she would be allowed to kiss him goodbye. As she did so, she noticed that her husband's eyes were not covered. She knew at that moment that she would never see him alive again. In Argentina, when the blindfold is removed from a condemned man so that he can say goodbye to his loved one, his execution is imminent.

Cox sent the following memo to his editor at Newsweek:

> *The military's reason for imposing censorship on the local press so that it does not report the macabre discovery of slaughtered, usually tortured, bodies on rubbish heaps, is that people need a rest from fear. But fear still stalks Argentina. I hope to take a specific case of one of the victims of what has come to be known as death squads (the identity and place will have to be heavily disguised) and paint a picture of the climate in Argentina and the challenge the military government must face if it is to restore normalcy to a country wracked by an underground civil war fought by small but fierce and ruthless bands of guerrillas. Regards, Cox.*

The first case confirming that the military was participating in state terrorism came to Cox's attention as the result of a mistake. A few weeks after the coup, a death notice that had been telephoned in to the Herald was published with an error. News Editor Graham-Yooll learned of this when he received a letter from the family of the deceased requesting a correction.

The letter writers explained that their son-in-law died under mysterious circumstances. Cox and Graham-Yooll drove to see them at their home 20 miles north of Buenos Aires. They were English expatriates who had settled in Argentina many years before. The couple served tea on china brought from England while they explained what had happened. Their son-in-law, whose name both Graham-Yooll and Cox promised would never be made public for fear of reprisals against the family, had been the head of the laboratory at the U.S.-owned Squibb plant in Zarate, an industrial town 55 miles northeast of Buenos Aires. At 2 a.m., there had been a loud knock on his front door. Members of his family were used to receiving emergency visits regarding the laboratory because Zarate's telephone system was unreliable. Looking through the stained-glass panel in the door, his wife recognized the silhouette of a helmeted policeman. The uniformed visitors explained that they had been ordered to take her husband in for questioning. She was surprised but not afraid, assuming that he would return home soon.

He did not return. She became frantic and began a search for her husband. No one could or would tell her what had happened. Two days later, her husband was found unconscious in a ditch. He was taken to a clinic run by Catholic nuns, but they were unable to save him. His wife was notified. A large crowd attended his funeral.

The man had attended the local university at night to get an advanced degree in chemical engineering and often invited younger classmates into his home so that they could study together. Naval authorities stationed in Zarate became suspicious. He had been picked up for questioning because some of the students were identified as militants. He was tortured, as his wounds proved, but when authorities realized he was not a member of any anti-government organization, it was too late. He was bundled off several miles away from Zarate and dumped, half dead, in a roadside ditch.

On the day he was buried, several unmarked cars sped past the cemetery, and leaflets bearing the emblem of the Montoneros, a left-wing Peronist terrorist organization, were tossed from the windows. It was an obvious diversion designed to make it appear that the victim had betrayed the Montoneros and was punished appropriately.

"For God's sake Andrew, if we know this by a mistake, how many things don't we know about?" Cox asked his news editor as they drove back into the city. The story was published without identifying the man by name.

A month later, almost by chance, Cox learned more about what had happened in Zarate. He had befriended Monsignor Kevin Mullen, an Irish-Catholic priest and secretary of the Papal nuncio in Buenos Aires, whose embassy was in a huge mansion next door to Coxes' downtown apartment. Friends and family members of people who were missing went to the mansion seeking help in finding their loved ones. Cox and Monsignor Mullen often worked together on tracing the *desaparecidos* and developed a close friendship.

The Monsignor was horrified by the disappearances, kept careful notes and compiled an ever-growing list of names. He took the list with him when he called on military commanders and appealed for their help in securing information about the *desaparecidos*.

The generals called Monsignor Mullen "the little red priest" to his face. He was short in stature but lion hearted. He ignored death threats and shrugged off efforts designed to intimidate him. The threats included a suitcase bomb left outside the mansion that housed Vatican diplomats. The bomb failed to go off.

Cox met often with Mullen, and both men tried to remain optimistic. But one day, the Monsignor called Cox and said, "Bob, I must see you. There's something terrible that you must know."

They soon met inside the nuncio mansion, once an Argentine ruling family's sumptuous home, that had been donated to the Roman Catholic Church. The dark room, with its heavy drapes and bulky furniture, was like a tomb, Cox thought.

"Bob, I've got to tell you this, though it's hard to believe. A man came to see me. He was in a terrible state. He told me that on the day after the coup, the navy was out on the streets of Zarate, stopping everyone and asking for identifications. He said they arrested him, took him away, tortured him with a *picana electrica* (electric cattle prod) and demanded that he name all the people in the *orga* (short for organization)."

The man told the Monsignor that he was in such pain and so afraid that he gave his interrogators the names of every respectable person he knew in Zarate. He told Mullen he had no involvement with the guerrillas and neither did the people he named. He said some of them had since disappeared, and he feared that he was to blame. He hoped the Monsignor could save them.

It was hardly surprising that Mullen was soon contacted by the Vatican and asked to leave Buenos Aires. The generals demanded it because he was interfering in politics. The Vatican elevated Monsignor Kevin Mullen by naming him first secretary to the Papal nuncio at the embassy in Paris.

A month and a half after the new government came to power, Cox wrote two bylined stories that ran on the front page of the Washington Post, headlined "In Argentina: Despite New Rule, the Nightmare of Violence Continues."

Cox described the press censorship imposed by the junta and the continued killings by right-wing death squads, which obviously were supported by government authorities. He wrote about the torture and subsequent death of the chemical engineer in Zarate. He described how the man's family at first could not bring themselves to believe that security forces tortured and left him to die in a ditch. He wrote that a major objective of the Argentine Armed Forces *appears to be to 're-educate Argentina' and the press seems to be first in line.*

Soon afterward, as Cox was leaving the Washington Post bureau in the art deco Safico building on Avenida Corrientes, he was approached by a young woman who asked him if he was a correspondent. Most foreign correspondents assigned to Buenos Aires worked in the Safico building and Carmen Beatriz Frascotto de Roman knew it. She was a high-spirited woman in her late 20s, with dark brown hair and the saddest eyes that Cox had ever seen. "Yes, I am a correspondent," replied Cox. "How may I help you?"

Carmen Beatriz de Roman and Cox walked to a nearby café where she told him that armed men in unmarked Ford Falcon cars had come for her husband, bound and blindfolded him in front of her and their 8-year-old son, and then took him away. She searched for him in vain. She sent telegrams to Argentine authorities, including President Videla. No one responded. She went to Plaza de Mayo to a government office where missing people were supposedly being traced. She was handed a queue number and told to wait outside in the line. She decided to seek out Bob Cox because there was no one else to whom she could turn.

Cox wanted to write her story. He told her that if the Herald published the bare facts about a kidnapping and there was no doubt the victim was not *un subversivo* (a subversive), there was a chance her husband would be released or at least legally arrested. But Carmen Beatriz de Roman was scared. She needed time to think.

Soon afterward, Cox received an invitation for a meeting with President Videla. The invitation followed a highly publicized luncheon in Government House in honor of the nation's leading intellectuals, including the writers Jorge Luis Borges and Ernesto Sabato. Both men welcomed the new government, assuming the junta would bring terrorist violence under control. Borges thanked Gen. Videla for leading the coup.

Pretty much everyone felt this way. Everyone believed that the military would stop the right-wing death squads.

Years later, Borges was criticized for backing the coup, but Cox knew why he did so. Borges was old and blind. He could no longer read and relied on what others told him. One day after the coup, Cox visited Borges in his apartment near Plaza San Martin. It was breakfast time, and Borges' meal was spartan: a bowl of dry cornflakes. Borges explained that, for a blind person, dry cornflakes are easy to consume.

He scooped up the cornflakes with his hands from the bowl. Then he sat with his cat and caressed her belly. I enjoyed walking with him in the neighborhood and hearing everyone say hello to him.

"Mr. Cox," Borges said. "I am hearing all these things. Is it true what they are saying?"

"Yes. It is true and far worse than what is reported."

Borges respected the Herald … He was asking me if it was true about what was happening in Argentina. I often read to him and told him what was going on, and this is how in one way he was informed, and it later caused him to speak out in Spain against the military government.

On the day of Cox's appointment with President Videla, he was ushered into a small annex to the president's office where two other journalists waited. Cox realized the meeting, so soon following the luncheon for the intellectuals, would be another attempt to win over the press.

President Videla, wearing a grey suit with light pinstripes, was mild-mannered as he greeted the trio of journalists. He talked in generalities about the plans of the government to bring law, order and democracy back to Argentina. The other journalists took notes, nodded and murmured their assent. Cox, tormented by what he knew, blurted out:

But, Mr. President, the disappearances are still going on. Aren't you going to stop that?

Gen. Videla's confident demeanor disappeared.

I realized at that moment he was not in control. He did not want to face up to the problem. The man astonished me because he seemed timid. He reminded me of a rabbit that might run at any time. He was nervous. He was an awkward man, and he showed no commanding presence.

One of the journalists, an editorial writer for the Spanish-language daily La Prensa, tried to calm the president. "When in power you have to do things that you might not like," the journalist said and cited Julius Caesar as an example of a great leader who sometimes had to be ruthless.

It was too late to turn the conversation back to pleasantries. I had spoiled the little get-together, but I had been given an insight into the true nature of the military.

CHAPTER 7
FAMILIES SAVED
(1974-1977)

More than two months after her husband was dragged away by armed men and every effort to trace him had failed, Carmen Beatriz de Roman asked that his disappearance be reported in the Herald. She and Bob Cox hoped to draw attention of the top military officials to brutal right-wing groups acting outside the law. Perhaps an investigation would be ordered, and her husband would either be legally arrested or freed.

"Two months is a long time," Cox reminded her, "and they might not want to admit that they have been holding him that long, or they might be afraid of what he would say if they let him go."

Mrs. Roman knew this was the last chance she had of saving her husband, if he was still alive. A story in Buenos Aires by the respected English-language newspaper might bring him back to her.

It was carefully written piece. Rosa Amuchastegui, the most trusted member on the Herald staff, took time off from running the classified advertisement department to translate the article into Spanish. On the Monday after it appeared in print, Cox took the translation to Government House and delivered it in person to Col. David Ruiz Palacio, the closest aide to Gen. Albano Eduardo Harguindeguy, the interior minister in charge of Argentine security forces.

"You are helping the subversives with these stories," Col. Palacio snapped at Cox.

"Just the opposite," Cox said. "We are helping you to restore law and order. President Videla himself has repeatedly said these lawless groups must be brought under control. Here is a case that will help you crack down on them. These goons surely aren't police or military because they maltreated this woman and her little boy and also stole $500 from her."

The Colonel picked up the four typed pages and read the first line of the story:

"Hace mas de dos meses que Carmen Beatriz de Roman vio a su marido por ultima vez. (More than two months ago Carmen Beatriz saw her husband for the last time.)"

The Colonel dropped the papers on his desk and stood up. The interview was over. As Cox was hustled out of the office on the ground floor of the Casa Rosada, he was adamant: "I want Mr. Roman to appear. What I want is for these cases to be brought out into the open. People should be arrested and tried if they are suspected terrorists. If they are innocent, they should be freed. The government can't go on allowing them to disappear as if they were non-persons."

Carmen Beatriz de Roman's husband was never found. She became a close friend of the Cox family, and when she lost her job, Cox hired her as a translator, which helped support her mother and son.

Cox had been receiving help from the U.S. Embassy in pressuring the military to respect human rights and trace missing people. He also befriended U.S. Ambassador Robert Hill, who was appointed to the post in early 1974 when the country was on the brink of being taken over by leftists capable of mobilizing thousands of young people for street demonstrations.

Hill angrily reported to the State Department that Argentine Foreign Minister Adm. Cesar Guzzetti was euphoric following his meetings with U.S. Secretary of State Henry Kissinger; he, along with other top state department officials, advised Guzzetti to finish the terrorist job quickly. "Guzzetti went to the United States fully expecting to hear strong, firm, direct warnings on his government's human rights practices. He has returned in a state of jubilation, convinced there is no problem with the U.S. government over the issue."

Ambassador Hill was furious. He told Cox that his concern for Argentine and Uruguayan human rights was in opposition to U.S. policy as applied by Kissinger, who had no intention of discouraging the Argentine military from using dirty-war tactics against citizens. This was confirmed in recently released classified U.S. State Department documents.

"An Uphill Battle for Bob Hill," was the headline of an article Cox wrote upon the ambassador's arrival. Hill was a distinguished U.S. diplomat with considerable experience in Latin America. He had served in Mexico, El Salvador and Spain.

He was a wonderful man who took everything with enormous

cheerfulness. While he was in Argentina he was a prime target for terrorists. I remember him telling me one day: 'I was tired of being caged in the embassy residence, so I decided to go to a restaurant for dinner. When the other diners saw me come in, everyone started leaving. They were scared that my presence would invite a terrorist attack.'

There were several attempts on Ambassador Hill's life, including the time when a sniper was spotted aiming a rifle from the window of an apartment building overlooking the garden of his residence and was quickly subdued. Early on, Hill warned the junta that the United States did not approve of human-rights abuses. On May 24, 1974, three Americans were picked up and tortured by Argentine security forces. They were fortunate to be released as a result of diplomatic pressure from U.S. Embassy officials. The Herald played a role in bringing these cases to the public's attention as well.

Overshadowing all else at that time were the killings of two respected Uruguayan senators, Zelmar Michellini and Hector Gutierrez Ruiz, who were living in exile in Buenos Aires. One was kidnapped from a downtown hotel and the other from an apartment in the exclusive Barrio Norte. Their bullet-riddled bodies were found inside a car along with those of two other exiled Uruguayans. Ambassador Hill sent a telegram to the State Department asking for instructions from the highest level on how he should express U.S. disapproval about what had happened to the Uruguayans. He wanted authorization to request an urgent meeting with Argentina's Foreign Minister. He proposed to ask the following:

> The U.S. very much sympathizes with the moderate policies announced by President Videla and had hoped to be helpful to Argentina in her process of national reconstruction and reconciliation. We fully understand that Argentina is involved in an all-out struggle against subversion. There are, however, some norms that can never be put aside by governments dedicated to a rule of law. Respect for human rights is one of them. The continued atrocities of (the government's) Triple A-type death squads – which have recently murdered Michellini, Gutierrez Ruiz and dozens of others and have just kidnapped a member of the Fulbright commission, Miss Elida Messina – are damaging the Government of Argentina's generally good image abroad.
>
> These groups seem to operate with immunity and to be connected

with the Argentine security forces. Whether they are or not, their continued operation can only be harmful to the Government of Argentina itself and cause consternation among Argentina's friends abroad. In view of the pace of developments, I would appreciate reply by immediate cable.

Although Hill disapproved of methods the Argentine military used against suspected opponents, the U.S. Embassy was expected to focus only on protection of U.S. citizens in the country. The concern Hill expressed about the death-squad-style murders of the Uruguayans and others went beyond official U.S. government policy.

The murders of Michellini and Gutierrez Ruiz were as blatant as they were gruesome. Their bodies were left like hunting trophies inside a small red car. The two other victims were identified as a young married couple exiled from Uruguay. Cox attended the funeral of Sen. Gutierrez Ruiz and was horrified to learn from his family that several of the kidnappers, members of the Uruguayan security forces, were in attendance.

Two days after the funeral, a man with silver hair who identified himself as Dr. Juan Pablo Schroeder came to the Herald to speak to the editor. Schroeder was a prominent lawyer from the Uruguayan capital, Montevideo. He had come to Buenos Aires after learning that the bodies of his daughter and son-in-law were found with the murdered senators. "I accept the fact that my daughter is dead, but I will not rest until I find my grandchildren," Schroeder told Cox.

Schroeder said he had tried in vain to get information from the Argentine government, military and police about his missing grandchildren. He received no help from the Uruguayan Embassy in Buenos Aires. He had contacted several local newspapers, radio stations and television stations, but no one seemed to care, he said.

Cox agreed to write and publish a story with photographs of the grandchildren on the Herald's front page. Pictured were Maximo, 3 months old; Victoria, 18 months old; and Gabriela, 4 years old. The article was headlined, "Help Me Save the Children."

Maud Cox noted in her diary:

Bob asked Dr. Schroeder for photographs of the children, and then and there he decided he would publish the story. It ran on Page 1 the following morning and the telephone rang continuously.

Government officials asked Bob why he published lies. But he told each government official that the story would be printed in a more prominent form until the children re-appeared.

Interior Minister Gen. Harguindeguy summoned Bob Cox to Government House.

"We want those children to appear," Cox told the general. "We will not stop writing about them until they appear."

"But Señor Cox, you are being taken in by these lies."

"You need to find those babies," Cox said. "Their grandfather isn't asking much – only for the return of his grandchildren. He isn't asking questions about his daughter."

"You are mistaken about this," insisted the general, his face purple with rage.

"No, you are mistaken. We will continue to publish the story until the children appear."

The next day, Cox published another story with another photograph of the children as well as a letter from Schroeder asking the kidnappers to return them. The following day at 8 a.m., the Coxes' home telephone rang. On the line was a journalist from another newspaper who said the children were found on the steps of a clinic in a suburb of Buenos Aires.

"Missing Children Safe and Sound," the Herald reported the following day.

> *I saw the children yesterday afternoon as they played with toys strewn around a room in the home of a cousin. They appeared healthy and happy, despite their ordeal. The 4-year-old has not said anything about what had happened. But she told one member of the Schroeder family that Daddy was looking after Mummy, who was sick.*

In a letter, Schroeder thanked Cox for saving his grandchildren:

> There are times in our lives when we walk down a path and encounter problems of a great magnitude which bring us face to face with dark depths. At such times even one's best friends disappear from our sight, but also great friends emerge, and such friendships last forever. To the heralding of the trumpet, and adhering to the cause, your name has now been forever imprinted in my life and my family's. When I returned to Montevideo, I was accompanied by the portrait of my daughter and the photographs

of the rescued babies that appeared on the front page of your newspaper.

I have never forgotten that my father – who honored his mother as 'the most English of the English' and who kept her last name Hosking – stated that simple acts go hand in hand with the greatness of the soul. For this reason, I want to express in these sentences, in my name, my wife's and my children's, and particularly on behalf of Gabriela and her brothers, that here in Montevideo our house on Millan Street 3835 awaits you every day from this moment on. There will be no need for you to announce your intention to visit us; the doors and our hearts will always be opened. With great affection, I salute you, Juan Pablo Schroeder.

Cox knew the press could play a key role in saving lives. He had to be careful, however, as he continued to press military officers to stop using illegal methods to round up and interrogate suspects.

It was a difficult relationship talking to some of them but I only did it when I knew I could help an individual case.

Meanwhile, Carmen Beatriz de Roman told Cox that people trying to trace their loved ones were going to an office in Government House where there were supposed to be records of prisoners transferred from one jail to another. The problem, she said, was the military officer in charge would see only 10 family members a day. Numbers were issued at 8 a.m. to the first 10 people in line outside. Each morning in front of Government House, a crowd gathered, and the line grew bigger by the day. On May 30, 1976, after returning home from work, Cox told his wife at dinner that he planned to take a nap before going to the Plaza de Mayo to talk to the people waiting for the place to open the following morning.

"What is it that these people want?" she asked.

"They are searching for loved ones taken away by unidentified armed men who appear to be members of the security force."

"But why do you have to go so early in the morning?"

"I want to be there when they start to arrive."

After taking a nap, he left the apartment and headed to the plaza. It was 3:30 a.m.

"Don't forget to take your medicine," Maud said.

Cox, who had been having severe asthma attacks, took a taxi to the plaza. The humid winter air assaulted his lungs, so he used his inhaler. The driver parked at a corner near the plaza. Cox got out and walked to a group of people waiting in line. Two women at the front said they had been there since 1 a.m.

Cox waited quietly in the queue. By the time the plaza clock struck 7 a.m., conversation was flowing freely among those waiting in line about *los desaparecidos.*

"Who took your son away?" a woman asked a man in front of her. She was dressed in a custom-tailored fur coat. "Was it the army?"

"The neighbors said it was the Army," the man said. "My husband, a lawyer, was picked up on the day of the coup by the army after he asked about a friend who had been arrested. You should go to *Regimento Uno* (Regiment One). Have you tried the federal police headquarters?"

"I went there to ask about my son. They told me he was all right, that he was being held under a special decree. They gave me the number, but my lawyer later told me it was the number of the wrong decree – the one that appointed the mayor of Buenos Aires."

Several people in line scoffed, knowingly.

"Then I went to the police headquarters, but they won't give you the time of the day there," he continued.

"Is he involved in politics? What is his name?" another woman asked.

"What do you want to know for?"

"I just want to help. My husband's on the boat, and there are 48 people with him. They might know about him," she said, going on to explain about a prison ship on which members of Isabel Peron's government and other political leaders were kept under house arrest.

"How is your husband doing?" another man asked the woman.

"They are well treated. They say some people have been given tremendous beatings in the police stations, but they haven't touched my husband on the boat. I've been here several times. You don't get anything out of them … It's always the same reply. There are no charges against my husband, only *presunciones* (presumptions)."

Cox waited with people desperately trying to determine what happened to their loved ones. And it wasn't only mothers who came to the Plaza. Men were among the first to gather in Plaza de Mayo when the initial disappearances occurred. Only later would the mothers become the dominant force in the nation's most famous human rights movement.

Soon after Cox's early morning visit to the Plaza, word spread that there was an Englishman, an editor at the Buenos Aires Herald, who deeply cared about the missing. Lines then formed early outside the Herald office, too. Each day, Cox interviewed as many friends and relatives of *los desaparecidos* as he possibly could.

To protect his reporters, Cox himself covered the story about *los desaparecidos*. One man affiliated with the Herald who was critical of Cox was an Argentine minority stockholder who played golf at a club frequented by army officers. Cox ignored him. When the mothers of missing people visited the newspaper office, they were met with some hostile stares from staff. But most of "the Herald family" was proud of their role in reporting what the other newspapers were covering up.

Meanwhile, Walter Klein, a top official in the Economy Ministry with daily contact with the military commanders, told Cox that he overheard expressions of their disapproval about what the Herald was doing.

"Bob, they think you must be a terrorist," Klein said. "Please be careful."

As a result, Cox decided to become better known in official and diplomatic circles. Perhaps this would help dispel rumors that he was a terrorist. The Herald was an international newspaper, and its editors were welcomed at most embassy receptions. Until then, Cox attended only major events. Along with his wife, who was of a well-known Argentine family, Cox increased his social contacts to gather information and to demonstrate that he and other members of his staff were simply doing their jobs by reporting the news.

One of those stories was about the abduction of Monica Mignone, a daughter of a former government official and devout Catholic who served in several military administrations. Mignone had been kidnapped because she worked with a "suspicious" group of nuns who ministered to the poor of Buenos Aires. Her father, Emilio Mignone, was devastated when she disappeared and upset that the local Catholic hierarchy, whom he knew well, ignored his pleas for help.

> *I had gone over to see Emilio Mignone and met him when he was trying to get the military to release his daughter. He knew that they had taken her to the infamous ESMA, the navy training school used as a clandestine prison and torture chamber. He could not believe his church would not help his daughter. The loss of his daughter caused him to devote the rest of his life to the cause of human rights. He was a wonderful man who deserved the Nobel Prize.*

It would be three decades later when both the New York Times and the British Broadcasting Corporation reported the conviction of Christian von Wernich, the Catholic chaplain, to the police. He was convicted for complicity in "seven murders,

42 abductions, and 31 cases of torture during the 1976-1983 'Dirty War,'" revealing only the tip of the church's involvement in that war.

Emilio Mignone would found the Center for Legal and Social Studies, the most effective human rights organization in Argentina. Mignone's first priority was to get the information out about people who were missing after being taken away by armed men. The major newspapers refused to publish reports about missing people, so he decided to purchase advertisements listing names of people who had disappeared. He collected enough money from the relatives of victims to purchase a full-page advertisement in La Prensa, which published the list as a *solicitada* (solicitation), which cost double the normal rate and freed the editor of responsibility for content. When the owners of La Nacion saw that La Prensa published the list, they also agreed to accept such special paid advertisements.

> *Most of the newspapers accepted the money. At the Herald we did not think it was right to do so. We would do anything in our power to save people, and we weren't going to take money for it. In the face of the newspapers' self-censorship, Dr. Mignone had found a clever way to make public what the government most wants to be hidden.*

The case of Monica Mignone again demonstrated that mere suspicion by the government qualified individuals to become *desaparecidos*. The kidnappings were often indiscriminate, subject only to the whims of anyone with a degree of authority. Sometimes, the kidnappings were retaliatory. The thirst for revenge seemed unquenchable.

Two months later, Montoneros terrorists detonated a bomb that had been smuggled into a dining hall full of police officers. Eighteen officers died in the blast, and 66 others were injured. Cox remembered the date because it coincided with an anonymous death threat he received against his own life.

Cox received a tip that the military planned to go on a killing spree soon. He called home and left instructions with his wife that Victoria must not go to a party with her classmates. "We've been told that they took a prisoner to the Plaza and machined-gunned him to death at the Obelisk. Victoria should not go out tonight," he said. "More killings are expected."

Bill Montalbano, the Miami Herald correspondent and close friend of the Cox family, wrote a story to draw attention to the risks the editor of the Buenos Aires Herald was facing, hoping it might help protect him. "Editor Keeps Head in Argentine Lion's Mouth," the headline said.

Montalbano's story summed up Cox's reporting on the disappearances. The article described Cox as a lonely voice of sanity in Argentina. Montalbano quoted the great writer Borges, who expressed admiration for Cox: "A man does what he must do, Mr. Cox. I count myself among your admirers."

Cox had become, as Montalbano put it, a legendary figure, adding that other newspapers would run stories about the Dirty War only if the Buenos Aires Herald printed them first. One of Cox's editorials – titled "Just Imagine" – attacked the military's use of unmarked cars without license plates during abductions:

> *Imagine for a moment what would happen if those Ford Falcons without number plates suddenly disappeared. And imagine what would happen if there were no more arbitrary arrests? Would it make a great deal of difference if those people suspected of being involved with terrorist organizations were arrested by uniformed policemen, identifying themselves, showing arrest warrants and informing relatives where they intended to take their prisoners?*

But the situation worsened. The telephone rang at 8 a.m. at the Cox residence on the day the Miami Herald published the story: "Bob, Bob. It's a terrible thing. Terrible. They've killed the priests," someone screamed through the phone line before hanging up.

Among Cox's best friends was a group of Irish-Argentines who put out a venerable weekly newspaper called the Southern Cross. Its editor was Father José Richards, a feisty Irish priest. Known and beloved as "Father Joe," he and Cox had established a strong relationship that grew even stronger as they shared their concerns about the violence in Argentina.

Father Joe had asked a friend to call Cox and tell him about "the St. Patrick's Massacre," which was an apparent retaliation for the bombing of the police dining hall. A right-wing death squad targeted the priests and seminarians at St. Patrick's Catholic Church in the upper-middle-class Buenos Aires neighborhood of Belgrano.

Cox called Bill Montalbano: "We need to go right now to St. Patrick's. It looks like they've killed all the priests there." He picked up the Miami Herald bureau chief at his hotel, and they drove to the church. A crowd of parishioners gathered there said armed men smashed the glass door of the parish house where three priests and two seminarians lived. The gunmen dragged them from their beds, made them kneel as if they were praying and shot them dead. Two messages were daubed in blood on the walls: "This is how we take revenge for our fallen comrades" and "This is what happens to those who poison the minds of our youth."

The youngest of the priests, Father Alfredo Kelly, had preached about the need for social justice in Argentina. His sermon upset certain members of the congregation. One of the seminarians had been a member of a Peronist youth movement aligned with the Montoneros. The two older priests were well-known conservatives. The next day, Cox's editorial and a front-page story stated that security forces were the killers and not "subversive terrorists," as the police were saying. The Buenos Aires Herald was the only newspaper in the country that reported in detail what had happened.

Shortly after the St. Patrick's Massacre, Maud Cox used her influence as a native Argentine from a highly respected family to support her husband openly in the quest to stop the killings. She knew full well her decision was a renunciation of her status as a privileged person. It put her life and the lives of her family at risk. The murders of the priests convinced her that Argentine armed forces were massacring innocent people.

"I was sickened by those murders. I was indignant. I decided at that moment I would stand by my husband on whatever he had to do," she wrote in her diary.

The following day, she accompanied her husband to the funeral mass at St. Patrick's for the slain clergymen. The church was packed. The bodies were placed in open caskets near the altar. The congregation walked past them while taking Communion.

Maud and Bob Cox joined the throng of sobbing parishioners who came to pay their respects. They solemnly filed past the five caskets in which the three priests and their two young assistants were lying, the victims' faces as pale as their shrouds. The mutilated bodies had been lovingly cleansed and blessed. They viewed the hypocrisy of the high-ranking military officers who attended the mass as a moral crime.

When the service ended, Bob and Maud left the church and went immediately to the U.S. Embassy. It was July 4, 1976. Neither spoke during the ride. Both were still in shock. They reached the embassy residence in time for the midday reception. Inside the main salon was Papal Nuncio Pio Laghi, who was talking to Ambassador Hill. Next to the ambassador was Argentine President Jorge Rafael Videla, standing erect in his crisply starched army uniform.

Surely President Videla would crack down on the Triple-A death squads now, Cox thought. After greeting Ambassador Hill, Cox turned to the president. "What has happened is appalling," he said. "We have come here directly from the funeral service at St. Patrick's. We are praying that you have the necessary strength to end this horror."

The President looked down at the floor as he shook Cox's hand. He could not look the editor squarely in the eyes.

When the reception ended, the Coxes walked out of the residence with its gold-and-cream furnishings, glistening mirrors and plush carpets. It was a lovely day. They departed through ornate wrought-iron gates and walked to their car, which was parked nearby. Standing there in front of them on Libertador Avenue was one of Argentina's best-known journalists. Traffic was heavy and he was hailing a cab. They offered him a ride, which he accepted. The Coxes tried to engage him in a conversation about the church massacre, but the journalist changed the subject.

"Did you notice that he didn't want to talk about what happened?" Bob asked Maud after they let him off.

"Yes. I wonder what is going on in his mind. It was strange," she replied. "This will be the attitude of most people now."

Many people who were once close to the Cox family had expressed similar disinterest in what was happening. The government propaganda was as effective as it had been in Nazi Germany when citizens pretended all was well. As long as it did not affect them directly, they did not seem concerned.

The official story was that Argentina's *desaparecidos* were terrorists who had fled to Europe with large sums of ransom money collected for the release of kidnapped business executives. Anyone who questioned the government or discredited the official story was *un subversivo* (a subversive). It was virtually impossible for any military officer to question what was alleged to be "state terrorism," but some did refuse to use illegal methods in the fight. Gen. Arturo Corbetta, commander of the Federal Police, was one of them.

Corbetta told Cox that, in the wake of the recent terrorist attack in the police dining hall, he called his men into a meeting at police headquarters and issued an order confining to barracks all those who were off duty. Their response was a mutiny. When he asked for help, the junta ignored him. His only choice was to resign. When he got home that day, he found his apartment ransacked. *"Terrorista"* was scribbled on a wall.

Maud wrote in her diary: "He was deeply upset. He told us that suspects were held in clandestine prisons and often moved around. He tried to stop the torture but was unable to convince the Minister of Interior, Gen. Harguindeguy, that the police must operate within the law."

Cox later learned that orders were given that all officers, including those with desk jobs, must take part in at least one military operation involving "Dirty War" methods so that all would have blood on their hands. Those who disapproved of the methods were forced to resign, then placed under surveillance. Corbetta was lucky. He was assigned to command a garrison hundreds of miles from Buenos Aires.

Illegal military operations to eradicate terrorism were massive in scale, but as daunting as the challenge appeared, at no time did Cox waver in his decision to do all he could to save lives. Threats against him multiplied. He was offered several opportunities to move to the United States but rejected them all. His focus remained on making the disappeared reappear.

The Buenos Aires Herald was virtually alone in reporting the truth in Argentina. Though the owners in Charleston, S.C., had maintained their support of the work of the Herald, Cox could not help but wonder if his job were in jeopardy or if the Herald would be sold because of the unrest. The answer came in a letter dated July 29, 1976, from Charleston:

> *Dear Bob: Bill Montalbano sent me a clip of his story about you and your situation, and needless to say it stirred both pride and unease in all of us here. I'm afraid I was guilty of assuming rather naively that one thing the military would be able to accomplish rapidly would be the re-establishment of public order. I want you to know of our continuing admiration and concern, and of our frustration that we can be of so little direct help to you and the Herald in a situation the grimness of which seems to be long outlasting our foolishly stirred optimism of a few months back. Peter.*

Cox folded the letter and placed it in his desk drawer. He was relieved to know that Peter Manigault was behind him.

Some members of the conservative Anglo-Argentine community complained that the Herald's editors were "bleeding-heart liberals" who were soft on terrorism. But the staff held firm to the newspaper's editorial line. Editorial writer James Neilson was caustic in his condemnation of the illegal methods used by the military. At times, Cox had to tone down Neilson's copy for fear of provoking the authorities unnecessarily.

The newly appointed Argentine ambassador to the United States, Arnaldo Musich, a respected economist, resigned his post in protest of the military's failure to respect human rights. There was some dissent among retired military commanders. Former Army Commander-in-Chief and ex-President Gen. Alejandro Lanusse told Cox the Argentine military was in a Vietnam-like morass, but he could not convince the junta to cease illegal anti-terrorist operations.

Meanwhile, the military's killing machine zeroed in on Herald staffers. News Editor Graham-Yooll was in mortal danger. Men were in an unmarked car and snapping photographs outside his home, his wife Micaela said. Several of the couple's friends had already gone missing. Graham-Yooll knew his life and the lives of his wife and three children were at risk.

In September and October 1976, the Herald published stories of more cases of the disappeared, a growing number of them children. Family members begged Cox to help them. Toddlers were not *"terroristas,"* so the Herald told their stories, and some were found as a result.

International pressure against the Argentine government intensified. Cox criticized comments made by Foreign Minister Adm. Cesar Augusto Guzzetti, who praised right-wing terrorist operatives as "antibodies" against left-wing terrorist "germs."

In the fall of 1976, a 19-year-old American Patricia Ann Erb, whose father was a Mennonite pastor, was abducted. Her father first met with U.S. Embassy officials, then contacted Cox at the Herald and asked that he publish a story on his daughter's disappearance. "U.S. Citizen Kidnapped," a front-page headline in the Herald proclaimed on Sept. 7. A photograph of Erb accompanied the story:

> *John Delbert Erb, a North American pastor, appealed yesterday for help in tracing his 19-year-old daughter. Patricia Ann was kidnapped on Monday night by a group of seven or eight heavily armed men. His daughter, who is a United States citizen, was taken from the family house in Floresta around midnight. Her father, mother and two brothers, aged 12 and 21, and an elderly woman who lives with the family were tied up and blindfolded while Patricia Ann was 'interrogated' in her bedroom. Before she was taken away, Patricia Ann asked to be allowed to say goodbye to her parents. The kidnappers refused.*
>
> *Neighbors said they saw a fleet of cars parked near the house on Belen Street. Mr. Erb, a Mennonite pastor, said the men painted signs on the patio of the house. They left the impression that they were*

terrorists taking vengeance against the girl for the death of one of their number. This conflicted with the behavior of the group. One of them was heard telling Patricia Ann that she had been traced through someone who was in jail.

Mr. Erb reported the abduction to the local police, who suggested he file a writ for habeas corpus. *He did this. The United States Embassy is working on the case.*

Patricia Ann Erb was released soon afterward.

Early in December 1976, Cox met with U.S. diplomats in La Cabana restaurant in Buenos Aires. One of them wrote the now declassified report about the case for the U.S. State Department that noted:

Mr. Cox is an Englishman of about 40 years of age who has been in Argentina some 20 years. His newspaper has been the most outspoken defender of human rights and democratic processes in Argentina. His wife, Maud, is an Anglo-Argentine lady of shrewd intelligence … Mr. Cox believes the government has not lived up to the moderate pronouncements it made on March 24. Cox described the situation as a terrible black night, which may be getting darker …

Bob Cox and his wife feel strongly that the United States has a positive role to play in all of this … They believe at the very least the Argentine Armed Forces would listen to the U.S. before they would listen to anyone else, and they felt that, if nothing else, the U.S. serves as a democratic example to the rest of the hemisphere.

Indeed, Robert John Cox clung to a slim hope – as the diplomat would observe – that President Videla was the most moderate of the junta, and if he were overthrown, the situation might worsen. But as 1976 drew to a close, it was clear the situation was not improving. Meanwhile, mothers of the disappeared, international correspondents, diplomats and others continued to come to the Cox home in Buenos Aires to get information about what was happening to *los desaparecidos*.

DAVID COX JOURNAL: JULY 2007

My brother Peter found peace of mind by playing soccer – with a tennis ball – which sharpened his athletic skills. Years later in South Carolina, he received a scholarship to play soccer at the College of Charleston. My sister Victoria loved horses and excelled at show jumping. She wore her equestrian uniform with pride and won numerous medals in competition at Highland Park. My brother Robert played the piano and mastered the music of Beethoven and Mozart. Our youngest sibling, Ruthie, adapted to her childhood as best she could while Mother reminded us that our sister needed special attention during those troubled times.

I played soccer and tried to do most of the things that children my age were supposed to enjoy. I also took it upon myself to stand guard over our family. I slept in the room by the back door of the apartment so that I could keep an eye on the back stairs. I volunteered for guard duty over our father's somewhat disciplined little army who used to line up shoulder to shoulder with mops and buckets in hand.

CHAPTER 8
DANGER AT THE FAMILY DOOR
(1 9 7 7 - 7 8)

Young Robert Andrew Cox, 13, walked into his parents' room and saw his father kneeling with left arm extended and his left hand clutching the top of the dressing table. With his other hand, he struggled to use his inhaler. The boy, frozen with fear, watched as his father gasped for air.

Bob Cox was more vulnerable to asthma attacks when under stress, and he was more worried now than ever about what was happening. Military officers told him there was no longer any point in his asking them about the *desaparecidos*. They were under strict orders not to discuss the matter with anyone from the Buenos Aires Herald. The fact that numerous diplomats, news correspondents, friends and others arrived at the apartment daily, all wanting to know more about the missing, made matters worse. The entire family was paying a tremendous toll emotionally.

"Every night as I prepared for bed, I thought I saw someone outside staring at me through the window," young Robert recalled. "I'd walk toward the window and pretend to be looking the other way until I reached the shutter strap. I'd grab it as quickly as possible, and the window would slam shut." He also stared for hours through the peephole in the back door to see if anyone was outside in the passageway.

Ruth, 6, timid and fearful, thought the large stones at the entrance to the apartment building were bombs that would explode at any second. Men in uniform frightened her. She heard more noises than ever outside at night. Were kidnappers coming?

One night, Cox told his wife that he had heard some grisly news and planned to check it out. "I heard that the Chacarita Cemetery crematorium is operating at night, burning bodies. I must see for myself if this is true."

"I'm coming with you," Maud insisted.

Soon they were en route to the massive cemetery, a 25-minute drive away. They drove past the gates and alongside a thick wall that encircled the burial ground. Despite the darkness, they could see a steady stream of smoke pouring from a tall chimney of the crematorium. They quickly turned the car around and left, saying very little to each other on the way home. Is this what was happening to the *desaparecidos*? Was this the fate of so many thousands of people who had gone missing?

Soon afterward, bodies, many bearing the signs of torture, washed up on the delta sands of Rio de la Plata between Argentina and Uruguay. Reports were filed by international news agencies, but the only mention of the gruesome discovery in the Argentine press was in the pages of the Buenos Aires Herald. Later, in what appeared to be a cover up, a paragraph in a Uruguayan newspaper mentioned that maimed and bound bodies of Asian sailors were found on the beach of a seaside resort. The general media in Buenos Aires reported this misinformation.

Rumors were rife because information released by official sources was sparse and often contradictory. Cox continued to meet with people who came to the Herald seeking help finding seized relatives. The junta believed the ends employed in their "Dirty War" against terrorism justified the means of doing so. "The battle we are waging knows no moral or normal limits, it is beyond good and evil," a high-ranking army officer was quoted as telling his men in a story that appeared in another Buenos Aires newspaper, which was as close as the media in general came to reporting what was really happening.

Cox wrote in an editorial that atrocities committed by Marxist and Peronist terrorists were no different than the government's use of similar forms of evil. Even he knew more than what he reported because several people who had been released from clandestine prisons begged him not to disclose his sources for fear of retribution. Incredibly, most Argentines lived within an illusion, trusting that the junta would soon bring the violence under control and return the nation to democracy through elections. The truth, hidden in large part by a complicit press, was that Argentina was experiencing its own Holocaust and few people not directly affected wanted to think about it.

Rodolfo Walsh, author of "Operation Massacre," an investigation into the ruthless suppression of a Peronist revolt in 1956 published in book form, had gone underground to run a clandestine news agency. On March 24, 1977, the first anniversary of the Argentine military coup, his newspaper ran an eight-page article he had written in the form of an open letter to the government. It itemized hundreds of incidents of torture and murder, and described the military's efforts to dispose of bodies by throwing them out of airplanes into the ocean. He estimated that 15,000 Argentines disappeared, 10,000 were imprisoned, 4,000 were killed and thousands more were forced into exile.

But Walsh's article, titled "I Accuse," appeared only in newspapers that circulated outside Argentina. The Montoneros, flush with ransom money after releasing kidnapped business executives, paid for his open letter to run as a full-page advertisement in the New York Times and major newspapers in Europe. The next day, Rodolfo Walsh was shot dead by Argentine security forces.

I sometimes think he willed his death. Walsh himself had taken up the gun, but at the end of his life he had returned to the "word." He was killed because of his words.

Cox received a telephone call from Jacobo Timerman. "Cox, where are they going to throw my body?"

Cox was surprised by the call. Timerman was the best-known journalist in Argentina. La Opinion was controversial because it was liberal editorially, yet Timerman worked hard to cultivate ties with the military in an attempt to expand his newspaper empire.

"I don't think you should worry, Jacobo. They won't touch you," Cox said. He knew that Timerman had close ties with the junta, as he had with past regimes. Timerman had earlier refused to receive members of a delegation sent to Argentina by Amnesty International to report on human-rights abuses. The delegation included British Lord Avebury and Father Robert Drinan, an Irish-American priest. Yet, much to the junta's displeasure, Cox and Timerman were tenacious in rooting out from others the military's darkest secrets of the "Dirty War."

Cox helped persuade Timerman to talk to the Amnesty International delegates. Afterward, La Opinion took a firmer stance on protection of human rights, often quoting stories and editorials in the Herald. Five months later, Timerman called Cox and said he feared for his life. Some of his writers were guerrilla sympathizers, and he knew it. Military intelligence officers had determined that a principal financier of La Opinion also managed the funds of the Montoneros. That night, Cox told his wife about Timerman's telephone call.

"Shouldn't he leave the country?" she asked.

"Why should he leave if he has done nothing wrong?"

A few weeks later, Timerman and several of his editors were picked up by security forces, taken to a clandestine prison and tortured.

Cox immediately launched an editorial campaign, which was soon joined internationally, to pressure President Videla to save Timerman, or at least make his arrest official. Soon afterward, Timerman was accused of being connected to terrorist activities through David Graiver, a part owner of La Opinion who was allegedly the financial brain behind the Montoneros terrorist organization. Timerman was moved to a cell at Federal Police headquarters.

Bob and Maud Cox were attending a reception at the British Embassy and discussing the Timerman case with friends when John Shakespeare, the British charge d'affaires, seemed surprised to see them.

"Bob, I have your telephone number and your address on a pad next to my bed," Shakespeare said, then hugged both of them.

Neither understood Shakespeare's unusual gesture at that time, but it all made sense a week later on April 24, 1977, when Herald staffer Betty Lombardo called the apartment and said:

"Maud, don't be frightened. I have good and bad news to tell you. They arrested Bob today but they have not made him disappear. They presented themselves with their credentials. He was taken to jail and ..."

Maud dropped the phone and ran to her father. *"Bestias! Bestias! Bestias!* (Beasts!)," she screamed before collapsing into Papito's arms.

Cox was jailed in the same cellblock at Federal Police headquarters where Timerman was lodged. At school the next day, some classmates told the Cox children that their father had been arrested because he was a Communist. The government's pretext for his arrest was the Herald's publication of reports of a news conference held in Rome by Montonero terrorists in which they announced they had formed an Argentine political party. The fact that Bob Cox had been jailed was immediately reported in major international newspapers, and editors as well as other worldwide figures sent telegrams to Argentine authorities demanding his release. The Miami Herald wrote: "In Washington, D.C. ... Newsweek, the Washington Post, the Christian Science Monitor and the Miami Herald, journals for which Robert Cox has written, have expressed concern to the Argentine Embassy and the State Department ... Cox's arrest came a week after army agents picked up Jacobo Timerman and Enrique Jara, editor and managing editor of the influential La Opinion."

The U.S. State Department wasted no time calling on the Argentine ambassador for an explanation of why Cox was arrested. U.S. Secretary of State Cyrus Vance spoke by telephone to U.S. Embassy officials in Buenos Aires, ordering them to act promptly to assure his release even though he was a British national.

Meanwhile, as Aunt Norma petitioned officials in Great Britain to help, the British consul general and the head of chancery in Buenos Aires went to Federal Police headquarters to talk to Cox. The police refused permission for them to see him but agreed to pass on his asthma medicine, which Maud sent, telling them it was a matter of life or death.

Peter Manigault was told of the Cox arrest as he was boarding a plane in Charleston. Bill Montalbano got an urgent message through to Manigault, who immediately canceled his travel plans and was soon on the telephone with U.S. Ambassador Bob Hill in Buenos Aires. It was an extended conversation that focused on the huge public outcry that was sure to come from the United States if Cox were not released unharmed.

Meanwhile, Maud called on Walter Klein, the Argentine government economist and family friend. She asked him to use his influence to get her in to see her husband. It was to no avail.

After 24 hours in a succession of prison cells, Bob Cox was taken before a judge, who was not happy about the matter. It was a Saturday, and he had been summoned to leave his *estancia* and report to Buenos Aires. The next day, Maud, who was waiting just outside the courtroom, was allowed to speak to her husband briefly. "Be prepared for the worst," he whispered in her ear.

At home, Ruth and David stayed in their rooms, and Peter sat crying in his grandfather's lap. Robert and Victoria were told that, since they were the oldest, they must look after the rest of the children as best they could until their mother returned. They had not seen their father in two days.

The judge heard the charges against Bob Cox: that he had violated press restrictions based on two Argentine laws relating to national security and subversion. The judge, influenced by mounting international pressure, opted to release him on bail. The "crime" carried a sentence upon conviction of six to eight years in prison. Soon afterward, Cox was escorted outside the courtroom to see his wife.

"I've been allowed to leave on bail, but first I have to go with these policemen to the station and sign my release," he told her.

"Right, and you leave from the front door, then disappear in the street … I'm going with you."

"Don't worry, Mrs. Cox. This time, he will not disappear," one of the police officers said.

Later that day, Bob Cox drove home to see his family and tried to calm them by making light of his stay in the *calabozo* (jail). Then he returned to work. He had another story to write in the next edition of the Herald.

> *I was dumped in the basement of the Coordinacion Federal (Security Superintendency). There I was made to strip while I was searched before being escorted to a prison cell. It was there, in the antechamber to the concrete boxes with steel doors in which top security prisoners were held in solitary confinement, that I saw the sign which symbolizes for me everything that has gone wrong since March 24, 1976. There in the antechamber was a huge swastika, emblazoned on the wall by the police themselves. Underneath was the word: Nazinacionalismo (Nazi-nationalism).*

The day he got out of prison, Cox also went to Government House and asked to see President Videla, whose press secretary, Navy Capt. Carlos Carpintero, said that would not be possible. Cox replied, "Well, tell him that if he wants to establish his authority and demonstrate that he believes in the rule of law, he should go down to the *Coordinacion Federal* with a brush and a bucket of whitewash and personally paint over that swastika. It is a symbol of mass murder …"

Capt. Carpintero laughed uneasily and said, "Don't expect him to do anything about it."

Cox had also seen another inscription on the wall of the jail's communal showers that is mentioned in Timerman's book, "Cell without a Name, Prisoner without a Number." The inscription read, "Yankee, Get Me Out of Here," which eloquently expressed the hope of many in Latin America regarding human rights in the wake of Jimmy Carter's recent election as president of the United States.

Cox was released thanks to pressure from the international press and from the U.S. and British governments. He called Ambassador Hill and other diplomats and thanked them. It would have been impossible for him to answer personally all the telegrams and letters of support that poured in. A week after his arrest, Cox wrote in the Herald:

> *I find it incredible that I should be the only person prepared to speak up and put in a good word for La Opinion editor Jacobo Timerman. If nobody among the many people he has helped over the years, none of the many partners he has had, and nobody on his staff feels moved to say something in his defense, then I feel morally bound to do so.*

President Carter was clear about his position on international human rights and thought he could make a difference in Argentina. He named Patricia Derian U.S. assistant secretary for human rights and F. Allen "Tex" Harris was assigned to the U.S. Embassy in Buenos Aires. Cox quickly realized that Harris was committed to saving as many innocent Argentine lives as possible. Harris' secretary, a Holocaust survivor, kept a card file of people who were missing. Harris used this data to pressure Argentine officials to disclose the whereabouts of the disappeared.

There was a slim chance the Argentine junta could be pressured into restoring the rule of law. The United States sought to bolster human rights in Argentina by cutting back on financial aid to the military regime. Simultaneously, Amnesty International openly accused the junta of authorizing anti-terrorism information-gathering techniques that included electric shock, sexual abuse and the dreaded "submarine," a water-boarding torture method that causes the victim to think he is drowning.

The U.S. Embassy secured the release of several Americans who were abducted, but it was not known until years later that Billy Lee Hunt and Jon Pirmin Arozarena, both U.S. citizens, were taken away by security forces and never found again.

Meanwhile, Patricia Derian's human-rights initiative and the work of diplomat Tex Harris at the U.S. Embassy in Buenos Aires were having an impact. The moderates in the military tried to establish greater control to protect their image and continue receiving U.S. aid.

Derian was an extraordinary woman who drew on her experience in advancing civil rights in the U.S. South to give human rights an international dimension. She was enormously brave in standing up to the military, particularly the most ruthless member of the junta, Adm. Emilio Massera, when they denied that people were being tortured and disappeared.

Harris took the place of Ambassador Hill in using diplomacy to defend human rights.

Harris had to fight against more senior diplomats who did not believe the United States should become involved in promoting human rights in Argentina and began to report, by a back channel, directly to Derian.

Hill's health was affected by the strain of living under constant threat from left-wing terrorists and the frustration of trying to persuade the Argentine military to return to rule of law. His embassy residence was rocketed and machine-gunned, yet he laughed in public at danger. He resigned in May 1977 and died of a heart attack in November the following year.

Hill was a Republican who fought communism in Latin America throughout the Cold War. He had numerous contacts, particularly in Cuba. He was one of the first Americans to warn that Fidel Castro was a communist while almost everyone else in the world lauded the bearded guerrilla as some sort of hero. Hill's close friend was South Carolinian Thomas R. Waring Jr., editor of the News and Courier in Charleston. It was from Hill that Waring learned early on about Castro's ideology. Waring was the first U.S. editor to warn that Castro was a communist.

"Mr. Hill, generally regarded as the best ambassador the United States has sent to Mexico in a generation, is an outspoken foe of communism in Latin America," Waring wrote in the News and Courier following Hill's death. "As far back as 1958, Ambassador Hill declared he was aware that Fidel Castro was pro-communist and that his brother Raul was regarded as 'one of us' by Moscow's leaders. Ambassador Hill's warnings to the U.S. State Department were largely ignored."

The same can be said about Hill's concern for human rights in Argentina. Cox had earlier praised Hill for his bravery in facing down the guerrillas when they appeared all too likely to seize power, as well as for upholding American values in his genuine affection for Argentina and its people. "Mission Accomplished," Cox wrote, summing up Hill's achievements upon his departure from Argentina. Before leaving, Hill scribbled "Thank You" on official stationary that was delivered to Cox by another U.S. diplomat stationed in Buenos Aires.

Cox also hailed the work of John Shakespeare, the British charge d'affaires who returned to the United Kingdom the following month. Before leaving, Shakespeare wrote:

> Dear Bob: Just before leaving for the airport today I was shown a copy of your editorial in this morning's Herald. Thank you very much ... I am really quite overwhelmed. One of the greatest pleasures of my time in Argentina was getting to know you so well in the last few months. You run the best newspaper in Argentina. Keep up the good work!

Early in 1978 shortly before he died, Hill returned to Argentina and had lunch with Cox at the Jockey Club. Hill told Cox about a brief conversation he had with Adm. Massera during an Embassy reception.

"I know that Cox is a CIA agent," Massera whispered to Hill, who led the admiral to believe he was on to something.

"I didn't tell him 'yes' or 'no.' I left him to wonder," Hill explained to Cox.

CIA agents were less likely to be accosted by Argentine security forces. Hill's response to Massera may have saved Cox's life.

But no one was immune from becoming a *desaparecido*. Rafael Perrota, editor and owner of El Cronista Comercial, invited Cox to lunch and confided his fears that he would be picked up by the military. Cox said he doubted that he would be a target because he had top military contacts. *There was hardly a general, admiral or brigadier who had not enjoyed Rafael Perrota's hospitality.*

Cox underestimated the paranoia of the hardliners. Perrota's fears were sparked because he was denied renewal of his passport. He had planned to visit his sister, who lived in Boston. "My wife insists I shouldn't worry. She said that if anything happens to me, all she has to do is call Adm. Massera and he will see that I am not harmed," Perrota told Cox.

Perrota disappeared a few days afterward and was never heard from again.

A few weeks later, Bob and Maud Cox encountered Mrs. Perrota at the Israeli Embassy residence. Ambassador Ram Nirgad had invited 12 people to dinner, presumably to gather information from a very mixed group about what was going on in Argentina. They were at a long dining table. At one end, Cox sat next to the Israeli ambassador. At the other end, Maud was among several prominent Argentines who were upset about international press reports of human rights violations in Argentina. Nearby sat an Argentine military officer who obviously was not happy that human rights was the topic of conversation.

"Who are you?" Maud asked the man.

"I am Adm. Santamaria."

"Well, you must be aware of what is going on. Innocent people are being killed."

"It is worse that you can imagine. We are desperate. We raid a house, and only a small task force knows about it. However, two hours later, another task force shows up, and makes a real mess of it," he responded.

"But how can you let these men do whatever they want to innocent people?"

"We have tried them in a military court."

"Well if that is so, you should clear up what is happening. The country should know that you are punishing the men responsible for these violations and that you are against the methods being used. They have even stolen from the homes. They go with trucks, and take everything away."

"No, we cannot expose them publicly," he said. "Who are you?"

"I am the wife of journalist Robert Cox. This silence will be interpreted as if the government agrees with the way these groups are acting. I don't understand how, after what you have told me, you believe that the international press is making up stories."

The admiral changed subjects, mentioning Timerman, whom he feared would become a martyr.

"Everyone knows the press lies and exaggerates," he said. "What they are saying is inconceivable."

Maud Cox was confused. Only a few minutes earlier, he had admitted that military task forces were involved in the kidnappings, but now he denied everything. She would meet Adm. Santamaria a year later at the wedding of his daughter to one of Maud's second cousins.

"I never brought up the subject again out of shame or lack of courage," she wrote in her diary.

DAVID COX JOURNAL: AUGUST 2007

Later that night, Mother sat down at her black baby grand piano. It was her most valued material possession, and it was in the living room placed at an angle that allowed her to have a view of the apartment's balcony and the city beyond. She began playing Franz Schubert's "Papillion." It was calming.

Afterward, we heard a metallic sound in the kitchen as our father banged away on his Olivetti typewriter. It was not.

CHAPTER 9
KNOWING A TERRIBLE SECRET
(1 9 7 7)

It was a typical hot and humid Friday morning in January 1977 as the Cox family left for their country home in Highland Park. They took Libertador Avenue out of the city. As usual, all five children were crammed in the back seat of the Peugeot, and the parents were in the front. Their travel bags were secured with rope on the roof rack. Cox had earlier demonstrated to his children how to tie the knots he learned in the navy.

A military truck ahead of their car stopped, forcing Cox to halt. The truck turned off the highway and through the open iron gates of a military compound. Two soldiers with guns got out of the truck, went to the back of the vehicle, opened the doors and ordered those inside to get out. Several young people exited, their hands clasped behind their necks.

"Oh my God," Maud exclaimed. The children stared. Bob said nothing as he drove past. Prisoners were being taken into a special navy training school that was used as a clandestine prison and torture center.

Two years would pass before what went on inside the sprawling buildings of the *Escuela Mecanica de la Armada*, or ESMA, became general knowledge. The school is adjacent to a stadium, home to the River Plate professional soccer team. The stadium property merges with Palermo Park, which stretches along the river from the heart of the city to its northern boundary. ESMA today is a museum of horror, featuring cells and torture chambers. People suspected of aiding guerrilla groups were tortured before being told they would receive a routine vaccination to prevent them from getting sick. Instead, they were administered a "routine vaccination" of Pentothal, a powerful sedative. They were taken to a nearby military airfield, herded onto transport planes, flown out over the Atlantic Ocean and dumped into the sea.

Meanwhile, the Mad Mothers of Plaza de Mayo were transforming their vigils outside Government House into regular protest meetings. Each Thursday, they marched around the plaza, and as each week passed, their numbers multiplied. They demanded that the government tell them what had happened to their missing loved ones.

They also gathered regularly outside the Herald building hoping to speak to Cox or members of the news staff. Some came to the Cox's downtown apartment as well. Renee Epelbaum and Helena Arocena were two of them. Maud served them tea and sandwiches.

"I remember you often and how much you did for us ... you were so kind and did so much for me," Helena Arocena, the wife of a Uruguayan diplomat, later wrote to the Cox family. "Peter Rabbit and Lady Mouse are very well, and keep me company."

Bob and Maud encouraged their children to give the *Madres* the toys they no longer used as a way of showing love and understanding. Perhaps the toys would somehow ease their suffering. The Cox children gave up their cherished dolls from the Beatrix Potter collection, which their father bought in London.

DAVID COX JOURNAL: AUGUST 2007

I visited Mrs. Arocena in her home in 1998 and saw our Peter Rabbit doll displayed along with her family mementos in the living room. She thanked me for the gift and gave me her diary.

In 1973, Mrs. Arocena's son Marcos, a promising playwright, was questioned by security forces because he had sub-rented his apartment to a man suspected of being a left-wing activist. Marcos was hooded, handcuffed and taken away as his neighbors watched. His mother later learned that he was offered his freedom. But Marcos asked that another prisoner, who had been held longer than he, be freed in his place. That man told Mrs. Arocena that Marcos saved his life. Marcos was never heard from again. She wrote in her diary:

> My darling, darling Marcos, come back soon, very soon. I pray for you every day and night, and I am still doing all I can to find you.

Three years later, she added these words:

> Marcos dearest, the trees in front of our house have flowered again, the third time since you have left, and you are not here to enjoy their sweet scent. My heart breaks every spring. The shiny green leaves on our trees, the flowers in the garden, the singing of the birds ... these are things that tear at my heart until your absence becomes a presence. I feel that I can hear your voice; that I have only to turn my head to find you standing beside me laughing. When will I know what has become of you?

In another passage, which she titled, "The Torture of Not Knowing," she wrote:

> For a mother, hope never dies. The battle goes on day in and day out. No matter how tired and disappointed, the will to fight increases with every defeat. ... Somewhere, somehow, someone will give me the information that I seek ... There is no retreat, no rest. Days end and begin again with the same empty feeling, and 'not knowing' only adds to the misery. Time does not heal. No one can tear a child from his mother's heart.

By September 1977, cases of missing people had increased dramatically. In October, Cox wrote an editorial about the *Madres:*

> *The 'Mad Mothers of Plaza de Mayo' got what they wanted yesterday. Police picked up 200 of them, along with six journalists who work for international news organizations, after a peaceful demonstration outside Congress. The story has gone around the world, drawing attention to their search for the missing ... this problem cannot be ignored. The government must take steps to end the nightmare some of these women have been living for more than a year and a half. The tragedy of many of them is that they simply do not know whether their sons, daughters and husbands are alive or dead. Their relatives have vanished into thin air. This situation can only be ignored at the government's peril. These women could be exploited politically. So far they seem driven by one aim only: That is to try and arouse the conscience of Argentina to their plight.*

As Cox wrote more and more about the disappeared, his stress became more manifest. His asthma attacks intensified, and his doctor recommended that he take a trip to the province of Cordoba, where the air is cleaner. The family soon left for the hillside town of La Cumbre, in hopes that the dry climate might restore his health. After staying a little more than a week, the pain in Cox's lungs abated, and the family returned to Buenos Aires. But his asthma soon returned. His breathing became so labored and shallow that he was bedridden for days. Maud gave him Prednisone by injection while he wrote from his bed. The letters from the *Madres* asking Cox to publish their stories in the hope of saving their children were forwarded from the Herald to his home.

To save time and make more effective the search for missing people, Maud kept a file of the correspondence with the help of daughter Victoria. They sat at the kitchen table and arranged the letters in order. Each told a different story, but the subject was always the same.

"Victoria," Maud said, "your father does not want to leave the country, but I'm worried about him. Maybe the time has arrived that I oblige him to leave. Can we get away?"

"No, Mom. If Dad wants to stay, I think we have to let him and accept the consequences. He needs to do what he thinks is right," Victoria said. She was only 15 at the time.

Harry Ingham also knew Cox was in trouble. After Cox returned to work at the Herald, Ingham often stopped by his office and asked if he would join him for dinner. Ingham realized that Cox's life was in danger. Once, he drove him home, parked the car and said, "My friend, I am afraid of what may happen to you over the Timerman case. It might not be worth pursuing."

"You're right," Cox said. "Nobody wants to defend Timerman. But what is he guilty of? He may not be liked, but he hasn't done anything wrong. They probably have it in for him because he is Jewish and successful."

Cox compared the Timerman case to the infamous Dreyfus Affair, a political scandal that divided France in the 1890s and early 1900s. Captain Alfred Dreyfus, a young Jewish officer, had been wrongly convicted of treason primarily because of his faith.

Another case that had international repercussions was the January 1977 disappearance of Dagmar Hagelin, a Swedish girl who was visiting Argentina. She was shot, wounded and abducted while visiting a friend whose apartment was raided by military police. Maud and Bob Cox were deeply concerned about her disappearance and went to see the Swedish Ambassador to Argentina, Karl-Anders

Wolter, at his residence.

They knew Wolter because his daughter attended Lincoln, an American community school in Buenos Aires, along with two of the Cox children. Dagmar Hagelin disappeared after being wounded by Capt. Alfredo Astiz, who headed one of the Navy's death squads. Astiz took her to the ESMA prison camp. She was seen alive there as she was recovering from her wounds. It was later learned that Navy officers drugged and threw her out of an airplane over the Atlantic. They hoped that by making Dagmar disappear they would avoid an international scandal.

Not all the stories had horrifying endings. Antonio Di Benedetto, a journalist and poet from the province of Mendoza, became entangled in a web of groundless suspicions spun by the commander of the local army garrison. Cox wrote about Di Benedetto's disappearance and confronted the government directly by demanding that he either be officially charged with a crime or freed. Di Benedetto was freed. He came to the Coxes' house and thanked Bob and Maud for helping save his life. He had been tortured and was incapable of describing the horrors inflicted on him. Upon his release, he was warned to leave the country. "In my cell, I thought that the newspaper owners for whom I worked were going to publish news of my arrest. I did not have any doubts about it because they knew me and knew of my opposition to terrorism. I was wrong about them," he said.

Before he left Argentina, Di Benedetto dedicated one of his books to Cox: "To Robert Cox, that sane idealist to whom I owe so much … and thank you Maud for receiving me so sensitively in your home."

Di Benedetto remained haunted by his torturers. Each time he thought about it, his legs shook uncontrollably. He never found out why he was abducted and always wondered why none of his own newspaper colleagues came to his defense.

The case of Alfredo Bravo, a human rights activist and politician, was similar. The Herald was the only newspaper to print the news of his disappearance and played a key role in securing his release.

DAVID COX JOURNAL: AUGUST 2007

Later, in 1998, Bravo asked me to thank *tu padre* (your father) for saving his life. "Please thank him for everything he did for me. Thanks to him, I am alive."

The Herald also covered the story of Associated Press writer Oscar Serrat, another *desaparecido.* In an editorial titled, the "Other Terrorism," Cox wrote:

> *The past disappearances of people such as Mr. Serrat who are above suspicion of any involvement with terrorism remain total mysteries. It is not impossible that they are all connected. We wonder whether the kidnapping of a top journalist working for a U.S. news agency was arranged to coincide with the arrival of a new U.S. ambassador in order to embarrass the government. The weight of evidence in past cases has suggested that the appearance of Mr. Serrat, as the result of the clear, decisive action by the government, would restore public confidence. Then it would not be wishful thinking to hope that it will be not too much longer before all the sinister black clouds that hang over Argentina are banished.*

Serrat was freed a few days later.

On Nov. 23, 1977, an earthquake measuring 7.4 on the Richter scale jolted Argentina. The epicenter was in the province of San Juan in the Andean Northwest region of the country. Sixty-five people perished. The Coxes felt the tremors at 6 a.m. in Buenos Aires as the family was having breakfast. First, a light fixture moved. Then, the entire apartment building shook. They thought at first that someone had detonated a bomb in an attempt to kill them.

Soon after the earthquake, U.S. Secretary of State Cyrus Vance came to Buenos Aires. He presented to the junta a list of 7,500 names of people who had disappeared and demanded that the government take immediate action to find out what had happened to them. One month later, French diplomats expressed similar concerns following the abduction of two French nuns, Sisters Alicia Domon and Leonie Duquet, outside the Church of the Holy Cross. They had taken part in a meeting to collect money to place an advertisement listing the names of missing people in a national newspaper.

Security forces also abducted several of the Mothers of the Plaza de Mayo at that time. The Coxes met and befriended Argentine attorney Horacio Mendez Carreras, who spent the remainder of his life searching for the missing nuns.

Yet there was some joy for the Coxes then, especially during their weekend retreats in Highland Park. The children loved playing croquet with their grandfather Papito, who missed shots intentionally. The boys played soccer with friends their age as well as grownups. That summer, Cox bought a bow and arrow for David, who pretended to be Robin Hood in Sherwood Forest while shooting at a target made of straw. He spent hours honing his archery skills while brother Robert and sister Victoria rode yellow Zanella mini-motorcycles, which Papito bought for them.

Papito hired an ironsmith to make a basketball hoop and a carpenter to construct a goal for the children. Few people in Argentina played basketball in the 1970s, and they considered themselves privileged to have their own court. The children still remember the walks through the garden in Highland Park with their grandfather, holding on to his fingers while listening to advice. They learned from him to be kind, innovative and strong.

But even at Highland Park, people's attitudes regarding outsiders were guarded as a result of the complex political problems that gripped the nation. The Coxes soon found themselves in the middle of a ethnic controversy in the neighborhood. Some homeowners wanted to restrict the number of Jewish families allowed to live in the gated community and convinced the neighborhood executive committee to call for a community-wide vote, which was set on a Sunday.

When Bob and Maud arrived to vote, they were shocked to see the number of their neighbors, even some prominent Jews who already lived there, in a long line of those who were in favor of the restrictions. Some friends tried to convince them that there was nothing wrong with restricting club membership, arguing that Jews had their own country clubs. The restriction was approved.

In December 1977, it was obvious that President Videla would not work with U.S. President Carter on improving human rights in Argentina. Just before Christmas, Videla announced that the military government would continue its crackdown on terrorism, adding, "In all wars there are people who survive, those who are incapacitated, some who die and others who disappear."

Videla's announcement was made on the same day the Herald published a scathing editorial on methods the military security forces used to combat terrorism. The editorial demanded that the government disclose who gave orders that resulted in the abductions of the French nuns and members of the Mothers of the Plaza de Mayo.

> *The seizure of a number of people connected in some way with the missing-persons' petition, or 'solicitada,' published – at the petitioner's expense – in last Saturday's La Nacion seems to suggest that we will be unlikely to enjoy peace by Christmas. This hope was inspired by some remarks made by President Jorge Rafael Videla during his successful visit to the United States when he suggested that normality would*

fairly soon be re-established in Argentina.

'Peace' does not merely mean an end to the depredations of left-wing terror gang thugs. It also means, or should mean, a return to the law and order without which organized society can scarcely exist, let alone flourish. It means an end to the 'grey zones' where legality acquires strange and novel meanings: an end to the use of unorthodox methods that accompany warfare against terrorism virtually everywhere but are nonetheless incompatible with the sort of society Argentina was and will once again become. It means an end to the sense of unease, of lurking terror that has haunted the country for far too long. It means, in short, clear evidence that the war against terrorism has really been won, as the military authorities say, and has not merely entered a new and sinister stage.

It would seem reasonable to assume, insofar as reason can be applied, that the people seized – who include some of the now world-famous 'Mad Mothers of the Plaza de Mayo' – were taken away by people who would rather their petition had not seen the light of day or were trying to intimidate those associated with it. Beyond this assumption, however, it is hard to go because it is here that the still unanswerable questions begin to crop up. Were the people who seized them members of the security forces or not? If they were members of the security forces to what department did they belong? Who gave the orders? Was the action in line with the official policy? Or can anybody above a certain level make up his own policy as the situation develops, even in some sensitive matters that affect the government's international standing? If the people in the unmarked cars did not belong to the security forces, how then could they operate so brazenly in one of the most tightly policed cities in the world?

Beyond these questions, needless to say, is a far more important underlying question. Who can possibly benefit from the prolongation of a climate of uncertainty that by now should belong to the past? It is inevitable that there will be public doubts about the government's ability to achieve its stated objectives if it cannot restore security and harmony in Argentine society. It is only in a framework of security and harmony with the return of the rule of law that the rapid economic, social and political transformation desired by the government and by enlightened public opinion can be achieved, and the longer this is delayed the fainter and fainter this objective will seem.

1936

Three-year-old Robert
J. Cox in Kew Gardens,
England, is pictured with
his father, mother and
sister Norma.

1945

Robert Cox, 12, holds his loyal companion Marcus in Churchfield Park,
Hanwell, England.

June 1954 (above)

Maud Cox with Juan Peron at the military club Circulo Militar two years after Evita's death. Although not a Peronist, her uncle was a top-ranking general during the Peron regime. According to one U.S. Embassy official, "Maud is an Anglo-Argentine lady of shrewd intelligence." Years later, such shrewdness helped save her family and narrowly escape abduction by state terrorists awaiting outside the family's apartment.

Circa 1957 (right)

A young reporter, Robert Cox is aboard a trawler in the port of Lowestoft, England. His newspaper story appears below the picture.

THE DRIFTER SKIPPER, Herman Muttitt, receives our reporter aboard the latest vessel of the Lowestoft fishing fleet.

A NIGHT OUT TO SEA WITH THE HERRING FLEET

Unending Search for the Silver Shoals

At the end of the voyage the fishing harbour had the air of Saturday. It was like jazz music played as recreation by shirt-sleeved musicians after a scrolling symphony.

Along the quays the whole of the drifter fleets were unloading their catches. The wicker baskets filled with herrings swung out from the ships on to the dock side. The masters of the drifters leaned out of their wheel-houses to exchange information about the night's fishing.

To-day and to-night was the re-spite from the endless, monotonous search for the herring shoals. It is a hard, wearying task. The fishing

Robert Cox, an "East Anglian Daily Times" staff reporter, gives his impressions of a day and a night aboard a Lowestoft herring drifter.

is carried out between anxious minute intervals to weather forecasts and news picked up over the radio of the fishing grounds with larger catches.

A week had ended for the Lowestoft-based drifter fleet. It had been a poor week. The herring in the most famous fishing grounds in the world for the East Anglian Autumn Herring Fishery had been elusive. The combination of skill and luck required for a good haul was lacking the luck.

"DREAM CONDITIONS"

I had heard something of the dream conditions needed to strike the herring: rich and heavy the morning before when I stood in the wheel-house of the "Norfolk Yeoman" with the skipper and one of the owners. The conversation was of winds and weather. I understood that when the moon was full and the wind Southerly the herrings moved by a natural volition into the miles of nets drifting behind the fishing vessels through the night.

The skipper himself preferred an Easterly wind in September. It was, I fancied a revolutionary theory. But there was no doubt that with the wind from the North-East we were in for a poor night's fishing and lots of "ground-swell" motion.

We waited for the inevitable weather forecast. The voice was dispassionate. It declared its disinterest in the rude elements outside Portland Place. The owner took his heavily overcoated figure away and the skipper was left to decide whether to sail or no.

Aware of the unpropitious weather and the threat of gales we left the harbour leaving the long line of moored drifters like a daring school-boy leaving an unadventurous class.

Nothing out of the drifter basin we disturbed the gulls who had been sitting on the water as smug as fat cats and passed another mass of gregarious gulls standing like a Roman Legion on one arm of the pier at the harbour mouth.

TO-MORROW'S GLEAM

The sea was grey and shifting as we headed out and away. I remembered the words of the skipper in the next boat as I felt the intoxicating fling signs of sea sickness. "Naar, you'll wish you was at the Palsy de Dance when you get out there," he said. I realised then that I was an amateur and possibly a Jonah.

Like the crew I had already begun to look forward to to-morrow and most of all to to-morrow night.

Later and about 20 miles out into the fishing grounds near Smith's Knoll herrings, the captain ordered me from almost hysterical nausea.

"You'll need to put this in your log," he said for I had kept a careful minute by minute note of the voyage. I had kept a note, at least, until I was forced to pour my stomach in faculties, fish the mal-de-mer, curse my fate and think of soothing things. I had been careful to watch a scientific depth sounding machine, possibly called a depthoscope. It

would indicate, I thought, the reaction of an experienced fisherman to scientific aids to his craft. The mechanism was supposed to give an indication of the presence of the fish for which we were searching. Would the skipper use it? Or would he prefer the instinct of experience?

INCURIOUS ACCEPTANCE

He was imperturbable. We were not really expecting to find herrings. The attitude was incurious: an acceptance of the fact that this was not the best of all possible worlds. The depthoscope seemed to have no place in the conjecture. The matter seemed only the concern of the figures in yellow oilskins and seaboots blanched the pallor of sea-washed men paying out the one and a half miles of nets and the captain at the wheel enjoying the waves.

So, we rolled through the evening and the early morning until the nets were manhandled aboard with the catch after four hours' strenuous haul. The catch was not good. About ten crans—10,000 fish—were in the hold. It was not so far a good season for at this, the peak time of the year, an average catch was 200 crans.

"Them herrings is very spotty. It looks like some of us will get rich while the others starve," said the skipper.

In hard cash it means that this year the East Coast drifter fleet have marketed about £200,000 worth of herrings less than the same time last year.

FEWER FOR FOREIGNERS

To Chinamen, Russians, Germans, Arabians and Creoles, it means fewer herrings for redding, kippering, pickling, canning klondiking, serving with sherbert and making into meal. Anyfishing and everything can happen to a herring if he is caught when the moon is full.

But the boatman himself simply wishes to deny the newspaper report that one of his kind would rather be at sea than in a feather bed. The captain was still laughing about that one when we went ashore for his afternoon driving lesson and to see his silent dog. He had had very perturbed about the dog.

BROADCASTING

HOME (330 m.: 93.5 Mc/s VHF)
6.25 a.m.—News; 6.20—Reports for Farmers. 8.30—Records. 8.55—Weather. 7.0—News. 7.15—Lent Orthodox. 7.50—Talk. 7.55—Weather. 8.0—News. 8.15—Market Intelligence. 8.30—Morning Music. 9.0—School. 9.5—Service. 9.35—Epistle Epilogue. 9.35—Choral Music. 9.55—School. 10.45—D-y Service. 10.30—Accordion. 11.0—School. 12.0—Any Answers? 12.30—Music Hall. 12.55—Weather. 1.0—News. 2.0—Schools. 3.0—For You Alone. 2.0—Welsh Orchestra. 4.30—In Chancery. 3.0—Children's Hour. 5.55—Weather. 6.0—News. 6.10—Sport. 6.20—Folk Songs. 6.30—Music Night. 7.45—The Great Detective. 8.0—Take It. 9.15—Current Affairs. 9.15—M'c's News (plain). 10.30—Shakespeare in Camera. 10.45—To-day in Parliament. 11.0—News. Summary and Weather. 11.5 app.—Market Trends. 11.15 app.—Close down.

LIGHT (1,500 m.: 247 m.: 89.1 Mc/s VHF)
8.0 a.m.—News; 6.15—Reports. 9.55—Story, Brain. Prayer. 10.0—Organ. 10.30—Anderson Band. 11.0—Mrs. Dar's Diary. 11.45—Story. 12.0—Vaughan. 12.0—Variations in Parliament. 12.15—Merry Band. 12.45—Northern Orchestra. 1.0—News with Mother. 1.5—Woman's Hour. 2.0—Oscar Rabin's Band. 3.45—Music with You Work. 4.15—Mrs. Dale's Diary. 4.30—Organ. 4.45—Trans-Antarctica Expedition. Langham crossings. Irene sprenkel. 5.0—Variety Orchestra. 5.30—Work Band.

6.0 a.m.—Frankie Vaughan. 6.25—Gene Finch's. Herring People. 6.30—Forces. 6.45—The Archers. 7.0—News and Radio. Newsreel. 7.30—Music Hall. 8.15—The Archie. 9.0—Grey River Boys. 9.15—Any Questions? 9.0—Friday Night is Music Night. 10.0—News. 10.15—Tune for To-Night. 10.30—Mike Band. 11.0—Band at Bedtime. 11.15—Serenade. 11.30—Music at Night. 11.55—News Summary. 12.0—Close down.

THIRD (464 m.: 194 m.: 91.3 Mc/s VHF)
6.0 Orchestral Concert. 6.40—Four Military of Thomas (talk). 6.55—Concert. 7.0—News. Japan (talk). 7.55—"Grande" (play). 10.0—Chamber Music. 10.45—Talk. 11.0—Close down.

MIDLAND (276 m.)
3.0 p.m.—Mid-Week. 3.15—Valeta Novel. 4.0—News. Sport. 4.30—Magazine. 10.30—Motoring.

TELEVISION
2.0 p.m.—Information Desk. 2.55—"Break Bag." by very McKechnIe. 3.30—Home Order. 3.45—Watch with Mother. 4.0—Film. 4.20—Contest. 4.30—Cookery. 5.0—News Round-up. 5.25—Children's. 5.40—Welsh Hymns. 6.15—Sport. 6.25—News. 6.50—Tonight. 7.0—Dixon. 7.30—Panel Game. 8.0—Spy. 8.30—Price Conference. 10.0—News. 10.15—Burns and Allen Show. 10.40—Cookery. 10.45—Weather and Close down.

March 1959

Robert Cox at the port of Tilbury, England, prepares to depart on board the *Highland Monarch* of the Royal Mail Lines to Buenos Aires, Argentina. Standing close by are his nephews Iain and Neil.

February 1970

The Cox children take a holiday in la Cumbre, Cordoba. Left to right are Victoria, Peter, Robert and David.

Feb. 16, 1978

The Cox family
visits Charleston, S.C.
The photograph
was published in the
News and Courier
to illustrate a story
written by Robert
and Maud Cox about
family travels.

Circa 1975 (above)

Publicity photograph was a gift from
actor Guy Williams (Zorro, at left) to
the Cox children.

1975 (right)

Guy Williams with Robert Cox's son
David at Highland Park.

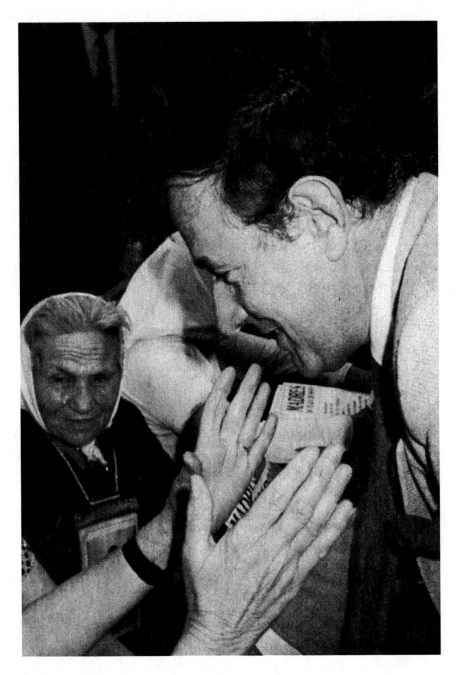

December 1983

One of the Mothers of the Plaza de Mayo reaches up to embrace Robert Cox when he risked a return to Argentina after President Raul Alfonsin was elected.

THE ROYAL BANK OF CANADA
Main Office
FLORIDA & CANGALLO
Branches
AV. CALLAO 291
AV. PUEYRREDON 1057

HERALD CENTENNIAL YEAR

Buenos Aires Herald

EL HERALDO DE BUENOS AIRES

THE ROYAL BANK OF CANADA

Founded 1876
100th year — 11.022

BUENOS AIRES, SUNDAY, MAY 30, 1976

16 Pages.·
Price: $30.

Had been provided for

Missing children safe and sound

by Robert J. Cox

THE missing children of a Uruguayan couple murdered by a terrorist "death squad" appeared safe and sound yesterday and were reunited with their distraught grandfather.

The children — a baby, Maximo, of two months; Victoria, aged 16 months; and Gabriela, who is four years old — were kidnapped along with their mother, Rosario Barredo, and the father of the two youngest, William Whitelaw Blanco, on April 13 from their home at Pasaje Matorras 310, in the Buenos Aires neighbourhood of Flores.

Neighbours pleaded with the kidnappers, who ransacked the house, stealing everything that could be removed, to leave the children in their care. The gunmen, who arrived in two cars with indistinguishable number plates and in a small truck, which was used to carry away their booty, paid no heed.

The mother, carrying the baby, was hustled away at gunpoint and the two other children were bundled into the waiting cars.

The couple was found murdered alongside the bodies of two prominent Uruguayan politicians, Zelmar Michelini and Hector Ruiz Gutiérrez — who had been kidnapped on May 17 — in a red Torino near the junction of the Ezeiza motorway and the General Paz.

There was no sign, or news, of the children until yesterday, when the chief of the Vicente López second section police station put a call through in the late morning to a telephone number left by the children's grandfather to announce that the children had been found.

The police officer said that the children had been left at the entrance of a clinic in Florida shortly after midnight. The clinic had apparently been notified and arrangements had been made for the children to spend the night when they were found on the doorstep.

When the children's grandfather, Dr Juan Pablo Schroeder Otero, a leading Uruguayan lawyer, arrived at the police station he found the children happily playing with the policemen there. The family dog, which had also been taken away, was not returned.

I saw the children yesterday afternoon as they played with toys strewn around a room in the home of a cousin. They appeared healthy and happy, despite their ordeal.

The four-year-old, "Gabriela", has not said anything about what happened. But she told one of the Schroeder family that her daddy was looking after her mummy, who was sick.

A relative looking after them said that they were hungry but that they had been given a change of clothes sometime during the fortnight they were in the hands of the kidnappers. They had been well cared for, she said.

Their release followed an appeal by Dr Schroeder to every inhabitant in Argentina to help him save the children. It was published by some, but not all, Buenos Aires newspapers after the Herald had drawn attention to the missing children in an exclusive story on Thursday.

Rosario Barredo was married to Dr Schroeder's son Gabriel, a member of the Tupamaros guerrillas who was killed four years ago. Their daughter was born a few days after his death. Mrs Schroeder was absolved of all terrorist charges and left Uruguay, eventually coming to Argentina, by way of Chile, where she has lived with William Whitelaw Blanco, the father of her two youngest.

Leaflets, attributed to a leftwing terrorist organization were found with the bodies of the four Uruguayans, but the kidnappings and murders bore all the hallmarks of rightwing "death squads" which have been active in Argentina. One of the Uruguayan parliamentarians, Michelini, was seized from his room in a central hotel by 16 heavily armed men who claimed to be members of a security force. Gutiérrez Ruiz was abducted by a group of armed men who used unmarked Ford Falcon cars.

The Argentine government has repudiated this killing and has ordered a full investigation to be carried out.

Lebanon near another outbreak

Beirut

CHRISTIAN and Moslem artillery duels pushed Lebanon to the brink of renewed full-scale war yesterday. One Christian leader accused the United States of "failing Lebanon in its need."

Security in the capital collapsed during a day of fierce fighting in Beirut and to the north, claiming nearly 100 dead and 155 wounded over the past 24 hours, according to casualty figures released by both sides.

Parliamentary deputies who met president-elect Elias Aarkis yesterday described him as pessimistic and fearful that the new military escalation may wreck his efforts to arrange peace talks.

"It is now definite that the peace conference will be delayed and not held within a week or two as hoped," deputy Ilus Ein Mansour said.

Palestinian sources said Christian mortars pounded a crowded outdoor market at the Palestinian refugee camp of Sabra on Beirut's southeastern outskirts, killing at least 26 persons shopping for the daily food and wounding at least 35 more.

The heaviest fighting was at the northern Akkar region near the Syrian border where rightists said two Christian towns came under a "genocidal" artillery attack. The rightists said leftist forces had completely surrounded Christian and cut off all roads and prevented Christian wounded from being taken to hospitals.

The Christians countered by shelling the Sabra camp and the Moslem suburbs of southeast Beirut.

Rightist forces defending the towns of Kobeyat and Andket, northeast of Tripoli, appealed to Syrian President Hafez Assad for "urgent and decisive action to save us from being massacred."

Christian Falangist Party leader Pierre Gemayel accused the United States of "failing Lebanon in its need" by restraining Syria from invading the country last January to impose peace by force. (UP)

'Help me save the children'

● From the Herald's front page on Friday, May 28.

Nadine returned home?

by Matthew T. Kenny

Mexico City

THE FAMILY of the kidnapped daughter of the Belgian ambassador predicted a "happy ending" to the abduction yesterday and indicated her communist kidnappers agreed to accept less than their original ransom demand.

"There will be a happy ending" a family spokesman said of the kidnapping of 16-year-old Nadine Chaval, daughter of Ambassador André Chaval, four days ago.

The spokesman indicated her abductors changed their minds at the last minute and accepted less than the 500,000 dollars they have been demanding under threat to kill the girl unless they got the full amount. The final payment was estimated to be nearly half a million dollars.

There were insistent but unconfirmed reports that the girl may have been released late on Friday night.

They were triggered by the arrival shortly before midnight of a compact car into the driveway of the house next to the embassy residence.

Witnesses said a blonde female "with the physical characteristics of Nadine" scurried into the house with two other persons as a Federal police agent blocked the driveway.

Family spokesman Ferdinand de Luy indicated the communist "League" which claimed the kidnapping and negotiated with the family, the abductors accepted the Chaval family's statement that they could not raise the demanded 800,000 dollars and decided to take what was available — estimated to be 480,000 dollars. (UP)

Yamani: No change

Bali, Indonesia

SAUDI Arabian oil minister Ahmed Zaki Yamani predicted the price of oil would remain frozen at its current 11.51 dollars per barrel until the end of 1976.

Yamani, who led the battle against price increases at the two-day conference of OPEC ministers, told an airport news conference that Saudi Arabia had the support of three other OPEC nations in its fight against any price rise this year and added

"No one can increase without Saudi Arabia."

"It is the Saudi Arabian crude that OPEC wants to increase and it doesn't mean they have the right to increase it without our consent," Yamani said.

The OPEC oil ministers wrangled over the price issue late into the night on Friday before finally deciding to conclude the meeting without any action at all.

"We just said 'no' because we believe this is in the interest of OPEC as well as in the interest of the whole world," Yamani said.

The current oil price freeze had been scheduled to expire July 1 and several members of the 13-nation organization had sought increases ranging between five and 15 percent.

Yamani said the next ministers meeting was scheduled for December in Doha, Qatar, and he saw no reason for any special meeting before then. (UP)

May 30, 1976

Stories on the missing children published in the Buenos Aires Herald.

June 1979 (above)

Robert Cox and Helena Arocena, mother of a disappeared son, on the television program Meet the Press, a few months before the Cox family was threatened and forced to leave the country.

1977

Robert Cox, second from right, appears on the television program Firing Line with William F. Buckley Jr. (far left).

Oct. 24, 1978 (left)

Robert Cox wearing a mortarboard and academic robe as he received the Maria Moors Cabot Award.

June 3, 1978

British Charge d'Affaires Hugh Carless honors Robert Cox as an officer of the Order of the British Empire (OBE) at the British Embassy in Buenos Aires.

December 1983

Robert Cox returns to Argentina for the first time since he went into exile and reunites with his close friend Harry Ingham at the airport.

1974 (above)

Peter Manigault backpacks in Bighorn Mountains, Wy.

1962 (left)

Frank Gilbreth was vice president of the Evening Post Publishing Co., a best-selling novelist and a popular Charleston News and Courier columnist.

1975

Peter Manigault, president of the Charleston, S.C.-based Evening Post Publishing Company, grooms a horse at a horseshow circa 1975. Evening Post Publishing Co. owned the Buenos Aires Herald from 1968 to 2007.

December 1979

Robert Cox hammers out an editorial in his apartment,
days before he leaves for exile.

December 1979

Cox family at the Ezeiza International Airport in Buenos Aires moments before leaving for exile.

March 17, 2002

Robert Cox with former President Bill Clinton at the Inter-American Press Association midyear meeting in the Dominican Republic.

November 1979

One of the photographs that Maud Cox had taken of the family so they could be
identified in the event of a forced departure – or worse. Victoria, Bob Cox, Peter,
Maud, David, Ruth and Robert Andrew.

CHAPTER 10
THE KISS OF JUDAS
(1 9 7 8)

It was dark when Maud Cox got out of the cab at the smoggy intersection of Paseo Colon Avenue and Alem Street near the Buenos Aires Herald building. She saw a long line of people, each wearing a white headscarf identifying them as the Mothers of the Plaza de Mayo. As she passed by the line, which was a half-block long, she was told that a contingent of the *Madres* had already entered the new Herald building at 455 Azopardo Ave. to meet with her husband. He absent-mindedly left his wallet at home that afternoon, and she was taking it to him. It was dangerous to be out at night without official identification.

At the top of the stairs, she walked past reporter Uki Goñi, 25, who was talking to one of the *Madres*. He was a son of an Argentine diplomat assigned to Ireland, where Uki was educated. Bob Cox tried to speak to everyone who came to the newspaper with a story to tell about the disappearances, but as the numbers grew, he asked Uki to help with the interviews.

In January 1978, the Herald was pressured by the government to tone down its coverage of the *Madres'* plight. Cox instructed his young reporter to find out as much as he could from the women, verify the information and secure writs of *habeas corpus* on as many cases as he could. Goñi was explaining to them how important it was for him to confirm information about *desaparecidos*.

"But how can we give you proof if it is the police that took our sons in the first place, and the courts will not take our cases?" one woman screamed in frustration. Cox heard the commotion, left his office and walked down the hall to where Goñi and the women were talking. He climbed up on a small marble table at the entrance to the newsroom and spoke directly to the *Madres* in broken Spanish.

"*Vamos a seguir luchando pero tenemos que hacerlo de una manera para lograr la justicia* (We are going to continue fighting, but we have to do it in a way to achieve justice)," he said.

The Herald was not turning them away, he said. Quite the contrary, the newspaper wanted to help them but could do so effectively by reporting only the facts and not conjecture. If the government managed to refute accusations in any one case, all the others could be placed in doubt, he said.

> *We can't lose confidence in the courts. One day all of this will end, and then all your presentations are going to be worth something. This is exactly what they want: for us not to believe any more in judges or in the law or in anything that we hold dear. We have to show that we are not going to give in and lose our faith.*

Cox climbed down from the table, removed a reporter's notebook and pen from his pocket and interviewed the women himself. When finished, he returned to his office where Maud was waiting. Goñi was awed. It was as if Bob Cox were the only person on earth who could get through to the *Madres*.

Goñi learned at a young age that Argentina had dirty secrets. His father told him about the Nazi connections between Argentines and Germans during and after World War II. He later wrote "The Real Odessa – Smuggling The Nazis to Peron's Argentina," a book describing the complicity of the Peron government in allowing German war criminals to hide in Argentina. Goñi was in his early 20s when he started working for the Herald. He soon became one of the best reporters on the staff. The reporter was fearless.

Goñi later described those difficult days in a book about Argentine Navy Capt. Alfredo Astiz, who infiltrated the Mothers of the Plaza de Mayo and spearheaded the abductions of founders of the movement and two French nuns who accompanied them. Astiz, who used the name Gustavo Niño as a cover, relied on his boyish good looks to befriend relatives of missing people who were raising funds to pay for an advertisement listing the names of *los desaparecidos* in one of the city's major Spanish-language newspapers. Astiz pretended that his parents were among the missing.

Astiz identified his victims on the day they were abducted by giving each one a kiss as death-squad members watched nearby. Several weeks before he gave the women "the kiss of Judas," Astiz was at the Herald in the guise of Gustavo Niño along with Azucena Villaflor, a founder of the *Madres*.

Soon after the abductions, Astiz was among a small group of *Madres* and their supporters who went to the Herald to tell Cox what had happened to their leaders and the nuns. Cox has the signature of "Gustavo Niño" on a list of participants in fund-raising activities held at the Church of the Holy Cross in Buenos Aires that was sent to President Videla. Those who were to be abducted were marked by Astiz on that list, which Cox still has in his files.

"Cox, *han desaparecido un grupo de madres y monjas de la Iglesia de Santa Cruz* (Cox, a group of mothers and nuns have disappeared from the Holy Cross Church)," a distraught mother told him that day at the newspaper office. He also remembers Astiz, as Gustavo Niño, pretending to be equally upset.

The Argentine government tried to cover up its role in the case by fabricating a letter that said the Montoneros were responsible for the abductions. The charge d'affaires at the French Embassy called Cox at home to tell him about the letter, written in French and signed by the nuns. It contained numerous grammatical errors and was phrased in such a way that there was no doubt that nuns had written under duress. French President Valery Giscard d'Estaing wrote to President Videla demanding that the government turn them over to the French Embassy.

Meanwhile, the Herald saved the life of a daughter of one of the *Madres* by publishing a story about her along with her photograph. What Cox did not know then, and which would later be reported by Goñi in his book, was that Horacio Elbert and Julio Fondevilla, two of the people kidnapped along with the *Madres* and the nuns that day, had been picked up by the security forces on their way to the Herald to denounce the disappearance of their relatives after meeting in the Holy Cross Church.

They were taken to the navy's concentration camp and tortured along with the nuns, according to others who were held there and later released. Although details of the fate of the nuns are still not known, there is no doubt that the navy officers who planned and carried out the abductions realized they made a mistake. But in trying to cover it up with the fake letter and by distributing an altered photograph of the nuns seated in front of a Montoneros banner, they only made things worse.

DAVID COX JOURNAL: SEPTEMBER 2007

Years later, when I was a Herald reporter, I met a young man who had been held at the ESMA center along with the nuns. He, like thousands of other young Argentines, took up arms against the government but after being captured and tortured, agreed to become an informant. My story, "The Broken Man," is an account of his torture and decision to save his own life by agreeing to become a prison spy. He said he had access to the prison files that identified those who had been interred in the camp. He said he saw the nuns after they were abducted and confirmed they were tortured and killed.

The disappearance of the nuns and the botched cover-up brought intense international pressure on the government to cease human-rights abuses. In response, the junta hired a public relations firm based in Washington, D.C. to help improve their image. It was especially important that they do so because Argentina was to serve as host for the 1978 World Cup soccer championship in June. The public relations campaign was designed to mislead the international media and, at the same time, convince Argentine citizens that reports of missing people were false and spread by the foreign press as part of a well-coordinated Marxist conspiracy.

The junta invited numerous well-known people to attend the games as special guests of the Argentine government. Former U.S. Secretary of State Henry Kissinger, an ardent soccer fan, was a personal guest of President Videla. Maud Cox remembered seeing Kissinger at a reception at the U.S. Embassy in Buenos Aires discussing with others the World Cup games. All she could think about at that time was Argentina's political turmoil and those who had disappeared.

It was also at that time that Maud took the children to see a live performance of the musical "Cabaret" at one of the theaters in downtown Buenos Aires. The songs – particularly "Willkomen," "Two Ladies," "Tomorrow Belongs to Me" and "Money" – were poignant, especially to those in the audience who knew what was happening in Argentina. Maud later discussed with Bob the setting for "Cabaret" – Germany's Weimer Republic in the 1930s prior to Hitler's rise to power. They noted the musical's striking symbolism and the sordid parallels with the situation in Argentina. "Cabaret" is the story of a nation's loss of innocence.

Soon afterward, Cox told his children they were going on vacation, first to see his sister in Wales, then to the United States for stays in New York City and Charleston, S.C. The family celebrated Christmas in Wales at a rural Victorian mansion that Cox's sister had rented for their stay. They walked the Welsh hills, enjoyed home-cooked dinners and gathered around a cozy fire each night. It was the first time the children had experienced Christmas crackers – small, highly decorated cylinders covered in colored crepe paper with a string on one end that, when pulled, exploded like a firecracker and ejected miniature toys.

Joining them at the mansion was Andrew Graham-Yooll, the former Herald news editor who fled Argentina in 1976 as government-supported death squads closed in on him and his family. He came from London with his wife and three children to spend the holiday with the Cox family. He and Bob Cox sipped brandy and talked for hours about the trouble back home.

After their Dickensian interlude in Wales, the Coxes boarded a plane for New York City. It was freezing when they landed at John F. Kennedy International Airport. Cox hired two taxis to take his family and the luggage to the Drake Hotel at 56th Street and Park Avenue in Manhattan. The lavishly designed and decorated hotel had been constructed in 1927. They rented a large suite with a small kitchen, which allowed them plenty of space to enjoy each other's company.

Cox was invited to visit the New York Times building, where he attended a daily news planning session conducted by Managing Editor Clifton Daniel, a North Carolinian who married former President Harry S. Truman's daughter Margaret.

Cox remembers Daniel as being autocratic in leading discussions about the news of the day. The lead story on Page 1A was about South African apartheid and the government's crackdown on dissenters. The Fashion and Style section featured an interview with eccentric novelist Truman Capote, author of "In Cold Blood," who had painted the walls of his Manhattan apartment blood red. Cox also had lunch with editors of Newsweek magazine and discussed human-rights issues in Argentina.

Later that week, the family attended a stage presentation of "Jack and the Beanstalk." Afterward, the children kept asking who exactly was the giant that smelled the blood of an Englishman? But the giant did not haunt their dreams while they were in New York City, which was covered that night by 17 inches of snow. It was the first time the children had seen snow. They built snowmen, threw snowballs and visited the F.A.O. Schwarz toy store.

"Look at the trains!" Bob shouted gleefully. The toy trains moved along, puffing out smoke, reminding the Coxes of the *Railway Children*, a film they had seen in Highland Park about three children who moved with their mother to the English countryside following the arrest of their father. In the movie, the children have all sorts of adventures as they play alongside the railway lines. They are finally reunited with their father, who was freed after being falsely accused of selling secrets to the Russians.

Cox was animated by their visit to the toy store. He purchased for his family a train set as well as a model of James Bond's Lotus Spirit car, which was added to their collection of Agent 007's miniature vehicles. After a week in New York City, the Coxes leased a Chrysler and drove to South Carolina.

CHAPTER 11
AN INTERLUDE IN CHARLESTON
(1 9 7 8)

The Cox family passed the time en route to Charleston playing not-so-typical travel games and singing. The musical tales about a venturesome turtle named Manuelita, written by Argentine author Maria Elena Walsh, were favorites. They included "The Kingdom of Upside-Down," "The Country of I Don't Remember" and "The Queen of Sweet Potatoes" – all of them reflections on Argentina's on-going political problems. The children did not know exactly what the underlying messages of the songs were. They simply enjoyed singing them all the way across the Blue Ridge Mountains and into the pinelands of the Carolinas.

A favorite travel game was *Gran Bonete* (the Big Bonnet). Each of the children chose a different color, then Maud would start by saying that Mr. Bonnet had lost his bird, which she described, and then quickly shouted the color of the lost bird. The player who had selected that particular hue had to be first to deny it before accusing someone else. Maud loved to play this game, which she learned from her own mother.

After two full days of travel, the family arrived in Charleston, a port city more picturesque than any they had ever seen. Their destination was the Manigault family beach house at Sullivan's Island, on the Atlantic Ocean north of the Charleston peninsula. Peter Manigault had offered to let the Coxes stay at the house for a few days. As the car pulled into the driveway, it passed Manigault's 16-year-old son Pierre as he headed back to the house after a walk on the beach. The house overlooked a series of sand dunes that ran parallel to the ocean and were covered in a coastal grass called "sea oats." It was winter and few people were on the wide beach.

Peter Manigault stopped by for a visit that that afternoon and welcomed his visitors from Argentina. He was a native of Charleston and a Southern gentleman.

After a few days at the beach, the Coxes moved into a hotel across the harbor at the heart of Charleston's Historic District. A family photograph was taken at that time of Cox standing with a cup of coffee in hand while Ruthie sat on her mother's lap beside a small table surrounded by the other four children among a pile of unopened travel bags, a box kite they flew at the beach, Raggedy Ann, Peter Rabbit and Mopsy.

The photograph was published in the Feb. 16, 1978, issue of the News and Courier to illustrate a story written by Bob and Maud about their trip to South Carolina. The article was titled "Traveling with Children," and offered the following advice:

> *The secret of traveling with children, and without tears, is to become something of a child yourself. You cannot expect to travel with children and relax at the same time. Banish any idea you had of sitting out on terraces sipping dry martinis, talking undisturbed to old friends about old times or reading* War and Peace. *You must realize early on that you cannot live full-time in an adult world if you have children to look after. Travel must be a shared adventure. It can broaden their minds and yours by giving you a glimpse of the world through their eyes. We have found that tolerance can be learned by the very young if you adopt the spirit of the Three Musketeers: 'One for all and all for one.' … We have thrived and flourished over the past 15 years through four long trips abroad with children. First there were two, then four, and on our last two jaunts, five children. Today we are on the road with Victoria, aged 15, Robert Andrew, 13; David, 11; Peter, 9; and Ruth, 6.*

The family's eight-day stay in Charleston stirred many memories for Cox, some of which he wrote about in another article for the local newspaper. He described his schoolboy days in London and how his father, a strident Conservative, enjoyed arguing with a dear friend who was a member of the British Labor Party.

> *Like all Conservatives, Dad thought he was always right. I played no part in the arguments, sympathizing with my mother, who hated these encounters so enjoyed by both protagonists. But I saw then that Dad, while not always right, was almost always right.*

The article also touched on a journalist's responsibility to be objective:

My father's vitriolic views made me somewhat antagonistic to ideologies and ideologues. They made my sister a Socialist. She even came uncomfortably close to joining the Communist Party. But my father considered Communists beyond the pale; he wouldn't even allow them into the house to argue with him. So my naturally contrary sister was not thrown into the arms of her Red friends by my father's argumentative ways. She steered away from Communism out of natural antipathy long before Stalin's murderous purges proved my father right again. I never became a Conservative with a Capital C, or, for that matter, a believer in any political ideology that uses an upper case.

It was also during this visit that Cox took a stroll along Meeting Street and came upon an odd building – a gas station that had been built to blend in with nearby historic houses. A plaque near the door explained that bricks and masonry from a demolished pre-Civil War home that belonged to the Manigault family were used to construct in the 1920s a new automobile service station on the site. More than 50 years later, the members of the Historic Charleston Foundation transformed the old corner station into a quaint gift shop and community meeting room. Charleston is a city of many "firsts" – among them being the first municipality in the nation to establish zoning laws designed to preserve the city's unique character.

It was impossible not to fall hopelessly in love with a city that set out to transform one of the horrors of the 20th century into an architectural gem.

The beauty of Charleston and the pride of its citizens reminded Cox of England's Frinton-on-Sea, where he spent his teen-age years. Charleston also captivated Maud Cox, who was impressed by how polite the people were. She loved the cleanliness of the city, as well as the curious joggling boards on many of the porches of the old houses downtown. Each member of the family took turns sitting down and bouncing on a joggling board, which is a long pliable plank supported by wooden stands mounted on rockers. Joggling boards originated in Charleston in the 1800s. They are particularly known as a favorite of young lovers who start out sitting at either end and slowly bounce themselves sideways until they meet in the middle.

Bob and Maud were also impressed by the fact that women had jobs that were reserved only for men in Argentina during the 1970s.

> *The youngest of the family, 6-year-old Ruth, has decided that she wants to be a Charleston policewoman, with a police uniform, a police gun, a police car, a police boat and a police airplane.*

Charleston captured Cox's heart:

> *I would need a lifetime here to explore the city's historical by-ways. Perhaps I would be disappointed to find that all has been discovered before me. But I would like to have the time to become something of an authority on this fascinating city. I certainly feel inhibited about writing anything based on a scant two weeks spent here …*

The Coxes fell in love with the S.C. Lowcountry, too. They visited the country home of the Evening Post Publishing Company's chief financial officer Hall T. McGee and his wife Peggy north of the city at an area called Sewee, named after a tribe of Native Americans that once settled there. Cox met with Assistant Publisher Frank B. Gilbreth, Editors Arthur M. Wilcox and Thomas R. Waring Jr., Managing Editor Ernest Cutts and Business Manager Joseph Smoak. Support for the Buenos Aires Herald by the company's top executives never wavered.

On March 4, 1978, a few days after the family returned to Argentina, a letter arrived for Cox from Gilbreth:

> Dear Bob: I don't know how the Herald got promoted to the biggest daily in Buenos Aires, but I guess you know how these things happen! Hope your trip was a success and that all the Coxes will be back to see us soon. Sincerely, Frank.

Gilbreth's note referred to an Associated Press story describing the Herald as the most reliable source in the world for news about Argentina. The newspaper, with a circulation of 20,000 readers, had developed an impressive international reputation. If Cox had been told before departing England at age 26 that he would become editor of such an influential newspaper, he would have laughed. His goal at that time was quite simple: to become a good reporter, remain single and see the world.

Two days after Gilbreth's letter arrived, three prominent members of the U.S. National Academy of Sciences Human Rights Committee arrived in Buenos Aires to press Gen. Videla for the release of physicist Elena Sevilla. She had been arrested in 1975, but never charged, three days after giving birth to her son. To help secure her release, the department of physics at Cornell University offered her a teaching post. The delegation from the National Academy of Sciences stressed to Videla that Sevilla's release would smooth the way for participation by U.S. researchers in the World Cancer Congress set for October in Buenos Aires.

Coincidentally, it was also at this time that Beatriz Rosalia Iparraguirre de Weinstein, an internationally known blood-disease specialist, was abducted by men armed with machine guns. They broke into her Buenos Aires apartment, took money and passports from family members, whom they locked in a bathroom, and left with Dr. Weinstein in a Renault automobile. The Herald published the story the next day on the front page.

As U.S. State Department declassified documents later disclosed, embassy officials learned of the case from the Herald story and immediately pressured the junta to release Dr. Weinstein. Her husband later confirmed to Cox that she was held by Argentine security forces. Tex Harris at the U.S. Embassy in Buenos Aires and Patricia Derian, assistant secretary of state for humanitarian affairs in Washington, D.C., worked closely to pressure the Argentine government on this and other human-rights cases. Argentine military officers, who called her "the Dragon Lady," hated Ms. Derian. But Cox praised her in a Herald editorial:

> The violation of human rights by terrorists does not justify the violation of human rights by those fighting the terrorists. Ms. Derian quoted Secretary of State Cyrus Vance as saying: "You do not violate human rights to protect them."

Alfredo Bravo, a socialist and human-rights leader who was abducted, had already been saved from becoming another *desaparecido* thanks to Cox and Harris. While Bravo was being tortured, his captors repeatedly attempted to get him to talk about his human-rights connections, including alleged meetings with Ms. Derian. Meanwhile, as Cox pointed out in an editorial, the general Argentine press persistently attacked her character.

In an editorial titled "Black Day," Cox recounted hundreds of killings, disappearances and other acts of violence that had occurred in Argentina since March 1976, when the junta came to power. He focused on the cases of Edgardo Sajon, Rodolfo Fernandez Pondal and Hector Hidalgo Sola, all highly respected Argentine citizens who had become *desaparecidos*. He asked why no one seemed to be concerned about the fates of these men and the others.

He cited the disappearance of Edgardo Sajon, who had served as press secretary for Argentine President Gen. Agustin Lanusse:

> *Mr. Sajon's disappearance should have sounded alarm bells. His disappearance, like the horrific abduction and murder of Gen. Aramburu in 1970, should have been considered a warning of more to come. Indeed since April 1, 1978, such terrorism has claimed others, notably the military government's own ambassador to Venezuela, Dr. Hidalgo Sola, and young journalist, Mr. Fernandez Pondal, who have both disappeared.*

It was later confirmed that Hector Hidalgo Sola and Rodolfo Fernandez Pondal were abducted, tortured and murdered by right-wing death squads as part of a power struggle between two of the branches of the Argentine armed forces. Both men knew that Adm. Massera, who headed up the Argentine Navy, was negotiating with the Montoneros to advance his own political ambitions. He wanted to take Gen. Videla's place as the president of Argentina and was willing to kill anyone who stood in his way.

In the case of Fernandez Pondal, Cox worked closely with the journalist's family to find out what had happened to him. Pondal's wife Marisa, who assumed her maiden name Presti for fear that she too would be targeted, later wrote a novel based on the long, fruitless search for her husband. The book was titled "Anne Frank is Argentine."

> *The public, generally, takes the view that anyone who was kidnapped must have done something to merit it. This callousness, this wish to remain uninvolved, is a national tragedy ...*

Catholic human-rights activist Adolfo Perez Esquivel was arrested as he tried to renew his Argentine passport and was imprisoned on April 4, 1977. The Buenos Aires Herald reported his arrest in detail, and subsequent editorials sparked what became an international campaign that secured his freedom. Perez Esquivel was later nominated for the Nobel Peace Prize.

"Who is this man Perez Esquivel? Nobody knows him," Argentine Interior Minister Gen. Harguindeguy asked Cox.

"This man, who you are holding in jail without any trial, has been nominated to receive the Nobel Peace Prize," Cox responded.

Mairead Corrigan and Betty Williams, co-founders of the Community of Peace People, had earlier been awarded a Nobel Prize for their organization's help in bringing an end to the conflict in Northern Ireland. Cox contacted the women and told them about the jailing of Adolfo Perez Esquivel in Argentina. Both Corrigan and Williams nominated Perez Esquivel for the prize and called Maud Cox to tell her about it.

In May 1978, a few days after Perez Esquivel's nomination became public, Cox met again with Gen. Harguindeguy and asked him about similar human rights cases. Much to Cox's surprise, the General no longer acted like a bully. He said the disappearances would soon end. Cox left that meeting extremely optimistic, thinking that perhaps he had misjudged Harguindeguy. But he soon learned that his "change in attitude" was a ploy.

Cox's meeting with Harguindeguy coincided with U.S. Undersecretary of State David D. Newsom's arrival in Buenos Aires to meet with President Videla on the subjects of human rights and creation of a nuclear free zone in the Southern Hemisphere. Soon afterward, Newsom spoke with Cox, who explained that the *desaparecido* problem was a time bomb and that the government did not know how to deal with it. He also told Newsom about the on-going political struggle among members of the junta, including the ambitions of Adm. Massera. Cox said the United States should insist that the rule of law be returned to Argentina. He also asked that the United States do all it could to support Argentine political moderates over the nation's hardliners.

The United States was working on several fronts at that time to resolve human-rights abuses in Argentina. U.S. Sen. Edward Kennedy had publicly cited high-profile cases such as that of former Argentine President Hector Campora, who holed up in the Mexican Embassy in Buenos Aires after being refused diplomatic immunity so that he could leave the country. Sen. Kennedy also asked for an accounting of the missing Swedish girl, Dagmar Hagelin, as well as an explanation of the disappearance of Marcelo Gelman, a son of Argentine poet Juan Gelman.

Meanwhile, the junta planned to use the upcoming World Cup soccer games in Argentina to convince other nations, and particularly the United States, that reports of human-rights abuses had been grossly exaggerated. They hoped that the construction of new soccer stadiums and an elaborate opening ceremony for the games would show that left-wing terrorists had been defeated and that the streets of Buenos Aires were safe.

They gave one group of British journalists an all-expenses-paid trip to Argentina that included a guided tour of the ESMA prison to prove that no atrocities had occurred there. The facts were, however, that more than 1,000 people had been tortured and murdered at the camp by then. Those who survived were transferred to a jail on an island in the Tigre Delta. Meanwhile, the journalists were feted by their navy hosts, and most subsequently reported the government's lies.

DAVID COX JOURNAL: OCTOBER 2007

Peter and I were ecstatic about the World Cup tournament being contested that year in Argentina. We learned about soccer at very early ages from Papito, with whom we listened to matches broadcast on his AM radio. Our games at school intensified as the opening match of the World Cup neared.

When we chose the teams among our schoolmates, we quickly selected for ourselves the names of Argentina's top players and pretended to match their skills on the field. Adjacent to the school playground was a building with a small balcony on the second floor where errant tennis balls often landed. A tennis court was located just below. We often used tennis balls when we played soccer because they helped us to improve our skills.

"Wonder how many balls are up there?" I asked Peter, whose face lit up in mischievous delight. He knew what I was thinking. The balcony had no door, only a tiny window. Hall monitors guarded the stairs to the balcony. We enlisted the help of our friend Richard, with whom I often played spy games. He agreed to distract the hall monitors while Peter and I slipped past. The plan worked perfectly. When we reached the window, I lifted Peter, who was smaller, up so that he could see what treasures had accumulated on the balcony.

"How many?" I asked.

"Tons, but I'm not sure if I can fit through the window."

"Yes you will," I said as I pushed him through the opening.

Once on the balcony, Peter tossed some tennis balls through the window for me and then hurled more down to the children on the playground. Tennis balls were imported into Argentina at that time and very expensive. The school's prefect saw what was happening and ran upstairs to get us, but by then, Peter had cleared the balcony of balls and crawled back through the window. We ran down the hall and escaped through another door. I had several tennis balls in my pockets, and we were quite cocky about our adventure for the rest of the day.

We also were confident that Argentina would win the World Cup. The games began June 1, 1978. Papito bought tickets to see Austria play Sweden. For a moment in time, it was if everything was normal again.

Cox covered the championship game at River Plate Stadium in which Argentina defeated Holland and won the World Cup. He, too, shared in the excitement, but reminded his readers that the respite from the disappearances and killings that had wracked the nation was only an illusion.

Soon after the World Cup ended and the focus of the world shifted elsewhere, acts of terrorism returned to Argentina, and the Herald resumed publication of the names of the latest victims. Julian Delgado, editor and founder of the nation's leading business magazine, Mercado, was among them. His colleagues told Cox about Delgado's disappearance before reporting it in the magazine.

It was at this time that John Illman, the first secretary at the British Embassy, paid a surprise visit to the Herald offices and asked to meet the editor in chief. Illman wanted to know if Cox would accept an honor for reporting on *los desapaecidos* to be bestowed by the Queen of England. Cox expressed his gratitude, adding he needed time to think about it.

Norman Ingrey, the former Herald editor and Cox's mentor, had stressed that journalists should not compromise their integrity by accepting government awards. But this was an unusual situation. Recognition by Queen Elizabeth II would help in the Herald's quest to find the missing. The Queen and the British government would demonstrate to the world that they supported the effort.

"This honors you, far more than me," Cox later told Illman and other members of the British Embassy staff. "I will accept it in the name of the Buenos Aires Herald."

A few weeks later on June 3, 1978 – Queen Elizabeth II's birthday and the 27th year of her reign – Robert John Cox, Esquire was named an officer of the Order of the British Empire on behalf of the Buenos Aires Herald during a special ceremony at the British Embassy. The Cox family gathered inside the Embassy residence, a splendid mansion atop a hill overlooking Palermo Park, the beautiful gardens and plazas of Buenos Aires. The Queen's words that marked the occasion are framed and on the wall today above Cox's cluttered desk in Charleston, S.C.

The presentation of the Order of the British Empire medal to Cox and the Herald served an important purpose. Recognition by the Queen of England made it far more difficult for the hard-line Argentine generals to sound convincing when they accused Cox of being a Communist. The honor that he accepted on behalf of the Herald produced a tremendous response from people throughout the world.

From Charleston, Peter Manigault, president of the Evening Post Publishing Co., joined the chorus of praises with the following telegram:

"Herald, Buenos Aires and Mr. Robert Cox: Congratulations from all of us at the Post and Courier. Peter."

Another message came from Holocaust survivor Irene Birbaum Goncrauski, who lived in Buenos Aires: "Best wishes, and congratulations ... I am a survivor from the Warsaw Ghetto and the Herald's constant reader since 1949."

More than 100 letters of praise came, including one from the secretary general of the Organization of American States, Alejandro Orfila. Others came from ambassadors and diplomatic representatives in Argentina as well as the New York Times, Washington Post, Associated Press and several English dailies.

DAVID COX JOURNAL: OCTOBER 2007

The next morning, Mother sat at her piano and filled the apartment with the haunting sounds of Beethoven's "Piano Concerto No. 1." Her fingers moved smoothly along the ebony and ivory keys. Again, her music gave us respite.

CHAPTER 12
A WORLD CUP, A PLOT, A ROYAL VISIT
(1978)

"It's that the noise again!" Cox whispered one cold Saturday night at the country home in Highland Park.

"Maybe it's the wind," Maud said.

Cox got up to investigate.

DAVID COX JOURNAL: DECEMBER 2007

As usual I could not sleep. I heard my father stirring around, so I went into my parents' bedroom to investigate. Theirs was next to the one where Peter and I slept. My brother Robert Andrew had a bunk bed in an adjacent room and my sisters' bedroom was down the hallway.

As I entered the room, my father was standing near the window with a fire poker in his hands.

"David, go back to bed," he whispered.

I did as I was told and pulled the blankets up around me. Peter was asleep.

My father passed by our bedroom and shuffled around the house checking the windows and doors. The wind howled. Seldom did any of us sleep soundly at that time, not even at Highland Park.

We arrived earlier that day and noticed the furniture was moved, although nothing appeared to be missing. None of the windows were left open and the locks were not damaged.

We already knew that our phone in the apartment in the city

was tapped. My father had picked up the receiver one day and overheard someone saying, *"Hola. Superintendencia de Seguridad"* ("Hello. This is the Superintendent of Security").

Superintendencia de Seguridad – also known as SS – directed the work of government death squads.

Also at that time at Highland Park, our pet rabbits were missing from their cage in the backyard. We searched the neighborhood but to no avail. It wasn't until 30 years later that I learned from a family friend what happened.

Someone broke into the cage while we were not there, killed the animals and strewed their bloodied carcasses on the front lawn. I asked my father if this was true, and he said it was.

"Why did you not tell us?"

"How could I?" he asked.

The Cox children lived in constant fear. They alternated their route home from school to the apartment, sometimes taking the train and other times riding the bus. According to recently declassified U.S. State Department documents, about a week after the Herald reported the disappearance of magazine editor Delgado, the co-owners of the publication expressed disappointment to the Argentine government that the story had been made public. Members of the ruling junta were angry with the Herald and summoned Cox to Government House for a meeting with Interior Ministry Chief Harguindeguy, who told him that Delgado had committed suicide. This meeting occurred one month after the General assured Cox and the U.S. State Department that the disappearances would end.

"Gen. Harguindeguy is like the Nazi Hermann Goering. He is a bully," Cox later told Maud.

Harguindeguy's claim that there would be no more mysterious abductions was another lie. Hundreds of people continued to be picked up, tortured and killed, and their bodies were burned, dumped into the Atlantic Ocean or buried in mass graves.

Cox stayed in contact with Harguindeguy so that he could get as much information as possible about the disappearance of people considered enemies by both the junta and the Montoneros. Cox wrote at least two letters to the Interior

Ministry's second in command, Col. Ruiz Palacios, requesting information about *los desaparecidos* whose families had asked the Herald for help. One was dated June 12, 1978 – only 10 days after Cox and the Herald were honored by the Queen:

> *Dear Col. Ruiz Palacios: Regarding the telephone conversation we had recently, I hurriedly sent you information of the three people kidnapped in the home of the Eroles family by 15 heavily armed men.*

On June 14, he wrote again:

> *Dear Colonel: The parents of Alejandra Naftal, a 17-year-old student, came to see me. The girl disappeared after 10 or 15 men visited her parents' home.*

He also asked the Colonel for information about six other cases of missing persons, and, again, if he had any news of the disappearance of the three members of the Eroles family.

On June 25, 1978, at 3 p.m. when Argentina faced Holland for the final of la *Copa del Mundo* ("the World Cup"), the Cox boys were as knowledgeable as most adult football fans about the game. The winning team would receive a golden trophy, and the most outstanding player would get the "Golden Boot" award. The Cox family, along with some of their closest friends, watched the championship game on the color television at Papito's house.

Both teams opened strong, but in the 38th minute, Argentina's striker Mario Kempes, known as *el Matador* ("the Killer"), scored the first goal.

"Goooooooooal!" millions of people throughout the city screamed in unison.

DAVID COX JOURNAL: JANUARY 2008

As the first half of the game drew to a close, I admit that I too cheered Argentina's goal while wearing an orange Dutch jersey emblazoned with the same No. 14 of Holland's star player Johan Cryuff, who refused to play in the World Cup as a protest against the junta's human-rights abuses.

Later, with only two minutes left in the 90-minute regulation game,

Holland's Dick Nanninga scored the tying goal. That meant the match would continue with a 30-minute overtime. Argentina scored a second time in the 105th minute, and Daniel Bertoni kicked the national team's third and final goal in the 116th minute.

Argentines everywhere erupted with joy. The national team had won the World Cup. Men, women and children danced in the streets and jumped into city park fountains amidst a cacophony of car horns. The Cox children were among them, weaving through the maze of jubilance. Bob Cox, who covered the game from inside the stadium, returned to the Herald to write his story. It was the first time Argentina had won the World Cup since the tournament began in 1930:

> *The biggest crowds in Argentina's history poured into the streets of cities, towns and villages throughout the nation last night to celebrate a sparkling 3-1 victory over Holland in the World Football Cup final. The jubilation was so great that the massive victory celebrations in Europe in 1945 seemed pallid compared with the frenzied joyfulness that gripped the country's 26 million inhabitants yesterday. For the record books, it was an historic moment – Argentina's first World Cup. But it meant far more than that to Argentines.*

> *When Argentina's captain Daniel Passarella was carried around the reverberating River Plate stadium on the backs of frenzied fans, the World Cup trophy glinting in the light of the arc lights stood for a much greater national triumph. Although the football was good, with moments of greatness that will assume epic proportions in years to come, the delirious cheers were for everything that led up to that moment when 77,000 hearts stood still as the final whistle blew after 120 thrill-packed minutes and Argentina had emerged as world-beaters … In the euphoria of yesterday's fiesta, anyone could be forgiven for thinking that they were ushering in a new lifestyle – of success – for the nation.*

> *An hour after the game, spectators in the stadium were still loath to go home. Thousands went down on to the sanctified playing area and kissed the turf. Then they plucked stems of grass to carry home as mementos of Argentina's shining hour.*

Indeed, high spirits, humor and tolerance prevailed. Not once did the victory degenerate into violence as a result of rowdy behavior as was the case in other countries whose national teams had won the coveted trophy. It was as if Argentina had suddenly become a place where all was clean and pure and decent. There were no leftists or rightists, no Peronists or anti-Peronists, no pro-government or Montonero terrorists on the streets of Buenos Aires at that time. Argentines proved to the world that they could get along with one another. They were unified as a nation of citizens from all walks of life.

Or so it seemed.

DAVID COX JOURNAL: JANUARY 2008

Although I was only 12 years old at the time, I was acutely aware of what the government had been doing to people considered to be a threat to the ruling junta. My fear and disgust was so keen that I found myself pulling for Holland to defeat Argentina in the World Cup soccer championship. My friends could not understand why I had switched my allegiance. Somehow, I thought, if Holland defeated Argentina, the killings would end, and we would not be abducted and murdered.

But the spirit of soccer, imbued with nationalism, had taken hold of Argentina. Billboards, newspaper and magazine advertisements and television commercials expressed support for the national team. There was no way to escape soccer fever. Peter and I often practiced kicking penalty shots downstairs in the garage. Sometimes, we walked to a nearby park to play with boys who lived in nearby shantytowns. Most were children of low-income families who came because the park was large, with grassy fields. We learned from them how to excel in the game. Soccer consumed their lives. They knew the secrets of "the beautiful game" and shared them with us.

Later, after we moved to South Carolina, we played on the Middleton High School soccer team and became well known locally. Once, when I set up Peter for the victory goal in a state championship game, the Post and Courier headline declared: "The Cox Brothers do it again!"

Not long after Argentina's World Cup victory, a woman who never went public with what happened to her was abducted by government agents and tortured. Her "crime" was that she looked like the wife of the Argentine national team's coach, Cesar Luis Menotti, who had spoken out against the harsh tactics of the junta in its fight against the Montoneros.

She was a friend of Harry Ingham, who said she was severely tortured before her abductors realized it was a case of mistaken identity and set her free. Ingham was disgusted with the Argentine leaders. He recalled the heart-rending decision of his own father to move with his family from his native Germany in 1933 after Hitler came to power. Ingham vowed to do all that he could to support Cox and the Herald in the campaign to stop the government's human-rights abuses.

Meanwhile, Walter Klein, as second in command at Argentina's Ministry of Economy, pressed for financial reforms despite resistance from powerful sectors of the military. He maintained his skepticism that the junta was coordinating massive abuses, arguing that the national economy must be fixed before worrying about rumors surrounding the governing faction.

Throughout this period, Maud Cox tried to maintain some sense of normalcy for the family. She took the children to the park daily. They also went to live shows at the theater and to movies at the cinema. She created special occasions.

Once, she dressed all five of them in Scottish outfits that included berets, kilts, green velvet jackets and *sporrans*, Gaelic for purses. They saw a performance of "Hansel and Gretel" at the Teatro Colon, Buenos Aires' grand opera house, where they sat in a box overlooking the stage.

At home, she introduced the children to the strident rhythms of a different type of music, *La Cumparsita*. It reminded her of when she was young and danced the tango with friends. Her oldest son Robert, who later became an accomplished concert pianist, learned the root music of the country from her at that time.

On weekends when it rained, the family did not go to Highland Park because the road became a river of mud that the old Peugeot could not navigate. When forced to stay indoors, Bob Cox encouraged his children to read, saying he spent many summers as a child during World War II immersed in books he found on the shelves of his grandmother's home in Rowsley, Derbyshire. He also encouraged them to write to their aunt in England.

They also went to the cinema on Calle Lavalle, a street lined with restaurants and movie houses with glaring neon signs that promoted the latest films that were cleared by the government. They saw "Grease," "Saturday Night Fever" and the "Sound of Music." The junta banned motion pictures considered to be subversive.

These films included "Last Tango in Paris," "A Clockwork Orange" and "Looking for Mr. Goodbar." Others, both foreign and Argentine, were censored so severely that they were not worth viewing. Censorship extended to numerous popular novels, too. "The Little Prince," by Antoine de Saint-Exupery, was one of them.

Argentine families hid or threw away many of their books for fear that having them might cause others to think they were anti-government terrorists. One family buried their books in large plastic bags because they had "Communist" red covers or included references to left-wing politics and philosophy. It wasn't until five years later, at the conclusion of the Falkland Islands War in 1983, that democracy was restored in Argentina, and the books were disinterred.

Most Argentines lived in an irrational fear of terrorism and of each other, resulting in a general feeling of indifference about the plights of others. Most members of Argentina's upper and middle classes became adept at denial. They refused to believe that people who were abducted in broad daylight by security forces were carried off to torture chambers and prison camps never to be heard from again.

Maud Cox often struck up conversations with taxi drivers to find out how much they knew about the disappearances. In her diary, she recalls a conversation with one driver who was taking her to the *Banco de la Nacion* (the National Bank) on Plaza de Mayo. She usually began these conversations with comments about the weather before moving on to the subject of *los desaparecidos*. But this time, she blurted out to the driver:

"What a disaster! What a terrible state our country is in!"

"Why do you say that?" the driver asked. "It's true that the economy is not doing well, but there have always been difficult moments in Argentina. There are cycles: some benefit from one cycle and then others benefit from the next."

"No, I am talking about the *los desaparecidos*. It seems that people are disappearing."

The driver said nothing until he stopped at the bank. As she was leaving the cab, he looked at her and asked: "Who are you?"

"I am the wife of a journalist."

The driver's eyes filled with tears, highlighting his grey hair and the deep lines etched in his face: "It's been more than a year since they took my son."

"Have you told anyone about your situation?"

"No madam. We are very scared. My wife had a small business, and my son worked with her. At night, he attended the university where he studied medicine.

He never missed class. We were surprised on the day he did not come home. We spoke to students at the university who knew him and they said some men stopped him as he was leaving class and took him away. My wife and I went to all the police precincts and asked if they knew what had happened. Nobody gave us an answer. We have been sick with worry, and a few months ago my wife suffered a heart attack. She is still in a very delicate condition.

"She cries nonstop. I work 13 hours a day to pay for her medicine. I am hopeful our son will return someday. Surely they will release him. He is a fine boy."

"You should contact the human rights organizations," Maud advised. "They may help you find him."

"I don't want to file a missing person's report. Surely they will release him."

He waved goodbye and drove away.

Many families ignored reality in such a way, but only by acting immediately to bring their loved ones' cases to the public would there be any chance that they would be saved. The ongoing power struggle within the armed forces often was a factor in the outcome of such abductions. In Timerman's case, for example, generals were divided about what should be done with him. Some thought he should be released. Others wanted him killed and forgotten. Fortunately for Timerman, stories about his abduction generated international pressure for his release. Once it became known that Timerman was in prison, the Argentine Supreme Court had no choice but to rule that his detention was illegal and ordered that he be held under house arrest in his own apartment just five blocks from the Coxes' apartment.

Meanwhile, Adm. Massera, the cunning navy commander in charge of the ESMA told representatives of the U.S. government that a list of the people who had disappeared should be made public. Massera thought President Videla would be forced to step down as a result. This would clear the way for Massera himself to assume the presidency.

Cox, who had written another editorial calling on the military to stop its power struggle and return the country to the rule of law, was in the middle of verbal crossfire.

Massera had heard that army Gen. Roberto Eduardo Viola might succeed Videla as president of Argentina and was infuriated when he read about animosity between the navy and the army undermining the future of the nation. Cox's files include a note from his secretary advising, "Massera wants to talk to you!"

When Cox arrived at navy headquarters, Massara complained to him bitterly, adding, "If you mention my name one more time in your newspaper, I'll put you away forever!" Cox held off on his commentary about Massera for a week and then referred to him as usual when he felt the occasion demanded. Massera was quite capable of carrying out his threat.

DAVID COX JOURNAL: JANUARY 2008
I once interviewed a man who was a member of the Montoneros organization in 1978. I was told that the Montoneros received word that a death squad was authorized by the navy command to murder my father at a reception he was to attend at the Sheraton Hotel in Buenos Aires. The Montoneros decided to protect my father by following him as he walked to the hotel and gathering around him as bodyguards when he entered the lobby. The Buenos Aires Herald's support of human rights was impartial in calling for a return to the rule of law in Argentina. The Montoneros apparently no longer saw him as a threat to them as they had in the past.

The newspaper consistently focused attention on the fates of children whose parents were abducted and on the disappearances of many of the children themselves. The Herald had helped secure the return of young children to their grandparents in 1976. The newspaper was also the first to report the founding of the Grandmothers of the Plaza de Mayo.

In the spring of 1978, Cox wrote the first story published in any newspaper about a group of grandmothers organizing themselves in the same fashion as the *Madres* had done previously. On the day after the story ran, one of the country's premiere news agencies, Noticias Argentinas, confirmed that the Herald broke the story about the new group known as *las Abuelas de Plaza de Mayo*. According to the Herald of May 17, 1978:

> *A group of women who say that they met by chance in the corridors of the law courts, on the pavement outside army garrisons, in police stations, before the altars of churches and finally in the Plaza de Mayo, have given themselves the title of 'the Grandmothers of Plaza de Mayo.' They number 13 and all have two things in common: They are searching for their children who have disappeared as well as their grandchildren.*

Cox later escorted correspondents of the Washington Post and the BBC to meet with the Grandmothers. The reporters were told that, in most cases when a military task force abducted the parents, the children were taken from them and issued false birth certificates. Then the children were handed over to military families to be raised in ignorance of their biological parents. The Grandmothers have since managed to locate more than 70 children who were abducted and adopted illegally. They used advanced DNA technology to establish the children's identities and have become an internationally known and admired human-rights organization.

But in 1978, most people treated them contemptuously, the same way that the Mothers of the Plaza de Mayo were viewed when they first organized. As the Grandmothers joined in the struggle to find the *desaparecidos*, Cox was nominated to receive the Maria Moors Cabot Award, the oldest international prize given to journalists who contribute to the advancement of Inter-American understanding.

He was jubilant about the news because he knew it would help in his campaign to make public information about those who disappeared. Meanwhile, he compiled a list of more than 100 journalists who were missing in Argentina. When he was selected to receive the Moors Cabot Award, he was particularly concerned about the unexplained murder of Horacio Agulla, editor of Confirmado, a leading Argentine magazine.

Agulla was gunned down outside his home in a posh neighborhood in Buenos Aires on the same day of the announcement. The following is Cox's letter to the coordinator of the Moors Cabot Award presentation at Columbia University in New York City:

> *Dear Mrs. Marwell: I saved myself the agony of having another photograph taken by discovering this portrait taken painlessly by a friend recently. I believe I look much the same, even perhaps a little less beaten-up. I include a pen portrait, which is very rough. I find it hard to write about myself.*

> *Please tell me if it is no good. I will, if you like, try to go back down memory lane and get some more interesting nuggets and polish them. But I am also enclosing a piece written by a former Maria Moors Cabot winner, which might be of some use.*

> *The most important thing about me is that I am married to a wonderful woman and have five heart-warming children… I will arrange tickets and reservations at the hotel. I am still awaiting my*

travel certificate from the police.

Am I expected to make a speech, please? Do forgive the scrappy typing, I am rushing this because I have to have a minor operation this morning and I wanted to get this off my conscience. Please let me know if I have been remiss in anything. Thank you.

Since Maud and *los chicos de Cox* (the Cox children) could not travel to New York, Cox requested that invitations to the awards ceremony be sent to Bill Montalbano, who had become the Miami Herald's chief foreign correspondent, and to Peter Manigault, president of the Evening Post Publishing Co. in Charleston. Soon afterward, Manigault called Cox and congratulated him. He also sent a copy of an article published Oct. 26, 1978, in the Charleston News and Courier that read in part:

> Robert Cox was recognized for his unyielding commitment to freedom of the press and human rights, and for his readiness to confront injustice regardless of the risk to his newspaper and himself.

A photograph of Cox wearing a mortarboard and academic robe as he received the Maria Moors Cabot Award appeared in the Buenos Aires Herald as well as several other international newspapers on Oct. 25, 1978. The next day, while he was still in New York City, a representative of the Mothers of the Plaza de Mayo went the Herald offices to congratulate him. Betty Lombardo, the Herald's secretary, relayed to him the message: "One came on behalf of all the mothers who have children missing to congratulate you for the prize and to say no one deserves it more. She was accompanied by her husband, who added, 'God Bless Señor Cox.'"

That note was in his files with hundreds of other letters of congratulations sent to him at the Herald. They are from people all over the world, including representatives of Reuter's news agency and United Press International, the ambassadors of the United Kingdom and the United States, human-rights leader Emilio Mignone and a member of the Hidalgo Sola family. Rabbi Marshall Meyer, an American and prominent Jewish religious leader in Argentina and a staunch defender of human rights, wrote:

> Dear Bob: I am proud to know you. I am proud to be your friend.
> I am happy and grateful that there are people like you in the

world. It makes it easier to live in such harrowing surroundings knowing that one can speak to Bob Cox on the phone and have lunch with him and have dinner with him and talk to him and be with him.

May God bless you together with Maud and your children, and grant you many years of life, vitality, creativity and the same exquisite sensitivity to justice and human suffering that has made you the person you are. We all love you very much. Congratulations!

Former U.S. Ambassador Robert C. Hill wrote from Littleton, N.H., only 21 days before he died of a heart attack:

My Dear Bob: Word has reached me through the Buenos Aires Herald that you have received the Maria Moors Cabot Award for distinguished journalism. I join with your thousands of admirers in congratulating you on this much-deserved award. As I look back on my years in Argentina, you and your wife were among the brightest experiences we had in your country.

A letter signed by more than 100 Mothers of Plaza de Mayo, noted Cox's:

… unwavering service to press freedom and human rights and for your will to confront injustice despite the risks for your newspaper and yourself. Today an act of justice has taken place. Those of us who daily feel heard, interpreted, understood and expressed in our desperate search, we cannot fail to join you in your happiness at receiving an award which has greater value because it transcends the journalistic acknowledgment and honors the supreme values of a man and his struggle for liberty and justice. Today the mothers of the 'non-people' say thank you! And continue! We pray God that the example of your 'journalism' is imitated by all those who have the duty to inform, and contribute like you to the peace that we all need.

Justice finally seemed to be on the Cox family's side.

DAVID COX JOURNAL: JANUARY 2008

When my father returned from New York City with the award
in hand, I was reminded of Caratacus Potts, the inventor in
the movie "Chitty Chitty Bang Bang." Potts' children, Jeremy
and Jemima, were amazed that their father could transform a
wrecked clunker in Mr. Coggins' junkyard into a magnificent
flying machine that was used to foil the evil doings of Vulgaria's
Baron Bomburst and the Child-Catcher. I, too, was amazed by
what my father had done.

Meanwhile, a real-life villain – a member of our own family – was
plotting against us, and we did not know it. He was a relative on
my mother's side who married the daughter of a leading Argentine
military officer. We trusted him completely and welcomed him
into our homes. It never crossed our minds that he was passing
information about the family to the military, but over the years,
we learned that he was primarily responsible for the tragedy that
would befall us.

What my brothers and I knew for certain was that when our
parents were not with us in the swimming pool at Highland
Park, he delighted in holding our heads under the water until
we felt as if we were drowning. He would pull us up and then
push us down, again and again. We tried to fight him off. He
would laugh and say it was only a game. When we were older and
told our parents about his behavior, they were shocked. We still
wonder if he was practicing on us that type of torture known in
Spanish as *"el submarino,"* also called "water boarding."

The Herald received repeated criticism from authorities and others for reporting
on the plight of the disappeared. Cox wrote an open letter to readers explaining his
decision to defend *las Madres:*

> *A number of readers have written to the Herald to question this
> newspaper's coverage of the Thursday demonstrations of the Mothers
> of Plaza de Mayo, who seek to draw attention to their search for
> missing children. Some readers have even gone as far as to suggest*

that we are guilty of anti-government propaganda because we show concern about those people who are searching for relatives who have disappeared.

Yet most readers have little or no knowledge of the suffering that people seeking missing relatives are going though. Their plight is almost totally ignored by most of the press. It is an issue people prefer not to face. And while the government has set up machinery in Government House to cope with people reporting disappearances, there has been no major initiative to pierce the mystery that surrounds thousands of disappeared.

Another disappearance similar to the unsolved cases of Sajon, Fernandez Pondal and Delgado came to light soon after the assassination of journalist Horacio Agulla. The Herald editorialized on the danger facing journalists:

Four of these men are distinguished journalists who have vanished without a trace. The fifth, Dr. Hidalgo Sola, was serving as Argentine Ambassador to Venezuela when kidnapped by gunmen in two cars. For each of these compelling tragedies there are thousands more. In some cases it is easier than others to guess why someone has disappeared. Indeed, it is clear that a large number of kidnappings are carried out by people so powerful that they are above the law. On the day Dr. Agulla was murdered, it was reported that another newspaper editor, Juan Ramon Nazar, who was kidnapped over a year ago, had reappeared. There was even the hint of recognition of some strange quasi-legality in his abduction in the report, which described him as having recovered his liberty.

After the ordeal of terror that the country has lived through, the public appears willing to accept the fact that unexplained, uninvestigated 'disappearances' might be part of the price that has to be paid to defeat terrorism. But unless victory is declared one day, public opinion will soon realize that all that has happened is that subversion is being replaced by institutionalized terrorism.

A long list of inexplicable disappearances could be drawn up. One day there will be an overwhelming demand for them to be investigated. The disappearance of innocent people, supporters of the government, even some who hold high posts in administration, cannot be forgotten. Their families will never forget them and they will haunt the memory of every good citizen in Argentina. You cannot wipe people from life like chalked names on a blackboard.

In choosing journalists as victims, the terrorists (clearly from the right as well as the left) are compulsively digging their own graves. Dr. Agulla's murder is another clarion call to the press to react and arouse the brutalized conscience of Argentina to the continuing terror. This latest case emphasizes the need for prompt government action on two fronts: a new crackdown on people carrying guns and the setting up of a special investigation department to probe past kidnappings and prevent abductions and assassinations. The security forces must be mobilized and redeployed to deal with ALL terrorism.

The United States expressed increasing concern about violations of human rights in Argentina. At the U.S. Embassy in Buenos Aires, human rights officer Tex Harris was compiling an official list of people who had disappeared and was meeting regularly with the Mothers of the Plaza de Mayo. In Washington, D.C. Patricia Derian testified before the U.S. House Foreign Affairs Committee and charged the Argentine government with systematic tortures and summary executions.

As now-declassified documents show, the U.S. government had detailed information about the methods of torture. The U.S. Embassy in Buenos Aires reported "physical torture continues to be used regularly during the interrogation of suspected terrorists and so-called criminal subversives who do not fully cooperate." Torture used to intimidate and extract information included "electric shock, the submarine (prolonged submersion under water), sodium pentothal, severe beatings, including 'el Telefono,' in which a simultaneous blow is delivered to both ears with cupped hands."

In addition, a 1978 Amnesty International report on the Argentine government's human-rights abuses described incidents of "cigarette burns; sexual abuse and rape; removing teeth, fingernails and eyes; burning with boiling water, oil and acid; and castration." Cox knew that torture was routine but did not know the extent until 1983 after democracy was restored in Argentina and more information emerged in the new government's Report of the National Commission on the Disappearance of Persons.

The Herald and the U.S. government also defended the rights of the nation's Jehovah's Witnesses religious organization, which was banned in Argentina soon after the junta seized power in 1976. Members of that faith suffered repeated attacks at the hands of junta operatives. In December 1978, church leaders were arrested, and more than $100,000 worth of their printed materials confiscated.

The Herald had already launched a strident editorial campaign in support of the Jehovah's Witnesses' freedom-of-religion rights. Soon after the arrests of the church leaders, the U.S. State Department condemned the Argentine government's actions. Official persecution of the church eased somewhat, but harassment of individual members of the faith continued until Argentina's return to democracy five years later.

Cox later learned that his defense of the Jehovah's Witnesses' rights to practice their faith in Argentina helped save his own life. The superintendent of the apartment building on Avenida Alvear was a Jehovah's Witness who called when he saw suspicious men in the vicinity and sensed an imminent threat to the family.

In November 1978, King Juan Carlos of Spain arrived in Buenos Aires for a state visit. The Argentine government hoped this would improve its increasingly tarnished international image. The King's visit did just the opposite, and strengthened Cox's resolve to confront the junta directly and press for democratic reform. The junta obviously did not understand that King Juan Carlos was a hugely symbolic figure in the ongoing effort to spread liberal democracy throughout the world.

Carlos was instrumental in bringing an end to Spain's military rule in 1975 following the death of Generalissimo Francisco Franco. Spanish military officers had assumed Carlos would support them. Instead, he shocked the world by committing the monarchy to Spanish democracy.

Cox was surprised when he received an invitation to attend a reception given by the military government for King Juan Carlos and Queen Sofia at the Concejo Deliberante, a beautiful edifice in downtown Buenos Aires that houses the city council. The glittering reception for the royal couple would be the biggest Argentine social event of the decade. Cox was one of only a few journalists invited, and his primary interest in attending was not social. He held the King in the highest esteem because of the crucial role he played in leading the transition of the Spanish government from a dictatorship to democracy.

Editors of several large Spanish newspapers questioned whether it was a good idea for Carlos to go to Argentina because of the junta's ugly human-rights record. But, as would soon become clear, he did not intend to butter up leaders of Argentina's military government.

As Cox stood at the reception inside the palatial Concejo Deliberante and waited for the arrival of the King and Queen, he kept his eye on President Videla and Adm. Massera. Both were decked out in formal military attire, and both were nervous. They were even more so when Spain's dashing young monarch walked in wearing a dinner jacket and black tie instead of his usual dress uniform. Queen Sophia was beautifully attired in a simple evening gown with a pink cape, which she handed to a nearby presidential aide. The contrast between Spain's confident Royal Couple and Argentina's cowering military elite was striking.

> Two very important things happened next that had enormous significance. The King gave a speech and chided the military government, explaining that human rights and democracy played a central role in Spain. I saw that, when the King spoke, the Argentine officers became more rigid. When they heard him praise democracy and emphasize that 'the inviolable rights of the individual' must be respected in the quest for 'order and social peace,' they could scarcely control their anger at his words. The other important event is the fact that somebody stole the Queen's cape.

"Who walked off with Queen Sofia's diaphanous evening cape?" Cox asked in an article that appeared in the Herald the next day.

> It's the secret everyone in the country seems to be in on, but that the general press withholds in order to save a certain lady of a traditional family of property from embarrassment ... Everyone is behaving like characters in a Galsworthy novel, except, of course, Dr. Alberto Ruben Coronel, a local lawyer who demands an investigation into the disappearance of the Queen's cloak.

The royal cape was retrieved from "a lady of distinguished aspect" at her home at 3 a.m. the next morning and returned to Queen Sophia. Meanwhile, Dr. Coronel's request for an investigation was denied by a local judge who said, "Only the Supreme Court can handle a case involving a foreign monarch because only the highest court in the country can deal with matters to do with ambassadors, ministers and foreign consuls."

The junta did not take Cox's commentary lightly. He received no more invitations to government functions.

DAVID COX JOURNAL: FEBRUARY 2008

We celebrated Christmas for the last time at Highland Park with our grandfather Papito. We gathered around the piano and sang as usual, each of us playing a maraca, triangle, bell, castanets and pandereta in accompaniment. Dinner featured the carving of a large turkey that my grandfather bought from the exquisite Las Violetas Café. This was followed by the showing of Christmas movies outside, under the stars, on the club lawn.

David asked his younger sister Ruthie what she remembers of that year:

> I remember Papito. Peter and I walked to his apartment many times. He was very important in our lives. I was very little when the military government came to power, but I remember many events and feelings I had about what was going on. Despite the darkness that surrounded us, we did have many moments that were very happy.
>
> As I look back, the two most important people that have taught me about how to live a good life are my parents. My father is a talented writer. He was able to help others by giving their story a voice when so many did not. He had courage that many did not have. If you talk to him, you know that he just did what he thought was right.
>
> My mother is a fighter. Her whole life she has fought. I have never seen someone with so much strength. She stood next to him, telling others that what was going on in Argentina was wrong. Some stood by my parents. Many did not. My mother left Argentina when she was almost 49 years old. She left her father and her home. She took her five children to a country she did not know. She began again from nothing. She went back to school and got her doctorate.
>
> My parents have taught us many things, but the most important lesson was to do always the right thing.

CHAPTER 13
LIVING WITH FEAR
(1979)

The year 1979 started with a bang. The Fariña family, which included five children, swung open the white wooden gate of the Cox home at Highland Park with military precision and drove a Jeep into the yard. Sitting on the vehicle's roof were the older Fariñas brothers, armed with *bombitas de agua* (water bombs). Packed inside were the other siblings, each shouting menacingly. Carnival had begun!

Within seconds, the Coxes were soaked as they stood on their patio. The Fariñas won the war, which always commenced by such a surprise attack. Most families who were at Highland Park during Carnival were careful to supply themselves with buckets of water balloons.But the Fariñas were masters of the game.

The only time this particular Carnival tradition turned serious was the year one of the Cox children – no one remembers who–tossed a water bomb randomly at a passing car and made a direct hit on the front windshield. Normally, victims of such assaults take them in stride. But this time, the driver of the car slammed on the brakes, got out and threatened the children. The man walked up to the house and issued a string of profanities, which got the attention of Papito, who demonstrated precisely how hot an Italian temper can get.

"Leave them alone. They are only children!" Papito warned. The children's grandfather, who stood more than 6 feet tall, was never intimidated, and this encounter was no exception. The intruder soon left the scene. How easy it would have been if all the family's problems could be solved in such a way.

Papito grew up in Buenos Aires as part of an upper-middle-class family. When young, he befriended members of the notorious Palermo Barrio gang, a group of toughs that, as Argentine author Jorge Luis Borges noted, was adept at winning knife fights. Although Papito was a gentleman as an adult, he maintained his ability to project a street-wise aura when necessary. In fact, to the dismay of Bob and Maud Cox, he owned a snub-nose revolver, which he showed to his grandchildren occasionally while vowing to use it on anyone foolish enough to bother them.

The Coxes built a guesthouse for Papito on the property in Highland Park, and he normally kept the pistol in his bedroom under lock and key. But sometimes while driving, he slipped the gun into the glove compartment of his silver-grey Peugeot 504. Unlike the old blue Peugeot 403, Papito's car was a sleek gem. Fortunately, he never had to use the pistol to defend his grandchildren.

Automobiles, of course, were a big attraction for the children, who took any criticism of the old Peugeot seriously. Unfortunately, this occurred often because the car was a clunker. On one occasion, an Argentine police officer took one look at the car and told Bob Cox, "Well, it's obvious to me that no one will ever accuse you of benefiting from corruption."

The Peugeot eventually died and was replaced by a white Dodge Polara, the Herald's company car. It was the envy of everyone except Cox, who described it as a "bathtub on wheels." But to the children, the vehicle was sheer luxury because all seven members of the family fit comfortably inside. Air-conditioning was rare at that time in Buenos Aires. Riding around in the Polara with the windows up during the summer reminded the children of their vacation in the United States, and especially of hot and humid Charleston.

But vacations were the last thing on the Coxes' minds in 1979 because the national economy was failing, and they had begun paying private school tuition for all the children. Inflation was high, despite the government's promises that prices would soon stabilize.

Early that year, Cox had a long discussion with Argentine Economy Minister Jose Martinez de Hoz, who said he was having difficulty convincing members of the junta to ease the financial stranglehold that choked the nation. All three armed services owned factories and other business enterprises with lucrative jobs filled by retired officers. Almost 60 percent of the economy was controlled by the military. This included all state-owned oil, steel and mining operations.

Martínez de Hoz cited the ongoing power struggle within the junta and told him that he and other Argentine economists had been threatened by hardliners opposed to privatization of state-owned companies.

In January, journalist Jorge Fontevecchia, 23, was ambushed by armed men in six un-tagged Ford Falcons and taken to a prison called El Olimpo. Fontevecchia founded La Semana, a small magazine that featured interviews with members of

Argentina's entertainment community. One was Mercedes Sosa, an internationally known folk singer whose name was on the junta's blacklist. Soon after the abduction, Cox wrote a news story and an editorial about the young editor. The publicity helped secure Fontevecchia's release.

"I personally owe my life to Robert Cox. Thanks to the Herald, which reported my disappearance, newspapers throughout the world published the story and international press organizations pressured the dictatorship to free me," Fontevecchia later wrote. Today, he owns a major Argentine media company that publishes several influential magazines as well as the newspaper Perfil.

In 1979, as Cox was forewarned by Argentina's minister of the economy, the "Dirty War" was taking on a more ghastly dimension. The factions within the dictatorship and the branches of the armed forces openly turned on one another. It was obvious that the most dangerous man in the nation was power-hungry Adm. Massera. He had been forced to retire as navy commander when his term as a junta member expired in September 1978. Yet he remained firmly in control of the nation's naval forces. This included the notorious ESMA torture center and death camp. Massera, who wanted to be Argentina's new president, was secretly in contact with exiled Montonero leaders for the purpose of forging a secret political alliance.

Elena Holmberg, a young diplomat assigned to the Argentine Embassy in Paris, found out about Massera's covert contacts and flew to Buenos Aires to tell President Videla about it in person. She never made it. Her body was found floating in a river outside the city. Cox worked closely with Tex Harris, the U.S. Embassy's human-rights officer, on the Holmberg case. Both men soon realized that Videla was too much of a coward to intervene for fear he would upset military hardliners. One of them was Gen. Guillermo Suarez Mason, el Carnicero ("the Butcher"), who was army chief of staff.

Suarez Mason, who directly oversaw the nation's prison camps, often bragged about the number of death sentences he signed daily. It soon became known that Suarez Mason was eager to sign the death warrant for Cox as well. Cox began tape recording his notes, thoughts and feelings about desaparecido cases he was following, including his coverage of Timerman, under house arrest a few blocks away from the family's downtown apartment.

Timerman was desperate to be free. Rabbi Marshall Meyer visited Timerman at his home and later told Cox he feared Timerman would soon have a nervous breakdown. Timerman was watched closely night and day by police guards who often ate the family's food and left the kitchen in a mess. They stole anything in the house that they fancied, the Rabbi said.

Timerman was a victim of blatant anti-Semitic acts perpetrated by members of the Argentine armed forces. Although official charges that Timerman had ties to the Montoneros had been dismissed and the Supreme Court ordered his release, the military hardliners refused to let *el Judio* ("the Jew") go free. President Videla worried that his own life was in danger because he had succumbed to international pressure and allowed the Supreme Court to rule in Timerman's favor.

As complaints from Government House about the *Herald's* editorials and news coverage intensified, Cox was regularly summoned for *un cafecito* (a coffee break) with Gen. Antonio Llamas, the government's secretary for public information. Cox knew a noose was slowly tightening around his neck and recorded as many notes and details as he could in case something terrible happened to him.

> *Today is March 9, 1979. I was called in by Gen. Llamas, who complained about a series of editorials – the usual complaints, except this time with a warning that the government was not going to accept my writing any more about human rights.*

The General complained he was being blamed for what Cox had written and abruptly left his office, leaving an open folder on the desk. It was a dossier of complaints about Robert John Cox's coverage of Argentine human-rights abuses, especially stories he had written for Newsweek.

It was, in fact, a subsequent story he wrote about Timerman that appeared in Newsweek that prompted the next call from Government House, only this time Cox was summoned to meet with Gen. Eduardo Crespi, the president's closest aide. Crespi complained that Cox had quoted an unidentified source about President Videla, saying that the fact that Timerman was Jewish didn't help his case. The article gave the impression that the President was weak and unable to maintain discipline in the armed forces. Crespi then asked Cox to identify his source. Cox declined, adding:

> *It is not the article that is damaging the country's image. It's the government's continued detention of Timerman despite the fact that the Supreme Court cleared him of all charges.*

Shortly afterward, Cox went to the U.S. Embassy to meet with Harris. He told him about the conversation he had with Gen. Crespi and noted an interesting irony that Cox later included in an editorial:

> *Externally, the military wants to project an image of a strong executive, but internally wishes to project the image of a weak president who needs the support of all thinking people against the hardliners arrayed against him.*

Cox told Harris about a new interior ministry strategy designed to cover up what had happened to the *desaparecidos*. The objective was to convince the Mothers of the Plaza de Mayo that their missing children had been killed in attacks on military forces. The *Madres*, however, never accepted such lies.

Cox also met repeatedly with Israeli Ambassador Ram Nirgad to discuss the Timerman case. The Ambassador said he must handle the situation delicately because of the extent of anti-Semitism within the Argentine armed forces. Rabbi Meyer had already told him that Timerman had been tortured and might soon begin a hunger strike if not released. That action could very well seal Timerman's fate.

On April 27, 1979, Cox wrote an editorial titled, "A Political Prisoner," that again demanded Timerman be freed because there were no legal grounds for depriving him of his liberty for more than two years.

Soon afterward, Bob and Maud Cox were invited to join a group of Argentine intellectuals for a human-rights seminar in Maryland organized by Georgetown University. Participants included Jeanne Kirkpatrick, foreign policy adviser to President Ronald Reagan and Samuel P. Huntington, author of the "Clash of Civilizations and the Remaking of World Order." Kirkpatrick and Huntington were considered to be sympathetic to Argentina's military regime.

At the conference, Cox stressed the importance of the Timerman case and described how "the two terrorisms" – one leftist inspired and the other by right-wing government agents – were destroying Argentina. A correspondent for La Nacion, Argentina's leading newspaper, quoted only what Cox said about left-wing terrorism. The story gave the impression that he supported the military completely. When they returned to Argentina, Gen. Harguindeguy called Cox and congratulated him for "defending Argentina."

In those anxious times, when fear and ignorance about "the two terrorisms" resulted in numerous misunderstandings, the Coxes were careful to maintain an image of being objective. They steered clear of most social engagements with people who obviously were pro-left or pro-right. They were surprised and concerned when they received an invitation to a dinner party from a couple they knew were close to key members of the government. But they accepted after agreeing to avoid any political discussions.

The dinner guests were influential people and included a prominent local banker. As they dined, the conversation kept returning to the plight of the *desaparecidos* no matter how hard the Coxes tried to talk about less controversial matters. Suddenly, the host slammed his fist on the table and asked: "Bob, what is going on in our country? Talk to us about human rights."

Cautiously, Cox described the situation, keeping it as close to the official version as possible. He said unfortunate excesses had occurred in Argentina's war against terrorism, adding he was hopeful the government would return to a strict observance of the rule of law. Then, quite unexpectedly, the host burst into tears and lamented the fact that some of his best friends had vanished and were surely dead. He explained that he had been critical of Cox in public before because he did not want anyone to know his true feelings about the military government.

"He became a very good friend of ours," Maud wrote in her diary. "That night, we realized how people operated on two levels in Buenos Aires."

Bob Cox realized that some members of Argentina's elite were against the military government's tactics of fighting terrorism with terrorism. He also was encouraged that the United States responded aggressively to Argentina's dictatorship. The growing concern in the United States about atrocities committed by the Argentine military was promising.

This was dramatically confirmed when B'nai Brith – the well-known Jewish human-rights organization – contacted Harris and suggested that a representative of the Mothers of Plaza de Mayo come to the United States to tell her story. Harris asked Cox for a recommendation. Renee Epelbaum, whose three children had disappeared, would be perfect, but she could not physically undergo the trip. So Cox asked Helena Arocena, whose son had disappeared, if she would accompany him instead. She agreed to do so.

They arranged to fly together to Washington to appear on NBC television's Meet the Press. On June 6, 1979, shortly before their departure, an article by Cox titled "Coming to Terms with History" was published in the Herald:

> *If we are to win the peace, then we must recognize the reality of the war. The price has been tremendously high. At least 5,000*

people (to take the lowest possible, most conservative estimate) have disappeared. Another 5,000 people (the figure is based on estimates by the military) have died. Between 1,500 and 2,500 are in jail, most of them without charges.

It would help, for a start, if the government would disclose the number of people reported missing – those who have not been traced – through the Ministry of Interior. This is the heart-aching, brain-numbing problem that we must all face. Gen. Viola made a brave effort to do so recently when he spoke about a new category of war victims: "Those who will be absent forever." To relatives, the statement seemed cruel. But it brought the taboo subject out into the open at last. The question that the Argentine press – with a few honorable exceptions – has ignored for so long has been raised at last.

Consider for a moment what the self-censorship that most of the press – the selfsame censorship that most of the media applied at the bidding of the Peronist regime, or because of the threats and intimidation of left-wing terrorists – has led to. Because the press refused to report thousands of disappearances over the past three years, countless innocent victims of a new kind of terrorism, which grew up in the image of the left-wing subversive groups, have vanished without a trace and hardly a whimper of protest. Some newspapers will only carry reports of kidnappings of journalists on their staff. Anyone else trying to trace a missing relative must pay to have the names listed in advertisements... Some requests for the advertisements have even been declined.

The result has been that for three years the country has been living an illusion. We have failed to come to terms with reality. Like all wars, this one has been almost unspeakably bloody. On top of that, it was hard for our natural allies to understand. No country in the world has ever suffered such an onslaught from terrorism. Think back to the horrors that we lived through: the appalling murder of the chief of police, Gen. Cardozo; the bomb in the canteen of the federal police security headquarters; the chain of cowardly assassinations of men in uniform – from humble police officers to highly respected admirals and generals to little children, who flitted in front of the terrorist gunfights while a fanatic continued to squeeze the trigger, to teen-agers blown apart by bombs. The catalogue of terrorist atrocities seems endless. They keep their prisoners chained like animals and treat them with bestiality. They tortured, blackmailed and terrorized. These were not isolated incidents. Horror has been piled upon horror... And there was no genuine national reaction of disgust and indignation or even unity.

So, when the coup came, it was natural – if totally unrealistic – to hope that the armed forces would turn black skies to blue overnight; that the disappearances, which had begun before the coup, would stop; that the courts would suddenly recover and impartial judges would hand down severe sentences. Capital punishment was introduced to deal with the terrorist murderers. But it was our society that broke down and the war went on and the innocent continued to die.

It was an unreported war – for sensible security reasons in some cases and, in others, because there is a feeling among the leaders of the armed forces that terrorists invariably misuse a free press. Out of such national suffering, a responsible press should have arisen to keep the country informed so that it could come to terms with history as history unfolded.

It may be said that the foreign press did not fully cover the terrorist onslaught on our society – which despite its imperfection, was, and still is, basically decent. The foreign press was not encouraged to report the terrorists then because the official view was that it was merely "a police matter." So the cover-up began.

But there were many brave foreign journalists who did report the terrorists' activities. When the local press was ignoring what was going on in Tucuman, Joe Novitski of the Washington Post was reporting from what was then terrorist-controlled territory. Many chose, then as now, to look the other way. And, as Michael Field of the London Daily Telegraph originally wrote, most of the foreign press came to report the second act of the Argentine tragedy without having seen the first.

What worries me now is that we, the people – and the government – have closed our eyes to a great deal of what has been going on in the second act. We haven't wanted to know. Virtually nobody – with a few honorable exceptions – has interviewed any relatives of missing people. The Thursday vigils of the Mothers of Plaza de Mayo were ignored by 90 percent of the Argentine press and media. The cry for help from the hearts of the people who have had someone dear to them snatched away by men claiming to the members of the security forces has gone largely unheard at home. But that cry is being heard abroad... The human rights movement abroad would hardly exist were it not for the pathetic, heart-rending appeals of people who have encountered only hard hearts and a stonewall in this country.

The problem of these suffering people is our problem. It should be faced and they should be ministered to here. They are being driven mad by the most terrible torture of all. Not knowing. After two or three years of the absence of a son or daughter – taken away from their homes in many cases after an apparent military officer or policeman explained that they are merely required for interrogation – they think they see the longed-for face in the street. They are perfectly genuine when they say that they only want to know whether to mourn or wait patiently for the return of their own flesh and blood.

The people of the United States have had to come to terms with horror after horror: The assassinations of the Kennedy brothers, of Martin Luther King Jr., of Vietnam, Watergate and, earlier, of the civil rights battles, which also had their disappearances. Britain had to come to terms with its colonial past, with its terrible record in Ireland and a continuing war against terrorism there today. The Germans had to come to terms with the Holocaust, and the Japanese with their cruelty during the last world war.

We must come to terms with our own Hiroshima. But because we lived a long way from the greater acts of violence that have shaped – although they almost destroyed – Western civilization, we insist on an attitude which is as patently transparent and ludicrous rather than cruel, as if President Truman had said that he did not know who dropped the bomb on Hiroshima.

Argentina must mature ... and come to terms with our history, with our shared guilt and our responsibility for all that has happened. We must come out into the light. We must release the prisoners of our darkness. We must accept the good with the bad, the joy with the despair. We must replace euphemism with fact and evasion with the truth. It is our own problem. There is no shortage of information abroad – exaggerated, in some cases; very often partial; only too often distorted by the terrorists through propaganda. It will not be easy to bind up wounds we have refused so far to recognize. But it can be done if we have confidence in the people and the country, and if we are honest with ourselves and realize that what we must tackle is a human problem.

The political consequences of the war can only be faced after we make the great effort required to end the suffering of those whose anguished cry that they simply don't know whether their nearest and dearest are dead or alive reverberates in every civilized corner of the earth.

Robert J. Cox

Cox was given a final warning about his coverage of the "Dirty War" when public information chief Gen. Antonio Llamas left the files open for him to see. Cox had received many warnings before, but this time it was different and he knew it. The fear he somehow managed to keep under control for more than three years had reached his soul. One afternoon, he turned on his tape recorder, and with the sounds of his children playing in the background, he said:

Today is Thursday, June 20, 1979. I want to document my fears.

Once again I woke up in the middle of my afternoon nap with an overbearing fear of what will become of my family. There seems to be no hope no... something very bad is going to happen... People treat me, I imagine, in the same way they would treat a condemned man, and this was something I could deal with previously through the years. At the Herald I often went to the first-floor to check the street, to see if there was a Ford Falcon waiting for me. I accepted back then that, if something bad happened to me, there was little I could do to save myself... I was much more concerned simply for my survival because it was like being in a war, and one could dodge bombs. It was a terrorist war and I expected that at anytime they would attack the Herald, and I thought they would come for me and would kidnap me, saying I was CIA or something or other.

I imagined I could enter the elevator, stop it between floors and be safe inside. I would plan different escape routes. ... Strangers entered the office with bags, and at times I was sure there were bombs inside

... Jim (Neilson) once confessed to me that he had carried a 'narvaja' (an old-fashioned cutthroat razor) in his pocket and was prepared to use it on anyone who came after him. He vowed that at least one of his abductors would fall.

One did not like to talk about these things, and I never dared tell anyone I was thinking about it before. ... Very often I thought that if they came after me, I would not know how to distinguish whether they were from the left or right or if they were police operating in disguise ...

Cox never told his family these things, yet they knew and felt his pain, his suffering, his anguish and his fears.

CHAPTER 14
SEARCHING FOR THE MISSING
(1979)

Bob Cox followed Gen. Harguindeguy to his office after a press conference at Government House during which the haughty interior minister tried to refute claims that the disappearances numbered in the thousands. Cox, with a small tape recorder in hand, had more questions. He often used the recorder when covering press conferences. He had forgotten to turn it off this time.

"How are you doing, Mr. Cox?" the General asked. "I congratulate you for what I read in the papers about comments you made during the seminar in the United States. You got all emotional. Sometimes you get carried away by that English romantic spirit, right?"

"Yes. That's right."

"But those articles you published today, you really hit us."

"It's not personal. Sixty journalists are missing."

"*Sesenta?* (Sixty?)," Harguideguy asked.

"Yes."

"There are prisoners, people who are involved in…"

"No. There are 60 journalists," Cox said.

"Only 60?" the General responded sarcastically.

"Sixty disappeared. I believe something has to be done…"

"Well, what you don't know is that there are a lot of disappeared," Harguindeguy snapped back.

"There are 60 journalists. Some of my colleagues have disappeared. You have to work to resolve this. This is a great problem." There was an audible tremor in Cox's voice.

"You are very sentimental," the General said.

"No. I am not sentimental."

"You are a great sentimentalist, a great sentimentalist... Then you go abroad and..."

As they entered the General's office, Cox continued his questions as his tape recorder ran.

"Can you help me a little?"

"We do help you, Cox. What do you think this is?" the General said referring to a document supposedly listing the names of all who had been killed that was on his desk.

"That's a lie!" said Cox, who had seen the false document before.

"Listen, I am not Jesus," the General responded in frustration. "I can't say, 'Lazarus get up and walk.' You know that."

The General's reference to raising Lazarus was his way of admitting that authorities had indeed murdered *desaparecidos,* and there was nothing he could do about it. Then, Col. Ruiz Palacios' voice broke.

"Cox, Cox, however, people have died ...".

"Yes, people have died," the General continued. "Many have died in this war, and there will come a time when the government will have to answer for them ... But we have to wait."

"Where is the military courage? Where is the military courage?" Cox asked.

"We do help you. I give you information ... but it is very different for me to express myself as interior minister than it is for you to write as editor of the Herald. Understand that we come from different worlds," the General said, adding that he, too, received letters and visits from people worried about missing loved ones.

"I see fathers and mothers and relatives and friends ... I see the generals, the brigadiers, the admirals, the colonels, the commodores ..."

"There are rumors now that 3,000 people have disappeared in the city," Cox said.

"They are crazy, Cox."

"How many have disappeared so far?"

"Listen, I've talked to you with great..." the general said hesitatingly.

"But, as you said, even military officers are disappearing," Cox continued, " ... you have to admit what happened."

Both Harguindeguy and Ruiz Palacios tried to convince Cox that most of what he had heard about the *desaparecidos* was not true. The General said the United States invented most of it in an attempt to discredit the Argentine government. He also warned that if the U.S. ambassador continued to press the government for an accounting of the disappeared, he would personally call every journalist in Argentina and explain that the United States was *mintiendo* (lying).

Cox told them their claims were ridiculous and cited the cases of journalist Fernandez Pondal and diplomat Hidalgo Sola.

Harguindeguy snapped back, stressing that excesses sometimes occur when a nation is at war.

"During World War II, American soldiers placed prisoners in a blockhouse and killed them all with grenades ..." he said.

Cox responded that there was no comparison between acts committed in World War II and what was happening in Argentina. Yet, the General kept insisting that Argentina was at war and obviously was irritated that the Argentine armed forces were viewed from abroad as violators of human rights.

"I get letters from all parts of the world about the disappeared. I get them from embassies; I get them from India, even from Ethiopia! One can improve the situation, but one cannot say, 'Lazarus get up and walk.' Nobody is able to say that!"

"*Las investigaciones sobre los desaparecidos son un chiste* (The government investigations of the disappeared are a joke)," Cox said in broken Spanish.

His war of words with Harguindeguy began in 1976 when Cox first asked the General about the disappearances. Their encounters were usually tense. But there were humorous moments, too. In December 1978, Gen. Harguindeguy sent Cox a letter that included 29 extracts from *Aunt Julia and the Scriptwriter*, a novel written by Mario Vargas Llosa that was banned by the Argentine government. The General asked that lengthy extracts be published in the Herald so that readers could see for themselves why the book was banned. Instead, noting that the excerpts would take up three full pages in the newspaper, Cox wrote:

> *I long ceased to be surprised by the new talents continually revealed by that many-sided man, the Interior Minister, Gen. Harguindeguy. I must say that if 'Aunt Julia' has been banned because of the extracts supplied to the Herald, the censor is going to have a very busy time in the future. Few modern novels will survive such strange and stringent censorship ...*

Yet most Argentine newspaper editors saw no evil, heard no evil and remained silent about the censorship. *Everyone had found a way to live, ignoring completely the problems of the disappeared, except some few exceptions.*

During a routine press conference at the U.S. Embassy, several reporters told Cox that the owners of their newspapers refused to allow publication of stories about power struggles within the armed forces. The Argentine judiciary was equally complicit. On June 24, 1979, Cox gave a ride to a judicial clerk traveling to his family's weekend house in Highland Park to Buenos Aires. They discussed many subjects during the drive, including the young man's work in a judge's office at the central law courts.

"Are you receiving a lot of *habeas corpus* writs for disappeared people?" Cox asked.

"There is a terrorist group that is obtaining lists of names and making these poor people present writs of *habeas corpus*," the clerk said.

"Look, people are desperate, and there was a time when no judge would take the writs. If they did, no one would take action on them," Cox said.

The young man changed the subject.

I told him he should understand that behind a habeas corpus *writ there is a person who is searching for someone whom they love. The young clerk admitted that he was the person in charge of receiving the writs from families whose relatives had disappeared. He confessed that he often felt like crying because he was so moved by their plights. I understood at that moment that he cared but that he had to do what he was told.*

Cox often wrestled with this puzzle. How could he break down the walls people built around themselves that allowed them to live in such denial? What could he do to communicate the extent of Argentina's human tragedy to the outside world? The answer presented itself less than a month later with the invitation to appear on Meet the Press at the NBC studio in Washington, D.C.

On Sunday July 8, 1979, Cox hurriedly packed his bags and rushed to the home of Helena Arocena. Soon, both of them were seated in an airliner bound for the United States for the Meet the Press interview. Mrs. Arocena was extremely nervous and appeared to be on the verge of a breakdown. She told Cox that she believed that CIA had kidnapped her son and that the agents followed her onto the plane to prevent her from exposing what they had done. Cox feared that she would not be able to join him on camera.

Upon arrival in Washington, Cox escorted Mrs. Arocena into her hotel room and urged her to rest. The following day, she seemed to have recovered, and they went to the studio. The moderator for Meet the Press was NBC newsman Bill Monroe and the panel consisted of James Nelson Goodsell of the Christian Science Monitor, Jeremiah O'Leary of the Washington Star and John B. Oakes of the New

York Times.

Monroe started the program by identifying Argentina as Latin America's leading human-rights violator. Between 5,000 and 15,000 people had disappeared there since the junta had come to power, Monroe said.

"Mrs. Arocena, I believe exactly three years ago tomorrow your son, Marcos, then I believe 36 years old, a writer, disappeared. What did your son's neighbors tell you about the circumstances of his disappearance?" he asked.

Mrs. Arocena's face blanched, then she said:

"He was supposed to arrive for lunch on Friday and stay a long weekend at home, but he didn't come. So I went downtown to his apartment to see what was the matter. Officers who did not want me to go inside surrounded his apartment. They said security agents had taken my son. I went inside anyway and everything was in chaos – his papers, everything, were scattered on the floor... So I went to the police station but got no information whatsoever from them. The neighbors later told me they saw a fleet of cars outside the apartment and that my son – hooded with his hands tied – was dragged out, thrown into a car and taken away."

She said security men arrived at his apartment at 3 a.m. and asked questions about someone to whom he had sub-rented his place during the summer. He told the men he did not know the tenant. Monroe asked if her son was involved in politics.

"Not at all. He is a writer but not in the least bit interested in politics," she said, then began to tremble as she had done on the plane.

At that point Cox looked into the eyes of each of the panelists and spoke very slowly: *In the chaos that came before the coup, we had one form of terrorism and it continued. An internal war was under way in Argentina in which no questions were asked of anything or anybody. The system of justice broke down completely and people such as Mrs. Arocena would go to the police but nothing was done.*

Argentine citizens became indifferent to violence that was committed by terrorists on the left and on the right, he said. *Argentina is a difficult county ...the only nation in the world that has been through an ordeal of total terrorism – an average of three assassinations a day. It's as if the murders of Martin Luthur King Jr. and both Kennedys occurred at the same time ... then continued through the 1970s until now. Yet despite all of that, there are some admirable people in Argentina... It has been very difficult ...*

The panelists appeared to be confused about what they were hearing. Cox explained that left-wing extremists committed numerous acts of terror and the military government cracked down on them by instituting a state-sponsored terror of its own. In the meantime, the majority of the nation's citizens looked the other way, thinking the government could handle the problem quietly and efficiently.

This is the other form of terrorism that people in Argentina don't want to face up to ... they don't want to face the fact that another form of terrorism had taken hold, that when you look into the eyes of the dragon, you become the dragon yourself ... Most Argentines are patriotic; they defend their country against accusations of human-rights violations.

Helena Arocena continued to tremble and Cox appeared exhausted as he called on conservatives and liberals throughout the world to help Argentina.

"What can we here in the Western world do now?" James Nelson Goodsell of the Christian Science Monitor asked.

"Speak out about it; try to make people conscious of what is going on," Mrs. Arocena said before turning to Cox.

Care about it without any political distortions. Insist on human rights without any ideological perversions ... appeal to the essential goodness of all Argentines, and of all people, to establish the kind of society that is necessary.

On the return flight to Buenos Aires, Cox thought about how much Argentina had changed since his arrival in 1959. People now live in their own little worlds. They have the illusion that what they do is not connected to others.

He had just returned from the United States where he had spoken out on national television about the Argentine military abducting, torturing and killing innocent people in its fight against subversion and emphasized that most of his fellow citizens were indifferent to what their government was doing. Cox later told his wife that he might be abducted and killed at any moment and that she should prepare for the worst.

I am getting nasty looks, Toopsy. People are asking me why I am still here.

"How can we protect the children?" she asked, and thought of grandmother Kathleen Boyle, who, although facing a very different circumstance, left her native Ireland in 1889. Maud asked herself if she could leave her own native country as her grandmother had before.

She decided that photographs should be taken of her family and of each member individually in case something terrible happened. So, as they walked along Avenida Alvear, a photographer took pictures of them together as well as close-ups of their faces. They walked to a nearby park and played on the swings and slides as the photographer continued to snap pictures. Only the eldest sister Victoria, who is looking away from the camera, has a trace of a smile on her face. All five photographs hang today on the wall of Bob and Maud Cox's home in Charleston.

The Coxes did all they could to protect their children and maintain some semblance of normality during those difficult times. Hearing their mother's piano as she played Claude Debussy's "Claire de Lune" helped them to escape into another world. The music carried them to a place where there was no sorrow, no stress – to a safe and beautiful world.

Or so it seemed.

The Argentine government was under intense international pressure to release Jacobo Timerman from house arrest. The new U.S. ambassador to Argentina, Raul Castro, paid Timerman a visit and explained that President Jimmy Carter was doing all he could to help. The American Jewish community also worked at many levels to secure Timerman's release. Nobel Laureate and author Elie Wiesel, himself a German Holocaust survivor, was in Argentina to speak on the subject of human rights.

Rabbi Marshall Meyer asked that he speak at his synagogue, and Maud Cox, who admired Wiesel's writing, was there to hear him. She was especially moved by Wiesel's story about the Just Man, which is included in his book *One Generation After*. It is an account of a man who went to biblical Sodom to convince the notoriously evil residents there to stop sinning and turn to God for guidance. But the killers went on killing and the rapists continued raping while the majority of their neighbors remained silent. A child eventually asks the Just Man why he is shouting.

"I'll tell you why. In the beginning, I thought I could change the people who live here. Today, I know I cannot. I still shout and I still scream to prevent them from ultimately changing me."

At the end of the lecture, Maud told Wiesel that she closely identified with the Just Man. Wiesel looked into her tearful eyes and said, "Someone in this society today feels the same way as the Just Man. His name is Robert Cox," then he gave her a hug.

Human rights organizations and the international media continued to pressure the Argentine government to stop the abductions and return the *desaparecidos*. The U.S. State Department even persuaded the junta to allow the Human Rights Commission of the Organization of American States to visit Argentina to investigate.

The members of the commission arrived in Buenos Aires two months later and read about a typical case of "Dirty War" tactics. Armed men who appeared to be members of a government security force took Maria Consuelo Castaño Blanco, 30, and her daughters, ages 3, 4 and 5, from their home. Neighbors witnessed the abductions and called Maria Consuelo's father, who went to the Herald and told Cox that his loved ones were missing. Her husband had been taken away earlier.

On Sept. 16, the Herald published the story and photographs of the children on the front page. On Sept. 19, the children were freed and left with a neighbor. The Herald stories prompted the intervention of the Organization of American States (OAS) Human Rights Commission. Maria Consuelo Castaño Blanco spent four years in an Argentine prison on trumped up charges, but her life was spared.

She later wrote a book about her ordeal titled *More than Human.* She wrote that soon after her abduction, she was taken to a government prison camp where she was identified only by the number A-11. She said she feared for her life daily. She often heard guards talking among themselves about how it was a pity that she was going to die at such a young age. Ten prisoners perished before she was transferred to another camp and forced to confess to a political crime she did not commit. But her imprisonment had been officially acknowledged.

She was sentenced to 24 years, which was reduced to 18 because she was a devout Roman Catholic. She was freed in 1983 and reunited with her children during the inauguration of duly elected Argentine President Raul Alfonsin. She later learned that the army had executed her husband, a Peronist, earlier at Campo de Mayo.

The 1979 visit to Argentina of the OAS Human Rights Commission was a sign that a return to the rule of law was possible. Rumors spread that that many people illegally held in secret prisons would soon be released. But Maud Cox knew better. In mid-September, U.S. diplomat Tex Harris arrived unexpectedly at the house.

"What's wrong, Tex?" Maud asked.

"Please pour me a whisky," he mumbled, adding, "I was with my wife and my kids at the park today. We had bought the children balloons and were enjoying the beautiful morning when, suddenly, we heard and felt explosions. A nearby building – which I knew was a clandestine prison – was engulfed in flames. Apparently, the authorities didn't want to leave any witnesses."

Cox arrived a few minutes later, saying he heard the military planned to kill everyone being held in the government camps. But he also had some good news: Jacobo Timerman had been freed from house arrest and placed on a plane bound for Israel, where his wife and children awaited him. He had been stripped of his Argentine citizenship, and all of his property was confiscated. Nonetheless, the U.S.

government considered his release a significant step in the restoration of the rule of law in Argentina.

Timerman's release appeared to herald a degree of respect for human rights returning to Argentina. Timerman was safe on a commercial airline bound for Israel, and the Coxes were optimistic that democracy was about to be restored in Argentina after three long years of military rule. But on Sept. 27, 1979, at 7:35 a.m., Harry Ingham called with urgent news.

CHAPTER 15
A FAMILY UNDER ATTACK
(1 9 7 9)

The phone rang.

Bob Cox answered. Harry Ingham"'s voice was strained.

"Bob, a bomb exploded in Klein's home," he said. "There are no survivors."

Within seconds of hearing that Walter Klein, the high-ranking government economist, and his family were dead, Cox dropped the phone, fell to the floor and covered his face with his hands. "No! Oh no!" he gasped. He could hardly breathe.

Maud helped him back to his feet, and he told her what had happened.

"We must go over there right now," she said. "Can you make it?"

They said nothing en route to the Kleins' house in the Buenos Aires suburb of Olivos as Cox's lungs slowly cleared from another asthma attack and he regained his strength. Upon arrival, they saw the smoldering rubble where the Kleins' English-style, two-story house once stood. Smoke was thick and water hoses snaked along the street as weary firemen took a break. A crowd gathered and Cox remembered his childhood days in London during the Blitz. A police officer walked slowly toward them.

"They were all taken out of the rubble and to the San Isidro Hospital. I think they survived," the officer said.

Bob and Maud left immediately and drove to Harry Ingham's house in the nearby suburb of Vicente Lopez. Together, they went to the hospital and upon arrival saw Perla Amoroso, Klein's personal secretary. She hugged Maud, whom she had known for many years. Perla was an accomplished singer who performed at the Coxes' wedding. Maud and Perla were members of the Sursum Corda Choir, an Argentine ensemble that had toured Europe. Maud soon realized that the tears that freely flowed from Perla's eyes were those of joy, not sadness.

"Maud, he's OK. They are all OK!" Perla said. "It is a miracle."

The entire Klein family had survived a terrorist attack in which carefully placed explosives wrecked their house. Only one pillar remained standing, and it was near there that all but the youngest child, Peter, huddled prior to the blast. Peter broke his leg while attempting to flee from the house.

Bob, Maud and Harry went to Walter Klein's room and were surprised to see he was composed and sitting up in his hospital bed. His face was pallid. His wife Pamela was sitting up in the adjacent bed. Klein explained what happened.

It was early and he was still in his pajamas when shots rang out in the yard. His bodyguards had spotted strangers outside and opened fire. Klein quickly gathered up Pamela and the children in a front room near a sturdy pillar of the dwelling. His son Peter tried to run out of the house when the terrorists let the servants leave by the back door. The gunmen shoved the boy back inside and tried to shoot him, but missed.

"Everyone must die inside," one of them shouted. The explosives were detonated; the house burst into flames. A Montonero task force trained by operatives of the Palestine Liberation Organization carried out the attack, Klein said.

Bob, Maud and Harry stayed for most of the day, then left to get something to eat. They stopped at a restaurant, and Cox left the table to call family housekeeper, Ester, who helped with cooking, cleaning and caring for the children. He said he wanted to tell Ester that everything was all right.

"It's not necessary," Maud said. "I left a note explaining what happened."

Cox called home anyway and son Robert answered the telephone.

"Don't come home Dad. They have come for you."

"Who has?"

"Men in leather jackets are waiting for you downstairs. The building superintendent said they are waiting to take you away."

Ester took the phone and confirmed what young Robert said. The superintendent, Victor, had told her that the men had been watching the building for several days. Victor told Ester to tell Cox that the men had claimed to be police officers. They said they wanted to question him "because Roberto Cox did not have his paperwork in order."

Victor said the men had earlier asked him about the family's daily routine – when the children went to school, at what time the school bus arrived to pick them up and other personal information. Victor said he was suspicious, adding that he told the men he was certain the editor of the Buenos Aires Herald would keep his papers up to date.

The Coxes knew their lives were in danger. Klein had earlier warned him that hard-line generals were angry about anti-government stories that appeared in the Herald. Cox was used to such warnings and gave little thought to the matter at the time because he knew it would interfere with his job.

After their meal, Maud insisted that her husband leave them and go into hiding. "Don't tell me where you're going. Just leave."

She returned home to find that 16-year-old Robert was extremely upset. She asked Ester to prepare her children a meal. Ester was a comforting presence. She was a nanny to the children in many ways and often read them bedtime stories. They loved the authentic Argentine dishes she prepared. Her *milanesas*, thin slices of beef fried in breadcrumbs, were excellent. She also made juicy *empanadas*, pastry envelopes stuffed with meat, herbs and spices. The children ate supper while Maud developed a plan of escape from the apartment. The men who Victor saw were still waiting outside in a Ford Falcon parked on the street near the entrance to the building.

Earlier that day in the town of Cordoba, the commander of the Third Army Corps, Gen. Luciano Benjamin Menendez, led an uprising in an attempt to oust Army Chief Gen. Roberto Eduardo Viola as well as President Videla himself. Gen. Menendez was supported by another hard-liner, Gen. Suarez Mason.

Menendez, Mason and others decided that Videla and Viola were too soft in the fight against left-wing terrorism. An extreme nationalist, Menendez also made no secret of his belief that Jacobo Timerman should not have been released. The Cordoba uprising was suppressed within 48 hours, and the coup failed. Menendez was forced to retire. He continued, however, to exercise enormous influence while Suarez Mason, who secretly supported Menendez, remained in power as First Army commander.

Meanwhile, Maud Cox, who was not aware of the attempted coup and did not know where her husband was, tried to reassure the children by saying he was staying at a friend's house. She also gave each of them special instructions.

"Be brave. I need to ask all of you to do something," she said.

She told them to put a change of clothing and toothbrushes in their school bags while Ester helped them pack. They left through the front door and walked in pairs to their grandfather's house as if nothing unusual had happened.

"Go straight to Papito's and don't look back."

Papito lived two blocks away. Peter left the apartment with Ruthie while the other two boys followed a short distance behind. Victoria stayed with her mother.

The children carried their school bags on their backs as if they were headed to their grandfather's apartment to do homework.

Maud filled three small suitcases with additional apparel as well as bed sheets. She left her bags in the living room so that they could be picked up later. Then she and Victoria walked to Papito's apartment. All arrived safely. Maud, trembling with fear, appeared to relax a little before telling Papito what had happened earlier in the day to the Kleins.

"*Sabe lo que paso? Lo fueron a buscar a Bob y ahora nos estan vigilando* (Do you know what happened? They came looking for Bob, and now they are watching us)."

Papito listened quietly.

"Here, I want you to hold on to our passports. We'll come and get them if we need to leave the country," she told her father.

Papito took the passports, went to his room and put them in a safe place.

Maud told her father that she thought it would be safer if the children stayed with her friend Susana Fernandez Beiro, who lived near the presidential residence. She called Susana's house, and her grown son Diego answered the phone. He said his mother was not at home. Maud explained that her husband left on short notice for a conference in the United States, and she did not want to be home alone with the children. She asked Diego if her family could stay with them for a few days.

Diego asked no questions. He said he would come to Papito's apartment as soon as possible to pick them up. Upon arrival, he parked his car in the underground garage and took the elevator to Papito's fourth-floor residence. Maud greeted him and explained what had happened.

She said it would be best if they left without being noticed by anyone watching from the street. They got inside the building's service elevator and went down to the parking garage. They slipped into Diego's car and hunkered down. The boys and Ruthie covered themselves with a blanket. Maud and Victoria got down as low as they could in the back seat. As they left, Maud spotted men in leather jackets waiting in an unmarked Ford Falcon near the exit. Diego drove past as if nothing was unusual. The men did not see his passengers.

Susana was waiting for them when they arrived. "What's happening, Toopsy? I got a strange call from Father Ratcliffe. He asked where you were."

Charles Ratcliffe was an Irish-Argentine priest who had been educated at a small school founded by Maud's grandmother Kathleen in San Martin, just outside Buenos Aires. He remained a close friend of the Boyle family through the years and officiated at the Coxes' wedding. He served as chief chaplain in the Argentine Navy, a rank equivalent to an admiral. He knew and admired Massera, having served on a battleship with the man who would later become head of the Argentine Navy and was responsible for the disappearances of thousands of his countrymen.

"Father Ratcliffe asked if Bob was in jail and if I knew where the family was," Susana said, adding that she did not give the priest any information. The Coxes later learned that he had telephoned Susana from the navy hospital. They never determined how he knew that Bob Cox was sought by the so-called "security forces" or why he wanted to know where the family was staying.

"Donde esta Cox?" ("Where is Cox?") Ratcliffe kept asking, Susana said.

Cox first went to the newspaper office and wrote the lead story about the bombing of the Kleins' house. Afterward, he called the British Embassy and asked for protection while he made arrangements to leave the country. He was convinced that if he went home, his family would be in jeopardy. The British Embassy dispatched a driver to the Herald to pick him up.

Upon arrival at the Madero House, the embassy residence, Cox explained his situation to Charge D'Affaires Hugh Carless, who invited him to spend the night. Cox had recently been asked to speak at the Woodrow Wilson Center in Washington, D.C., but declined because he did not want to leave at such a critical time. Carless and Cox agreed that he should go now, and arrangements were made for him to fly to the United States. That night, Cox read a book that he found in his room. It was the autobiography of Kim Philby, a master spy who betrayed Britain to serve the Soviet Union.

Carless called the U.S. Embassy and explained to officials there why Cox wanted to leave Argentina. They agreed that the temporary visit would be appropriate considering the circumstances. A recently declassified report by U.S. authorities stated that Cox "had been under extreme tension for a long period and needed a rest." It also stated that, "The tone of some of the Herald's recent stories and editorials have … attracted increasing critical comment in the Letters to the Editor column," adding, "The Argentine animals have been highly aroused by recent events, so Buenos Aires is not a healthy place for people like Bob Cox."

"The recent bombing of the Jewish seminary is a classic example of this situation," the report stated. It referred to an explosion at 3 a.m. in October 1979 designed to halt construction of a Jewish elementary school and seminary building. Both buildings were unoccupied.

After spending the night at the residence, Cox left the next morning in an embassy car with a diplomat as an escort. En route to the airport, they noticed that two Ford Falcons following them. Cox was escorted to the gate, and the plane left on time for Washington, D.C. He called home upon his arrival in the United States and told his family where he was. They had not heard from him in three days. They stayed out of sight in Susana's house the entire time he was gone.

Soon after Cox called home, Maud went into the city to have coffee with a friend, and during the course of their conversation, she decided to ask former Argentine President Gen. Alejandro Agustin Lanusse for help. Maud had talked to the retired general at a recent dinner party and was impressed by his honesty and his pride in the military. She knew that he had spoken often with her husband and expressed disapproval of some methods being used to fight terrorism. She also knew that Lanusse was not well liked by members of the junta.

She called Lanusse and he agreed without hesitation to meet with her. She wrote in her diary what he said:

"Never, ever make yourself an adversary. Make a point of crossing the street and talking to the person you think may be your enemy. In this case, go to the source. Go and speak to Gen. Harguindeguy and ask him what is going on. Ask him for protection. You do not know where exactly the threat is coming from. Let them find out who is after you and your family."

Maud telephoned Harguindeguy's office and spoke to his secretary, who said she would ask him to return her call. He never did. She was told later that Harguindeguy was too busy to see her.

She then called Gen. Lanusse.

"I think the message is clear," she told the former president. "We must leave the country."

Lanusse agreed, and after a long silence, added, "Mrs. Cox if there is ever anything I can do for you …"

"You have already done more than enough," she said before hanging up the phone and bursting into tears.

Unfortunately, Maud did not have the necessary paperwork to leave Argentina without being accompanied by her husband, so she called him in Washington and explained what had happened. Cox went to the Argentine Embassy in Washington and spoke to Ambassador Jorge Aja Espil, who was a cousin of President Videla, and asked for help in securing the required paperwork. The ambassador called President Videla, who said he wanted Cox to return to Argentina.

"The president has asked me to plead with you to return to Argentina,"

Ambassador Aja Espil said. "You are important in the struggle for democracy. I promise you that you and your family will have all the protection you need."

Cox called his wife and explained that Videla wanted him to return because the Herald had an important role to play in restoring the rule of law to the nation. The ambassador told him that if he left Argentina, it would be a victory for the terrorists and for the military hard-liners as well. Maud was not impressed by the ambassador's argument but agreed that her husband should come home, which he did on the next available flight to Buenos Aires.

Meanwhile, Gen. Harguindeguy's secretary called Maud and said the Coxes would receive around-the-clock protection by the federal police. At 11 p.m. that night, three armored police vehicles with guards arrived at the house where they were staying. The man who was second in command of the federal police had also come to take a statement. Uniformed officers with machine guns cordoned off the house.

Maud told the children to stay out of sight while she talked to the police commander. He was conspicuously annoyed the whole time. At 1 a.m., he asked her for the third time to repeat her story about the threats the family had received.

"I happened to notice that your last name indicates that your family is from Germany. When did you come to Argentina?" Maud asked the commander.

The officer glared.

"My father was German. He arrived here 30 years ago."

"Thank you," Maud said.

"I've been instructed to tell you that Bob Cox and his family should stay in Argentina for the good of the country," the commander said coldly, then left. She was certain the man was a son of one of the Nazi officers who fled to Argentina at the end of World War II, among them notorious war criminal Albert Eichmann.

Cox returned home and said President Videla reassured him that a uniformed policeman had been assigned to guard the Coxes' apartment building. Most of the buildings in the neighborhood had guards because many of the neighbors were government officials. The next day, the *comisario* (precinct captain) stopped by and told Maud that he had orders from the interior minister to safeguard the family day and night. He also gave her his "hot line" telephone number and told her she could call at any time.

"Don't hesitate to call me, any time at all, if you feel unprotected or sense danger," the *comisario* said. However, the officer assigned to protect the family was seldom at his post and the "hot line" often rang unanswered.

Several days later, Cox wrote a story for the Herald about Walter Klein's return to work in the Finance Ministry. It ran on the front page along with a photo of Klein, his arm in a sling. The government economist said he condemned the murders of his two bodyguards and thanked his neighbors for helping rescue him and his family.

> *The aim of the attack on the Klein family was to provoke an irrational reaction from all of us ... Although the terrorists did not succeed in their monstrous plan, there were people who momentarily lost their reason. The terrorists clearly hoped to see in our reaction a mirror image of their own nihilism. They wanted us to respond to the terror in our minds and the anger in our hearts by rejecting civilized values. They wanted us to show the same scorn for justice that they feel, the same cynicism about human rights and the same lack of respect for human life. They wanted us to become like them because they know that if we can be brought down to their level, we will have lost our only advantage over them.*

Not long afterward, the Kleins and Inghams joined the Coxes in Highland Park for an *asado*, a typical Argentine beef barbecue. While the adults were talking on the porch, one of the children tossed an aerosol can into the fire. The can exploded and fragments hit the wheel of a bicycle on which a man was riding past the house, knocking him to the ground.

Cox, Ingham and Klein heard the noise and came running. The man on the bicycle told the men he was not injured and left. Not long afterward, the children had a bomb scare of a different sort. Their school was dismissed early one day because someone reported that a bomb had been placed in a classroom. The principal received an anonymous telephone call that the intended victims were Klein's son and the son of the Central Bank president. It was a hoax.

A few days later while at the breakfast table, Maud told her husband, "I'm afraid, Bob. I sense that something terrible is going to happen to us."

"I feel the same way," Cox said, adding, "When I was in the United States, I met with our friend Mort Rosenblum, who is editor of the International Herald Tribune. He said that, if we are forced to leave Argentina, I could work for him in Paris."

"Why did you not tell me this before?" Maud asked.

"Because I cannot leave Argentina ... My work is not done here. I'm telling you this now so that you know that we have choices. There might come a time when we will have to move to Paris, but please do not tell this to anyone."

Not long afterward, Maud wrote in her diary:

"Bob came home from work tonight and said he has received confirmation from the owner of the newspaper in Charleston, S.C. that he could take three weeks off in December."

Peter Manigault was one of the most considerate people the Coxes had ever known. He knew that threats against Cox had intensified and did not hesitate to approve his request to take an extended break over the holidays. It was November 1979, and the children were delighted to hear that the family would soon celebrate Christmas in England.

DAVID COX JOURNAL: FEBRUARY 2008

That night, Mother sat at her piano and played a tango about two lovers and sang to us softly. The title was "A Media Luz (At Half Light)."

We were ready to leave the shadows.

CHAPTER 16
FLEEING FOR SAFETY
(1 9 7 9)

"Robert John Cox, editor of the Buenos Aires Herald, has been marked for assassination by hard-liners in the Argentine government," Rabbi Marshall Meyer told Patricia Derian.

They were meeting in New York City on Nov. 13, 1979. Meyer had excellent sources within the Argentine government and had been warned that if Jacobo Timerman, who was living in exile in Israel at the time, published articles about his years of captivity in Argentina, Cox and Timerman's brother Jose would be killed. This information had already been passed on to Jacobo Timerman, the rabbi explained.

"My source says Editor Bob Cox's time is up," Meyer added.

It was not the first time someone had threatened to murder Cox. But this treat was different. Men in leather jackets and driving unmarked cars had been following him since September. The family lived in constant fear. Son Peter, 11, was having an especially hard time sleeping. On Nov. 20, a letter addressed to Peter arrived. When everyone got home that afternoon from school, he was the first to enter the kitchen where Ester was preparing the meal.

"Peter," she said. "A letter arrived today and it's for you."

Maud picked up the letter from the counter and handed it to her youngest son. It was in an envelope bearing the St. Andrew's insignia and the school's address. It was sent by certified mail. She noted that it was addressed to *Ignacio Pedro Cox,* Peter's "official" name. Argentine law at that time did not allow citizens to have "foreign" first names.

Peter was delighted that someone had written to him. As he opened the envelope, brother Robert moved closer to see what it said.

"Mummy, I don't understand. Who are they?" Peter asked as he began to read it.

"Peter, the Montoneros have written to you!" Robert shouted.

Mother tried to snatch the letter away.

"Get me out of here!" Peter screamed, thinking it was a letter bomb. "Get me out of here! Get me out of here! Get me a helicopter!"

The letter fell to the floor.

At that moment Bob Cox walked through the door. Since the attack on the Klein family, he made a point of coming home from the office when the children arrived from school so that he could spend an hour or two with his family. He picked up the note and immediately recognized the symbol of the Montoneros, which incorporated an AK-47 rifle in the letterhead. He moved away and read the letter while Maud tried to calm everyone:

> Dear Peter: We write you this little letter because we know that you are worried about the things that have happened to the papas and grandfathers of some of your friends, and you are scared that something like that could happen to your 'daddy' and you ... But we do not eat little children for breakfast.
>
> Considering the fear that we know all of you feel and the scare you had when your parents began packing their bags and moving you out of the city, and because journalists of high quality like your 'daddy' are more useful to us alive and 'speaking out,' we have decided to send you this little note of advice ...
>
> For that reason, and in consideration of the peculiar work of your 'dad,' we would like to offer him (and all of you) the option to seek exile due to the risk of being assassinated by the Videla dictatorship. You, Peter – like Victoria, Robert, David and Ruth – can choose what you want most and propose it to your 'daddy' and 'mummy.' You can sell your house 'Victoria' in Highland Park, sell what does not belong to your grandfather Agustin Daverio, sell the two cars (the Peugeot and Dodge) and use that money to buy half a dozen new ones in any country, and go to work in Paris with Rosenblum at another, bigger 'Herald'...
>
> Or, you can all stay and die fighting for liberty, for human rights, at the request of the good friends of the dictatorship ...We prefer the first option and we want to believe that you, your brothers, the friends of your Dad (Freeman, Friedman, etc.) and your uncles

that are waiting for you to spend a Merry Xmas in England prefer the same thing.

A great revolutionary greeting from friends of your papa – the Montoneros."

It was inevitable, Cox thought, as he read the letter again. He knew that it was not from the Montoneros. It was a death threat from the military hard-liners. For some time, he had been receiving letters on the Montoneros notepaper congratulating him on his defense of human rights and promising to reward him when they came to power. He assumed that the objective was to associate him with the terrorists and, at a future date, use the letters to incriminate him.

Cox could live with threats against him, but they were now directed at his children. Peter was most vulnerable, but no one outside the family knew it. Whoever wrote the letter knew details: the references to the murdered fathers and grandfather of Peter's classmates; the name of the house in Highland Park; the number and makes of the cars; the fact that the Coxes planned to visit relatives in England at Christmas; that Cox had a job offer in Paris at the International Herald Tribune.

When the news of the threat against Peter was published in the Buenos Aires Herald, Maximo Gainza, the editor of La Prensa, came to see Cox. He was worried because he had also received a similar letter that purported to be from the Montoneros. He knew the veiled threats came from the State Intelligence Service because one of his reporters, who moonlighted as an agent, saw the letters being typed on the Montoneros' stationary by colleagues in intelligence service headquarters.

Gainza feared that his son Santiago, who was in the same class at St. Andrew's as Peter, would also be threatened in such a way. He showed Cox the forged "Montoneros" letter he received, congratulating him for La Prensa's coverage of human-rights issues.

"Don't worry Maxi, that's the letter that I received a year ago, and I received many more after that," Cox told him. "Judging by my experience, it will be some time before they get around to sending a threatening letter to your son."

But the urgency of Cox's situation could not be ignored. He was willing to risk his own life to help save others, but this latest threat was different. The reference to a job offer in Paris came from a very private conversation held with his wife in the kitchen of their apartment. Surely, the apartment had been bugged.

The mention of "Freeman and Friedman" was also curious. It was a reference to Anthony G. Freeman and Townsend B. Friedman, both diplomats at the U.S.

Embassy in Buenos Aires whose names would never have been mentioned inside the Cox home.

Cox showed the letter to James Neilson, the Herald's assistant editor, who said it appeared to have been written by someone who was anti-Semitic. "Some people assume that you are Jewish," Nielson added.

Cox made an appointment to see Gen. Harguindeguy.

"So, Cox, what do you want me to do about it?" the General said after glancing at the letter and tossing it on his desk.

"Find out who wrote it and take the necessary measures."

The General laughed, saying his children received many such letters.

"They collect them in a scrapbook," he quipped.

"I am leaving you the original, and you have the obligation to find out who in the armed forces wrote it," Cox said.

"I am not interested," Harguindeguy responded.

"The letter was sent certified. It should be easy to trace. I know that the intelligence services send out letters like this with the seal of the Montoneros. You know who sent the letter."

"Cox, I have to leave, excuse me," Harguindeguy said as he left the room.

"I demand an investigation!" Cox shouted.

Later that day, Cox told his wife what happened, and she was adamant in her response:

"Bob, we have to leave!"

"I can't. This month they have taken an entire group of high school kids. I need time to find out where they are so that we can save them. Their parents are desperate, very scared, but have not yet agreed to let us publish their story."

The next day, Cox went to the U.S. embassy to tell his friends about the letter. They told him he was a marked man. He returned home immediately.

"It's bad," he told his wife, adding that President Videla has asked to see him. "If Videla says he cannot guarantee our protection, I will write to Charleston and ask for a year's leave of absence."

His meeting with the president was set for the next day at 11:45 a.m. On arrival, Cox was told that the meeting had been rescheduled for 4:45 p.m. When he returned to the president's office that afternoon, he was greeted by one of Videla's military aides, who criticized him for publishing two recent editorials about human-rights abuses in Argentina.

"After those two editorials, *suficiente*" (enough), the military aide warned. "If you don't desist, *los duros* (the hard-liners) will attack us for what you are writing."

While he sat waiting, an army colonel approached him: "Perhaps I shouldn't say this, but I admire you and respect you for the stand you have taken."

It was not the first time an army officer expressed gratitude to him for the Herald's defense of democracy and human rights.

"Thank you," Cox responded. "A lot of people don't understand the situation."

"I understand and want to tell you I agree with you."

Moments later, an orderly entered and said the president was ready to meet with him. The President's office was a long, spacious room with a row of large windows on the outside wall. All were shuttered, and the curtains were closed. President Videla, dressed in his uniform, sat at his desk. The orderly left Cox and the president alone.

"I am very sad to hear you are leaving. Please stay with your family," the president said.

"After everything that has happened to us, it is very difficult for us to stay."

"I know you think it was the armed forces that sent you the letter," Videla continued, adding that the intent obviously was to damage the government.

"I can see that," Cox said.

"Please stay," Videla said.

"I will try to convince my wife to do so, but I need strong guarantees from you for the safety of my family," Cox said, then described in detail previous threats, adding that the federal police had not fulfilled the President's promise to provide around-the-clock protection.

The President apologized, adding that he could not guarantee his own safety. "You must stay here because, if you leave, everyone will say that the government is to blame."

Videla said that the government almost fell after Timerman was released. Gesticulating with his hands and looking at Cox, he then said that, had the attempted coup succeeded, *un loco* (a madman) like Gen. Menendez would have assumed the presidency.

"*Me gustaria irme* (I would like to leave the presidency)," he said, but added that if he did, a general with blood on his hands would take over. "He is a general with a sword who has a thirst for vengeance ... The nation would be drenched in blood."

"My God, are things that bad?" Cox asked.

"I would like to give up and go home," the President sighed.

Cox now knew what he had always suspected: Videla was a coward. Cox remembered that when Videla became commander-in-chief of the army, another officer described him as a general who would never give an order unless he was certain it would be obeyed.

"*Señor Presidente* (Mr. President)," Cox said. "I urge you to resolve the question of *los desaparecidos*. If I have to leave the country, I intend to continue writing about this problem. You must resolve it or your government will surely fail."

He asked Videla to intervene directly and order the release of the children who had recently been abducted by government agents and taken to the ESMA prison. They are innocent, he said. The President said that he could not intervene because, the hard-line military officers engaged in the "Dirty War" would surely stage another coup. It was an admission that he was not in control of his own government.

Cox left the office, sat in his car and recorded notes of everything he had heard, including the fact that Videla could not guarantee his family's safety. As soon as he arrived home, he wrote the following letter:

> *To my friends at the Charleston Post and Courier: I request a year's leave of absence from my job here in Buenos Aires because of the events outlined in the accompanying folio sheets ... We have been living under these circumstances for roughly a decade now. I am reasonably proud to have had threats from both extremes, but this latest, very direct, detailed and evil one comes at a time when the trends are good and Argentina seems to be emerging from a very black tunnel. The difficulty for us now is that the menaces, which have to be taken seriously, are directed at the children and that the government has made it clear that it is in no position to protect them. After much thought, I ask you if I may take a year off from the Herald, without pay.*

He added that, after spending Christmas in England, he would find a place where he and his family could live safely. He said he hoped to return to Argentina after the political situation improved.

It was early December 1979. The family planned to leave Argentina on Dec. 17 but did not want anyone else to know the departure date. However, agencies in Argentina and elsewhere reported that the family was leaving. The Herald confirmed that the editor and his family would depart because of the threats. A flood of letters in support of the Herald and Cox soon followed.

One Argentine woman wrote that she had read the news on the subway that morning and had been crying ever since. His departure was a loss for all of Argentina, she added.

There were hundreds more. One man wrote:

> With heavy heart I read the news of your leave of absence in this morning's Herald. The past years have taught us not to be surprised at how low humanity can sink, but perhaps it is our salvation that we are still shocked when it happens again. Perhaps I am not being fair when I say how much your presence, leadership and acting as the public conscience will be missed. How selfish I am to have as a first reaction how much we will suffer ...

Another, from a mother whose son, a journalist, had disappeared, stated:

> It is with great sorrow that we have learned of your decision to leave the country. We cannot forget how kind you were when I went to the Herald for some advice about our son Enrique, and how through these long three years, we have felt, reading your paper, that somebody was understanding and supporting us in our plight ... We wish you and your family all the best and hope that your absence will only be temporary. The country needs more people like you – God Bless you all.

The following excerpts from the many letters sent in response to the family leaving the country tell an incredible story about the Argentine tragedy.

> A reader in Buenos Aires: "I am just one of many who are deeply disturbed after reading the news of your decision to leave Argentina. I want you know how much I have enjoyed, appreciated and approved of your leadership at the Herald ... Thank you, Mr. Cox! I wish you and your family all the best, and may God keep you safe and bless you in all you do."

> A Mother of Plaza de Mayo: "Through a telephone call made to me in Uruguay from Brazil, I learned the sad news of your departure. You will never know what this means for Uruguayans and Argentines. I implore you, do not abandon us. Continue publishing stories about us and let Amnesty International know what is happening. With your departure a piece of our heart leaves as well."

Canadian Ambassador D. W. Fulford: "May I join with Mr. Roth and others in expressing my regret at Mr. Cox's temporary departure. He has set a high standard for whoever may fill in while he is away. It is a pity that Argentina should lose at this juncture the services of a courageous journalist of recognized integrity."

A reader in Buenos Aires: "Thank you for everything you have done for me and for others. Thank you for having been able to show that decency and dignity had not vanished from our country. For many years I have read the Herald and for the last few there have been times I have done so in anger and despair. I have shared all the pain and humiliation of the persecuted, of the disappeared and of all those who are afraid. You have always stood for all that makes a human being human. You have fundamentally fought for a society free from fear, you and the courageous people at the Herald shared your sense of responsibility."

The Permanent Assembly of Human Rights: "The Assembly of Human Rights, after learning of the threats directed against your family, expresses publicly its condemnation to what represents a serious terrorist action. The Permanent Assembly of Human Rights joins the press, intellectuals and different political sectors that have expressed their profound sorrow at hearing the news of your departure. We could not be absent from honoring you, and we would like to stress our acknowledgment and respect for your work in clearing up the problem of the disappeared in favor of those arrested who are not granted due process and in your championing for human rights and a free press."

Telegram from a reader: "Please receive my full moral support in view of monstrous acts."

A reader in Buenos Aires: "There is not much we can add to the numerous letters you have received expressing the support and solidarity of freethinking men and women of our country, except that they interpret our own thoughts. We do wish that you – a foreigner and therefore subject to as many or more risks than we Argentines – have been an example to all of us in your courageous fight for the full application of our laws to all men and women regardless of their creed, race or ideological thoughts.

We are going to miss you but hopefully not for long, as we firmly believe that right will in the end triumph over might."

From families of relatives who disappeared: "In gratitude to who offers his most sacred value, his life."

From a family whose lives were saved: "My wife Beatriz and I wish you good luck wherever you may be."

From a staff member of the Argentine Foreign Ministry: "After trying to reach you several times on the phone (nearly always ringing to the right number at the wrong time), I have decided to send you a few lines to tell you how much we all in the Foreign Ministry thank you for being brave, for being honest, for speaking out when most of your colleagues remained silent. Elena Holmberg's case shall not be a closed one. We will, all of us, maintain it alive for as long as it remains unsolved."

From Helena Arocena, who never found her son: "After reading all those beautiful letters to you in the Herald, I find that I have nothing to add… I who owe so much to you."

From U.S. Congressman Robert F. Drinan: "I have admired your work immensely ever since I came to Argentina as a member of an Amnesty International team."

A mother who lost her child: "I am one of the Mothers of Plaza de Mayo – one of the 'Mad Mothers' for whom you have fought so much to defend our petitions. I am infinitely grateful because your brave editorials have served in our despair as hope in the midst of silence and indifference. Your fight has not been in vain because everything that is done in favor of liberty and justice will one day find its reward. Thank you."

From a reader in Buenos Aires: "As a great admirer of all you have done for the Herald and through the Herald, and all you have done for my country, I want you to know how sorry I am that you are leaving."

From an Argentine mother whose children disappeared:

"With all my gratitude I want to convey my sincere acknowledgment for your humanitarian help to the sad situation of thousands of families, and for trying to find a solution to a situation that you have addressed with honesty and courage, which is lacking in the majority of our own journalists despite the fact that many have lost their lives.

"As our last wish, we hope that you will be back with your family very soon to work in a climate of peace and security, and we will no longer have to pass by your office and cry out in our pain. We hope that in your farewell article you dedicate a small part to us by calling on the authorities to tell us where are our children, which is the only thing that will bring peace to their consciences. The way they have acted toward you, they are accusing themselves of the terror that they are committing.

"We also ask that you send to little Peter a big kiss. We want him to know that the tears of the boy will be transformed when he becomes a man in his pride for the greatness of the soul, the courage and nobility of his Daddy."

A few of the letters were mean-spirited, wishing the family good riddance. Adm. Emilio Massera sent a cynical note saying he regretted that we were leaving, adding the time was not yet right for him to speak from his heart.

One of the letters was a homemade postcard sent by one of the first people he helped Carmen Beatriz Frascotto de Roman. The postcard is a depiction of her son Federico and herself waving goodbye, with a white handkerchief in hand, to a departing airplane. It includes the sad face of a yellow sun in the heavens. It says, "To the Cox family. We wish you a happy Christmas and a happy New Year. Have a good trip, and we hope to see you again. With much love, Beatriz and Federico Roman."

Even *el Zorro*, actor Guy Williams, sent word that he hoped the situation in Argentina would soon improve so that we could return. He wrote that he was leaving for California and would return to Argentina in January. "I want all of you to know that I am thinking of each one of you, and that things will improve so that you can return soon. My very best wishes, Guy."

Shortly before the family was to leave, as Maud crossed the street en route to a grocery store, the drivers of two Ford Falcons without license plates screeched to a halt nearby. Three men with machine guns got out of the vehicles and surrounded her. She looked at them directly and said: "I am sorry. Did I inconvenience you in some way?"

The men appeared to be confused. They got back into the cars and sped away.

"I wonder, who they were going to kidnap?" she heard a passerby ask.

A few days later, a large envelope arrived at the Herald. Inside was a sheet of paper that looked like a military order. On it was a crude drawing of a leg attached to a ball and chain with the following message: "To Mr. Robert Cox, with compliments, Gen. Luciano Benjamin Menendez." Menendez was the *ultra duro* (the ultra hard-liner) who had narrowly failed to topple President Videla.

On Dec. 15, 1979 – two days before the family was booked on a flight to leave Argentina – Cox sat stoically at his typewriter. He had one more piece to write as editor of the Buenos Aires Herald. But the words would not come. Meanwhile, Harry Ingham called the Cox home and asked Maud and the children to join him for dinner at a restaurant near the Herald building. As they dined on steak and *papas fritas* (fried potatoes), Ingham left the table and called Cox at the newspaper office.

"Have you written it yet?" he asked.

"Not a word," Cox said, adding he had two hours left before deadline.

Ingham hung up the phone, walked over to the table and told his guests that he would return soon. He walked to the Herald and into the newsroom. He announced boldly that he was taking the editor out to eat. Assistant Editor James Neilson, who was supervising the news desk, protested. Ingham hustled Cox out of the room, promising he would bring the editor back soon so that he could write his farewell. Cox was sweating as he and Ingham sat down at the table in the restaurant.

"The most important person in Argentina has arrived!" Ingham announced to everyone in the room and then demanded that the best of everything on the menu be served his special guest.

Cox just sat in a daze.

"It is just not coming."

Wine was served and Ingham filled Cox's glass.

"It will come. It will come," Ingham insisted. "Just relax and forget about your article for a while."

A half-hour later, as Ingham filled Cox's glass a fourth time, and the waiter was clearing the table, he said:

"Drink up, Bob, you're ready. You have work to do."

"Yes. Yes," Cox responded and as he emptied his glass and stood up with a grin and swagger.

Exactly as Ingham had promised, the editor met his deadline.

I shall be only too glad to say goodbye to the 1970s – an appalling decade for Argentina and the world. I am immensely sad as I say 'au revoir' to Argentina. But it is 'au revoir' and not goodbye.

I am leaving today with my family for a sojourn abroad. We do not know how long we will be away; but we do know that we will back. And our return will be in a new decade – one I am sure will see the beginning of a new era for Argentina.

It is ironic that we are leaving because of a silly – although sinister – threat addressed to my young son Peter. The threat – a particularly nasty letter composed by someone who must be very sick – came on the heels of a number of disturbing events.

I would not claim to be among those in Argentina who have received the most threats. A friend, the late Heriberto Kahn, who was the greatest journalist this country has produced, received three in a day. But I have received enough to be able to weigh the risk involved in ignoring them.

Being threatened is a ludicrous, ridiculous experience. The best response – perhaps even the best security measure – is to laugh off the menace. It is like being in a very bad film. There is the crude note – pasted letters cut from a newspaper, usually. There is the sophisticated letter, typewritten, well phrased – a murderous heart beneath well-tailored clothes. There is the direct, spoken threat. Indeed, one feels like an actor in a bad movie. A bit-part player with his back to the camera, facing the gangster smile with the throw-away line '... I'll have you put away forever...'

The letter sent to my young son was hand-written. It was researched, drafted and penned by people who I have had no reason to doubt their impunity. It came directly from Argentina's heart of darkness. It came from that shady area of national life that nobody challenges and few people talk about.

At first, I could see no reason behind the letter. It did not scare me although I was sickened by the thought of people who have so departed from humanity that they choose children as their victims. I was not surprised, either. The greatest atrocities of the terrible decade of the 1970s have been committed against children. But over the past few days I have discerned an evil design behind the letter – coming on top of intensified intimidation and hostile propaganda. The idea, I believe, was to try and discredit the Herald. The plan almost achieved its object.

Rather than subject my children to the inevitable publicity resulting from a direct challenge to the group threatening us, I thought it would be better to leave Argentina in the wake of a brief and un-dramatic explanation of the causes of our departure. It was quite by chance that the threats against us became public knowledge. But I am glad, now, that they did because, despite the pain of the past weeks, we, my family as well as in the wider circle of friends (many of whom we knew nothing about), have seen the shadows over Argentina lift. We have seen and felt the real country – the people who are not afraid, the people who will not give in to lawlessness, the people who have stood up to be counted.

The greatest difficulty for a journalist working in Argentina over the past 10 years has been to tell readers what they didn't want to hear and to point out what they didn't want to see. Terrorism, to begin with, was only a minor problem – 'a police matter.' We were all supposed to look the other way. Finally, when we had to look terrorism in the face, it had taken on the proportions of a monster. The reaction of almost everyone in Argentina came too late.

So it has been with what we call, ambiguously, 'The other terrorism.' It, too, has grown to monstrous proportions. It has frightened people out of their minds. And with the country shadowed by terror from both sides, people have preferred to be blinkered. Some tragically mistaken people even believe that one form of terrorism can protect them from the other.

I believe that the moment has come – far too late, because the list of victims of 'the other terrorism' is maddeningly long – when we will see the beginning of a strong reaction to the terror tactics, regardless of their origin. The awakening of Argentina to the simple truth that what was wrong yesterday is wrong today must come with compassion and concern. The press must tell people the truth. The relatives of *disappeared people cannot be ignored as if they were lepers.*

We must face the reality of the cruelty of the past decade in order to bring about a change in the 1980s. We must care about all the victims of the war, which we must bring to an end. The threats against me, which I believe have made me a liability to the Herald, came from people who want to keep Argentina in darkness. But I have been enormously heartened by the response of Herald readers and of my colleagues. They have lit torches to lead the way to the new era.

I hope to be writing regularly from abroad. I will be writing to all of you who have written to me. I thank you all, particularly those of you who have addressed messages, drawings and even gifts to my children. I apologize for the incoherence of this message of leave-taking. But my feelings are chaotic. I can express only a tongue-tied-love – an inarticulateness born of the grief of parting. The Herald will continue to tell it as it is. There seems no point now in trying to tell it as it was.

The suitcases were packed, and friends and relatives came to see the family at the apartment. Papito said goodbye but was too sad to go to the airport. He looked at each one of his grandchildren and patted their heads as they left the apartment.

Upon arrival at the airport, the Coxes saw that a large crowd had gathered. Harry Ingham repeatedly embraced each member of the family and said goodbye. Two mothers whose children had disappeared and on whose cases Cox had worked until the last minute were among the well wishers. Also waiting was a contingent of reporters from the local and international press.

"I am leaving with great sadness but also with a lot of love, and I repeat that we will return as soon as we can to Argentina," Cox told the reporters.

He was asked if he was leaving because of what he had written.

There was a lot of news that I was hesitant to report because of the circumstances but I felt it my duty to do so, so I did it ... The families of the disappeared cannot be ignored. The duty of the press is to worry about all the victims. The reaction toward terrorism came too late in Argentina.

The Cox family boarded the plane and sat together in their assigned seats. A sense of relief enveloped them. They were safe, finally, and still together. That's all that really mattered.

CHAPTER 17
END OF A JOURNEY
(1 9 7 9 - 1 9 8 3)

DAVID COX JOURNAL: MARCH 2008
"I seem to have lost my bearings," my father said holding my
hand as we walked along a street in London.

It was this great city, the royal seat of kings and queens, that
was the setting for most of the children's stories my father shared
with us early in our lives. They were marvelous tales about secret
castle doors, magical stairways and ominous towers where young
princes and princesses were stashed away by aging tyrants. They
also included Dickens' waifs and James' giant peaches and Willy
Wonka's chocolate factory.

We missed our homes in Argentina but felt safe and secure now in
the country where my father was born. He showed us the house
at 47 Grosvenor Road, and we strolled with him along the streets
on which he played as a child. He pointed out houses where he
delivered groceries on a bicycle that had a back wheel bigger than
the one on the front to make space for his heavily loaded basket.
We saw the house where his grandfather, a jeweler who specialized
in clocks, lived. We imagined London in a different time as we
walked through his old neighborhood. We wondered what it was
like to sleep inside a bomb shelter as he did when he was young.

Christmas in England cosseted us. The snow covered the roofs
and softened the streets and cooled and buffered our minds.

On Christmas Eve 1979, Cox lifted his fountain pen and wrote to his closest friend:

> *Dear Harry: The send-off was memorable and our hearts are still heavy when we think of you all. But the children are happy and unworried, although they miss their friends and need no prompting to write. Everything has gone smoothly. We had a sympathetic reception and I was happy to see that I had no press party waiting.*
>
> *I've done one interview with the BBC and the interviewer was very understanding. Here I'm seen as Very Right Wing, which is a nice change. Much, much love. We think of you constantly and hope that things work out. Look after yourself. We can never thank you enough or repay you properly – except in heaven.*

Cox's letter was the first of many he wrote to Ingham through the years. The family spent Christmas Day in England with Aunt Norma and Uncle Donald in their home in Redditch in the southwest Midlands. The children played on thick carpeting and marveled at the floor vents of the house's heating system, which they had never seen before. Behind the house was "The Caravan," an old trailer that their cousins used to travel across Europe. It was "planted" in the garden now and used as a playhouse.

Cousins Neil and Iain stopped by for a visit. They were the little boys who waved goodbye to Cox as his ship left Tilbury long ago. Andrew Graham-Yooll, the former Herald news editor who left Argentina in 1976 and moved to London, also came to see them. Graham-Yooll worked for the Daily Telegraph and helped the Coxes find an apartment in London.

Cox visited the Royal Institute of International Affairs (Chatham House) in London to give a talk about what was happening in Argentina. He was also invited to the Foreign Office in Whitehall to meet with Nicholas Ridley, the minister of state who had followed the story of the Cox family's exile and wanted to know more about human-rights abuses in Argentina.

One of the boys' former Buenos Aires schoolmates whose family had moved to London, came to see the Coxes after they moved into their new apartment. His nickname was *Conejo* ("Rabbit," because his teeth stuck out). He brought with him two stink bombs. The boys soon decided that it was their mission to detonate the apparently harmless, bombs near some posh homes in the neighborhood.

Coincidentally, an alert had been issued that day warning that the Irish Republican Army might strike in the vicinity. Someone overheard the boys talking in Spanish about their malodorous *bombas* and notified the police. An officer followed them for a few blocks before stopping them and asking what they were up to. *Conejo* managed to convince him that their bombs were harmless and the officer let them go. It would have been different in Buenos Aires.

Jacobo Timerman was living in Israel at that time and read that the Coxes were in London. Timerman sent a letter to Cox and thanked him for all that he had done.

"We had the privilege to fight against all forms of totalitarianism, and to be accompanied by our families and some friends and be still alive … the fight continues," Timerman wrote.

DAVID COX JOURNAL: MARCH 2008
It was at that time that my father gave me a blue hardcover book that would become my first diary. I referred to it as my "newspaper," and I scribbled on the first page a vow to follow in my father's footsteps and become a journalist. I wrote about our visit to Shakespeare's birthplace at Stratford-on-Avon. I described the musicals the family enjoyed. They included "Evita," "My Fair Lady" and "Oliver!" I wrote about the London Zoo, the wax figures at Madame Tussauds, shopping at Marks and Spencer and seeing the movie "King Kong."

Soon the Coxes were on their way to Paris to stay in a hotel not far from the Eiffel Tower. In the mornings, after breakfast of croissants and brioches, they walked along the Champs Elysées and under the Arc de Triomphe. They visited several museums, including the Louvre, as well as the palace at Versailles. In the evenings at the hotel, Maud played her favorite French songs on a piano – songs she learned as a child that were written and sung by Charles Aznavour, Edith Piaf and Maurice Chevalier. One day, the family boarded *le Metro* for a visit to the Pompidou Museum where they saw an exhibition of Salvador Dali's paintings.

While in Paris, Bob and Maud Cox met former Argentine Sen. Hipolito Solari Yrigoyen, a human-rights activist exiled in the French capital. Afterward, they went to the Apostolic Nunciature to see Monsignor Kevin Mullen, who had been transferred there from Buenos Aires after criticizing the ruling junta. Mullen told the Coxes what happened to the French nuns who disappeared in Argentina in 1977:

"They were thrown into the sea," he said, gesturing with his hand that their bodies had been cut open at the chest so that they would sink faster.

"How do you know this?" Maud asked.

"Maud, there is such a thing as a confession for those who repent. I have sent what I was told to the Vatican."

Father Mullen later wrote to Cox and urged him to return to Argentina:

> "You are one of the very few who raised a voice in the name of humanity and civilization at an awfully agonizing moment in the history, and I remember that. I would grieve, really, if you could not go back to a country you patently love and have loyally defended in the best sense in which a nation is defended – by standing for the basic rights of its people. I think of you often and pray that you, Maud and the children are reasonably happy. I would be as sad as you would be frustrated to think that you were condemned to a nomadic life … "

Not long afterward, Cox accepted an offer to become a visiting scholar at the Woodrow Wilson Center for International Studies in Washington, D.C. When it came time to leave London, he took four of his children with him to a house he had rented in Alexandria, Va., while Maud and son Robert Andrew returned to Buenos Aires so that he could take his final high school examinations.

Diplomats at the Argentine Embassy in London warned her that it was risky for them to return. But she told them she would not let a few generals stand in the way of her son's graduation. As they got off the plane at Ezeiza Airport outside Buenos Aires, several security men approached.

"We are going to protect you," one said.

Minutes later at the baggage carousel, more men walked up and introduced themselves as state intelligence agents. They asked where they planned to stay in Buenos Aires and what they intended to do while there. She said she was going to see her father and that her son would take his high school exams.

"Un momentito" ("One moment"), one of the agents said. "I have orders from the top – from Gen. Martinez (commander of Army Intelligence) – not to let you out of my sight. Your father must visit you at your place, which will be secure. Your

lives are at serious risk. Let's hope God helps us in this mission. Listen to us and do exactly what we tell you to do!"

The agents escorted them to their downtown apartment and left. As Maud unpacked their bags, the doorbell rang. Another contingent of SIDE agents introduced themselves. Later, at 7 p.m., a man who appeared to be in charge arrived and said:

"Señora, we will now leave you with the federal police," explaining that officers inside three police cars parked outside of the apartment building would guard them day and night.

"Señora, look at me. I am 45 years old. I am Argentine," he said as he lifted his hands and showed her his palms. *"No he matado a nadie,* (I have not killed anyone)."

"I hope not," she said, adding she needed to run some errands and buy plane tickets for their departure in three weeks.

"As far as the tickets and the errands are concerned, we will take care of them for you. We will talk about the other things later," he said. "Where is your son taking his exam?"

"In Olivos, outside the city."

"My God! We are going to have to mobilize the entire security force in that area," he said, and motioned to Robert to come closer.

"How old are you?"

"Sixteen."

"Then you know what is going on here. You may even know better than we do," the officer said, then turned to Maud and said, "Right now, you are the government's top national security priority. Nothing must happen to you. Do you understand?"

He paused, then added: "Don't try to escape. If you decide to go anywhere, you must tell us several hours in advance so we can secure the area that you go to."

One policeman was posted outside the door of the apartment building, a second manned the second floor and a third stood guard in the ground-floor garage. When Maud asked permission to go shopping, they accompanied her. She sat in the back of the car between two security men carrying machine guns. Another police car followed. Some walked with her inside the supermarket while others stood at the door.

Agents also accompanied Robert to the school in an unmarked car. He sat in the backseat between two armed guards. The vehicle was escorted by two police cars, one in front and the other behind. Two armed officers stood outside the classroom while he took his exams.

Maud also asked to go to Highland Park. She had promised to give the family's furniture to friends, including the Kleins, who had lost most of theirs in the explosion. Her request upset the security chief because hard-line military officers controlled areas outside the city. He granted her permission after working out an elaborate security plan that he called "Operation Country Club."

Robert and his mother sat in the backseat of one of four cars driven in convoy to their country home. Ester, their housekeeper, rode in another car. Robert noticed that machine guns and grenades were on the floor of the vehicle. He also noted officers in vehicles posted at various points along the way. Several more were stationed outside the gates to Highland Park.

They were told to wait in the car while the house and yard were checked and cleared. Once inside, the two of them and Ester were not to open any windows or shutters. Maud arranged the furniture to make it easier for her friends to remove the pieces they had been promised, then made lunch for everyone. When Ester served some food to the security guards outside, they seemed surprised.

"Tell the Señora she can come out of the house, *la vamos a proteger*" ("we will protect her"), they said to Ester. Maud and Robert joined them outside for lunch. One of them said he had taken on this particular assignment because he needed money. He said he wanted to own his own taxi service some day. Another planned to retire early and go to the United States to live with his sister.

"You should try to feel free and take advantage of the days you are spending in your country," another said. "Tell your husband that you were well taken care of. If you have any complaints whatsoever, please let us know."

On the last day of their three-week visit to Argentina, a friend who had many government contacts visited Maud. "You know, they are not only scared of Bob; they are also scared of you," her friend said.

When it came time to leave, guards accompanied Maud and Robert to the airport and onto the plane, which was to take them to the United States. She thanked each of them before they left. She was convinced that President Videla had arranged for such heavy security out of fear that hard-liners would harm them to provoke an international scandal. When they landed in Washington, the rest of the family awaited at the airport.

She later wrote a letter to Andrew Graham-Yooll's wife, Micaela, both of whom longed to return to Argentina. "I am writing this to you because I don't think you should go now. Give it a year longer."

The trip home had been traumatizing for young Robert. He resented being surrounded day and night by security guards and having to ask them permission to come and go. Like Peter, who still had trouble sleeping, it had become obvious that Robert had been deeply affected by the events.

Things began to change during Bob Cox's stint at the Woodrow Wilson Center for International Studies. As a visiting scholar, he had more time to spend with his family. They had rented a house on a hill where the children played ping-pong in the basement and tasted peanut butter for the first time. They also made friends with people their age from all over the world.

Cox met many journalists and others while at the Woodrow Wilson Center. Some had lived through similar situations. The Peruvian writer Mario Vargas Llosa was one of them. Cox's time as a scholar there marked the beginning of a long healing process for the family. He became more reflective about what had happened, and had time to write a monograph on terrorism and the media, the *Sound of One Hand Clapping*. Maud liked Alexandria and quickly adapted to living in the United States.

After six months at the Woodrow Wilson Center, Cox was offered a year-long Neiman Fellowship at Harvard University, so the family moved to a new home in Cambridge, Mass. One day, a friend who had close contacts in the Argentine Embassy told Cox that terrorists planned to assassinate him, possibly on U.S. soil. He did not take the warning seriously at first. But that changed when he went to New York City and participated in a televised discussion about human-rights abuses along with Jacobo Timerman. A man who identified himself as Pastor Rodriguez Carmona, an Argentine intelligence officer, was in the studio audience.

Rodriguez Carmona said the plan was to wait until Cox returned to Buenos Aires, kidnap him in the street and take him to a place where a shootout with two Montonero terrorists would be staged. The Montoneros would be brought to the scene from their cells in a clandestine government prison and shot dead along with him. When police arrived, one of the officers would also become a casualty. Then the government would announce that the Herald editor had been killed when Montoneros terrorists tried to kidnap him. Alternately, they might use the forged Montoneros letters to claim that he was meeting the terrorists secretly when the police came upon them.

Prior to participating in the television discussion, Cox had written Ingham about returning alone to Buenos Aires to continue his work at the newspaper. But after telling Maud what the man in the studio audience said and hearing her objections to his proposed return to Argentina, Cox had second thoughts. He also wrote a letter to Peter Manigault in Charleston in which he described what he had been told:

> *The idea was to stage everything so that it would appear that left-wing terrorists had kidnapped me. While trying to rescue me, a policeman would be wounded. I would be disposed of and people would then believe the disappearances that I have denounced were all the work of left-wing terrorists.*

It was clear now that the Coxes would settle in the United States. Cox wrote to Ingham:

> *I'm restored to a state of health I didn't realize existed. I have no more asthma! I'm beginning to work reasonably well and have just the occasional, but very deep, bit of depression and gloom ... The children are fine.*

Cox often said that, not only did he feel free in the United States, but he could smell freedom each time he arrived.

Cox's Neiman Fellowship ended in July 1982. He had been offered jobs in the United States at newspapers and a professorship at the University of Chicago. He seriously considered applying for a job at the New York Times because living in Manhattan would be similar to living in Buenos Aires. The Miami Herald asked him to join the newspaper's editorial page staff. However, Cox wanted his children to grow up in a safer environment.

He wrote to Peter Manigault in Charleston for help. Manigault was an excellent employer with a genuine concern for the people of Argentina. He never wavered in his support. On Jan. 6, 1981, Cox wrote:

> *Dear Peter: I fear that you must rue the day you came to Buenos Aires and became star-crossed with the Herald. Cambridge and Harvard are wonderful and everyone is well and exhilarated. We remember you in prayers and gratitude.*

Cox told Manigault about the most recent assassination plan for him and enclosed a secret tape recording he had made of his conversation with the Argentine agent in New York. He asked Manigault if he could work at the Charleston newspaper until it was safe for him to return to the Buenos Aires Herald.

Our feeling as a family is that it would be unwise to return so soon after a change of president (Gen. Viola succeeded Videla on March 29, 1981). We hope this will bring a definite improvement within a year. All the contacts we have made indicate it would be better for us to wait. The only encouragement to return came from the Papal Nuncio, who wants me to come back immediately on my own. Maud says that if I do that, I would have to join the priesthood first.

Manigault offered Cox a job on the editorial staff of the company's flagship newspaper, the News and Courier in Charleston. He went to South Carolina to hear the details and to arrange for his family to move to Charleston. When he returned to Cambridge, he was overjoyed about his prospects. On Feb. 26, 1981, he wrote:

Dear Peter: A late but equally fervent letter of thanks for the time I spent with you all in Charleston. The good tidings were received with a fairly audible sigh of relief en casa (at home). The children are enjoying their American adventure and admit to fears about returning just now. As Ruthie expressed it for the entire brood: 'Quiero volver cuando no hay robones molestandonos (I want to return when there are no crooks bothering us).' Peter says in English that he wants to go back 'when the nasty people are no longer around.'

I profess to be as optimistic as ever about a reasonable outcome in the fairly near future. I only wish my arguments were more convincing to others. The situation looks unpleasant now, however, because the Martinez de Hoz plan appears to have smashed into a brick wall. As a friend who called said, 'It's a tragedy. Once again another economic program has gone down the tubes.' I think the fatal flaw is all too apparent – the Argentine disease of myth making. Instead of dealing with reality, Martinez de Hoz decided to create a myth and so created a false situation. The totally artificial exchange rate, in itself contradictory to everything Martinez de Hoz' team is supposed to believe in, characterizes the predicament. But there are many other telltale anomalies in the program. It remains to be seen what can be rescued.

I am more and more excited about the prospect of working for you and my list of stories grows. I thought some pieces on terrorism as a potential threat to the United States might be interesting for a start.

Cox ended his letter by informing Manigault of the visa requirements to work in the United States and thanking him for a lovely crab dinner served in Charleston.

The family rented a U-Haul for the move to Charleston. Cox drove the truck and Peter and David sat with him on the front seat. Maud, the girls and young Robert followed in their yellow AMC Hornet station wagon. They got lost on the way south when they failed to take the correct exit. They had no cell phones and no map, yet somehow found each other at another highway exit. Upon arrival in the South Carolina Lowcountry, they knew that they would like their new home.

Cox was named assistant editor of the News and Courier, and the family settled into their house west of the Ashley River, where he and Maud live today.

Sometimes, the worst possible conditions, like the war in England, bring out the best in people, and sometimes they bring out the worst. In Argentina, it brought out the worst in people, except for a few honorable exceptions.

From Charleston, Cox continues to write about Argentina. He never abandoned the families who sought his help. He contacted U.S. senators and congressmen and asked for their help and understanding. He introduced himself to influential people throughout the world and explained to them what they could do for the people of Argentina. He was instrumental in getting the United Nations to pressure the Argentine government to release prisoners who survived in the prison camps.

He wrote to then U.S. Sen. Ernest F. Hollings, a South Carolina Democrat, and Sen. Paul Laxalt, a Republican from Nevada, asking them to intervene to save the life of Miguel Angel Fagian, a Uruguayan held in a secret prison camp in that nation, which had similar troubles. To Hollings, a native of Charleston, he wrote:

> *I have just penned a letter to Sen. Laxalt. I am given to understand by Amnesty International that shortly after his visit to Uruguay, where he praised the present military government for improving the situation of human rights, a young man disappeared. I was given the bare details.*
>
> *His name is Miguel Angel Fagian and he vanished on his way to work at FUNSA tire factory in Montevideo on Jan. 29. The Amnesty people, who are all too sadly wise and experienced in these cases, are convinced security forces kidnapped him. In the past 'disappeared' persons have reappeared as prisoners in army camps (unlike Argentina). But there is always a period of great anxiety during which the clandestine prisoner is usually tortured and often dies ... I*

wonder if you could speak out to save a life. I doubt if the Uruguayan military will pay much attention to Amnesty International.

As a very new Charlestonian, I don't know whether I'm entitled to think myself a citizen of the Holy City yet. But I know that I do share the pleasure of all Charlestonians at your national prominence. It is heart-warming to see the media spotlighting someone for his commonsense and commitment to public service. I hope the nation takes you in to their hearts and minds as South Carolina has.

Despite the efforts to save the man, Fagian was never heard from again.

Meanwhile, Cox received more news. Before he left Argentina, he worked with the parents of two high school students who were abducted but had been allowed to call home from ESMA, the prison near the heart of Buenos Aires. The Herald tried to report the abductions, but the parents believed that they could secure their sons' releases with the help of relatives, one an army general, who held high positions in the government. Cox received the following message in Charleston from the parents of one of the boys:

Cox, scream and let the entire world know. I have been told unofficially that they have murdered my son. They had us believe they were going to release the children. Please, Cox, speak out!

Cox remains haunted by such voices. People he could not save still appear in his dreams. If only he had tried harder, perhaps one more son, one more daughter could have survived:

If evil is still in control, then one has to battle against it. I am convinced we didn't do enough in the past and really deserve to be whipped through the streets one day for not doing everything we could to halt the juggernaut.

Thoughts of the past are distant now but still remain for the Coxes. Those of the *desaparecidos* who never came home will never go away completely, Cox said as he walked recently with his son David through the lovely gardens at Magnolia Plantation on the Ashley River near Charleston. Such times that are supposed to be enjoyed in peace and quiet bring memories that interrupt his silence, demanding that he re-examine the causes in order for them to be completely understood, and to remember a time so painful and unreal.

Cox received death threats until Dec. 10, 1983, the day Raul Alfonsin was sworn in as Argentina's democratically elected president after approximately two decades of military rule. Soon after democracy was restored, Renee Epelbaum, a founding member of the Mothers of the Plaza de Mayo, visited the Cox family in Charleston. She had lost three of her children. Two young priests who had been imprisoned and tortured in Cordoba visited a few weeks later. In gratitude for all that he did, they built Cox an office in the space over his garage.

Harry Ingham also came to Charleston, as did caricaturist Menchi Sabat and Luis Moreno Ocampo, the assistant prosecutor who tried the military junta for mass murder from 1984 to 1985. The trial proved top officers like Jorge Rafael Videla, Emilio Eduardo Massera and others were guilty of crimes that included forced disappearances, torture and murder. To the great disappointment of a nation that felt a great injustice, all of them were later pardoned. New trials bringing new charges against the military officers continue to this day.

Former Miami Herald reporter Bill Montalbano, who became the Los Angeles Times bureau chief in London, stayed in touch with the Coxes until March 19, 1998, the day he died of a heart attack. The Coxes also heard from friends who had abandoned them when times were bad in Argentina. They apologized. They were afraid, they said.

The Coxes kept in touch with Mrs. Arocena, who never stopped looking for her son Marcos.

DAVID COX JOURNAL: MARCH 2008

Our grandfather passed away in 1983. I was with him in Buenos Aires at the end of his life. At his funeral, I stood in the rain, holding an umbrella. A drizzle fell on the pavement while the fallen leaves of trees that lined the cemetery absorbed the rain. My relatives were there dressed in black. They included a distant cousin, much older now, who sobbed like a child. At that time, we did not know all the hurt he had caused us when we lived Argentina. His tears that day seemed sincere.

My mother stood beside me as I held the umbrella that grey day. She watched as her father's casket was placed in the Boyle family vault. Stories of the family that passed from one generation to another were entrusted to us for safekeeping.

And as we grew older, there were new stories to add to the old ones. Mother told us of the time when she boarded a plane in Lima, Peru, on a flight to Buenos Aires. La Prensa editor Gainza Paz whispered to her: "Look who's over there," motioning toward a man in a seat behind her. "It's Suarez Mason."

She saw out of the corner of her eye the general known as the 'Butcher' who was responsible for thousands of deaths in Argentina as well as our exile. He turned and locked eyes with my mother as the plane landed. His bodyguards took a defensive position. She was paralyzed by fear and shock, and regretted not being able to tell him what she thought of him.

A few years later, my parents attended an Inter-American Press Association meeting in Santiago, Chile, and were followed by security agents while they remained in the country. The nation's dictator, Augusto Pinochet, spoke at the meeting, extolling the importance of press freedom, which he had extinguished in Chile. Mother refused to sit in the same room with the man, and my father joined her just outside in the hallway.

When Pinochet finished his speech and was marching out of the conference hall, Maud told him to his face he was *un asesino* (a murderer). Pinochet stopped, as did his bodyguards. He looked straight at her and then moved on silently.

"It is impossible to describe with precision that moment, and the expressions of hate and bewilderment of the men and women who accompanied him, as I watched stone-faced Pinochet stop for a one second and then continue his imperturbable march..." recalled Argentine editor Nelida Rajneri in an interview published in the *Story of the Inter-American Press Association*.

Letters of families whose relatives disappeared are piled on shelves in my father's office above the garage at his house in South Carolina. Most of the relatives of the *desaparecidos* have stopped writing. But a few still thank him from time to time. Like broken pieces of glass, recollections of a tragic past can cut if you are not careful when picking up the shards. But it is only through remembering that one can be free of the torment.

Through the years, each of us assimilated the experiences we had in Argentina. Each has returned to our native country, sometimes together and at other times alone. After graduating from the College of Charleston and the University of South Carolina with a master's degree in communications, I moved back to Buenos Aires and worked as a reporter for the Herald. I have since written three books about Argentina (this is the fourth), married and worked at the Kuwaiti Embassy in Buenos Aires. When our daughter Julia turned 2, my wife and I decided to return to Charleston to be closer to my family. About a year after our move, our son Agustin was born. We named him after my grandfather.

There is no getting away completely. When we are in Charleston, we miss Buenos Aires; when we are in Buenos Aires, we miss Charleston. Our minds are like ships sailing back and forth between the two, each time replenishing our souls with precious cargo.

I carry with me today so many good memories – of my late grandfather, Papito, and of so very many childhood friends and experiences. Memories of the good times at Highland Park represent all that is good and pure about Argentina. No terrorist – right wing or left wing – can steal these things away. Charleston provides a solid foundation on which to anchor ourselves as a family, and although we are grown and have new friends and families, we are never really apart. We know who we are. We are happy to be alive. We survived.

The terror of the past is a distant memory now.

Or so it seems.

EPILOGUE
DECEMBER 2007

Pierre Manigault, the only son of the late Peter Manigault, opened the glass doors of the Post and Courier building at 134 Columbus Street in Charleston, S.C., walked briskly to the elevator and took it to his office on the third floor. It was Friday, Dec. 14, 2007, less than two weeks before Christmas, but the season was far from festive. He was worried.

As chairman of board of the Evening Post Publishing Co., he had to resolve a number of problems before year's end. He was most concerned about the future of the Buenos Aires Herald. The newspaper, long considered a bad financial investment by the corporate managers, had been losing money and circulation for more than 10 years. The family-owned publishing company had expanded significantly since the early 1980s to include 12 newspapers, 15 television stations, a London-based news syndicate and thousands of acres of South Carolina timberland. His father, whose faith in the mission of the Buenos Aires Herald was unfailing, died in 2004, and most members of the company's board of directors were ready to sell the newspaper.

The matter was all but decided in October when unionized employees of the Herald threatened to strike over wages. It was the second time they had done so in 2007. Such labor disputes were unprecedented in the newspaper's previous 132 years of existence. Despite a significant boom in the Argentine economy for almost 10 years, the Herald's losses were significant, and it would take millions in capital investment to continue operations.

A buyer had been found, and the board was ready to settle the matter. Pierre Manigault was in a difficult situation, as his father had been when he faced similar challenges regarding the Herald's future. But under the chairmanship of Peter Manigault, the Evening Post Publishing Co. held the property for 40 years.

Pierre Manigault wrote the following to the board:

Under our ownership, the Buenos Aires Herald has become internationally recognized as one of the world's most highly respected defenders of democracy, human rights and journalistic freedom. I believe that as responsible stewards of the legacy we cannot in good conscience sell the 132-year-old Herald at this time ... It is our role 40 years later to more carefully consider how this important chapter in the Evening Post's history might end.

The board met as scheduled, and the vote was taken. Only two members of the 13-person board opposed the sale – Peter Manigault's son and Peter Manigault's widow.

AUTHOR'S NOTE

As dusk turns to darkness in Charleston, S.C., I'm reminded of chasing *bichitos de luz* across the yard in my far-off native land and seeing my grandfather in his usual linen pants and white cotton shirt standing tall on the front porch and pointing out the stars of the Southern Cross. Appreciated – like fireflies and guiding lights – are all who helped in this effort.

It would have been impossible to write this memoir without my sisters and brothers, my parents and grandfather. I dedicate this book to them. I am also indebted to my editor, John M. Burbage, who first sat with me in his home overlooking the celebrated Charleston peninsula to consider the importance of this endeavor. He read aloud the opening pages of my first draft, then stared out over the historic city before gently suggesting that some changes be made. I am grateful for his insight, his encouragement and his editing. Editor Susan Kammeraad-Campbell also shared her knowledge and provided valuable insights in the making of this book.

I am forever indebted to Pierre Manigault, chairman of the board of the Evening Post Publishing Co. in Charleston, for his decision to publish this book, and to his father, Peter Manigault, for standing firmly behind my father, Robert J. Cox, throughout the darkest days of Argentina's military dictatorship. The steadfast support for my father by Peter Manigault and his brother-in-law Frank B. Gilbreth allowed the Buenos Aires Herald and its staff to help save thousands of lives.

I thank my friend and colleague Damian Nabot of Argentina for his sound advice on how best to recall and relate my childhood memories; and our dear friend Harry Ingham of Buenos Aires, who gave me the letters he exchanged with my father from 1979-1983. I also thank the Mothers of Plaza de Mayo, the Grandmothers of Plaza de Mayo and the Children of the Disappeared for their courage and inspiration. I am most grateful to God for the love and support of my wife Maria and the precious gift of our two children.

For the writing of this book, the author and editors also consulted *En Honor a la Verdad*, by David Cox; declassified U.S. State Department documents on Argentina's "Dirty War"; the private papers and published commentary of Robert J. Cox; the diary of Maud Cox and her book *Salvados del Infierno; God's Assassins: State Terrorism in Argentina in the 1970s*, by Patricia and William Marchak; and Charles R. Rowe's *Pages of History: 200 Years of the Post and Courier.*

Robert and David Cox, father and son.

INDEX

A

Meet the Press 119, 165, 174

Africa, 45, 66

Agulla, Horacio, 151, 155

Aiken, 40

Aja Espil, Jorge, 185

Alberte, Bernardo, 69

Alfonsin, Raul, 117, 178, 215

Alvear Avenue, 16

American High School, 34

Amnesty International, 97, 101, 156, 195, 197, 213-214

Amoroso, Perla, 180

Amuchastegui, Rosa, 79

Andes, 27, 38

Anne Frank is Argentine (Pondal), 137

anti-Semitism, 35, 164

Apostolic Nuncio, 13

Aramburu, Pedro Eugenio, 30

Arc de Triomphe, 206

Argentina, 9-14, 16-21, 24-36, 38-39, 42-48, 50-51, 53-59, 61-64, 66-67, 70-71, 73-74, 76-78, 81-82, 87-91, 93, 96-97, 101-103, 107-112, 115, 117, 120, 127, 129-130, 132, 134-141, 144-153, 156-159, 162, 164-165, 168, 173-179, 184-187, 189, 192, 194-202, 204-205, 207, 209, 211, 213-217, 220-221

Argentine Railways, 33

Argentine Supreme Court, 12, 149

Argentinisches Tageblatt, 64

Arocena, Helena, 106, 119, 165 174-176, 197, 215

Arocena, Marcos, 106-107, 175, 215

Arosemena, Otto, 39

Arozarena, Jon Pirmin, 101

asados, 11

Ashley River, 213-214

Astiz, Alfredo, 109, 127
    See also Niño, Gustavo

Attwood, Lily, 26, 28

Aunt Julia and the Scriptwriter (Vargas Llosa), 173

Aunt Norma, 49, 60-61, 99, 205

Avalos, Eduardo, 28

Avebury, Lord, 97

Aznavour, Charles, 206

B

Barrio Norte, 81

Baths of Carcalla, 50

Beatles, The, 60

Beaufort, 40

Beiro, Diego, 183

Belgrano, 88

Berggrun, Joseph, 33

Bertoni, Daniel, 145

Besme, 69

Blue Ridge Mountains, 132

B'nai Brith, 165

Book of Imaginary Beings (Borges), 64

Borges, Jorge Luis, 57, 64, 77, 160

Boston Globe, 43

Boyle, Andrew Thomas Swift, 33

Boyle, Richard, 33

Boyle, Robert, 33

Brahmin, 57

Bravo, Alfredo, 109, 136

Brazil, 32, 36, 195

British Broadcasting Corporation (BBC), 86, 151, 205

Buenos Aires, 9-11, 13-20, 23-28, 30-34, 36, 38, 40-42, 44-46, 50-51, 53-55, 57-58, 61, 65, 67, 69-72, 74-76, 79, 81-83, 85-89, 91, 93, 95-96, 98-99, 101-102, 108-110, 115, 118, 120-121, 123, 126, 128-129, 135-138, 140-141, 146-147, 150-153, 156-157, 160-162, 165, 174, 176-177, 180-181, 183-184, 186, 189, 191-192, 194-197, 199, 205-207, 210-212, 214-220

Buenos Aires Herald, 9, 13, 15, 18-20, 23, 26, 34, 36, 40-42, 44, 58, 65, 70-71, 85, 87-89, 91, 95-96, 118, 121, 126, 135, 137, 140, 150, 152-153, 181, 189, 191, 199, 212, 218-220

C

Cabaret, 129

Caesar, Julius, 78

Café Society, 23

Campora, Hector, 51, 138

Canary Islands, 25

Capote, Truman, 130

Carless, Hugh, 120, 184

Carnival, 17, 160

Carpintero, Carlos, 100

Carreras, Horacio Mendez, 110

Carter, Jimmy, 100, 177

Casa Rosada, 70, 80
    See also Government House

Castaño Blanco, Maria Consuelo, 178

Castro, Fidel, 25, 46-47, 102

Castro, Raul, 177

Catalano, Armando, 56
    See also Williams, Guy; Zorro

Cathcart, William, 27

Center for Legal and Social Studies, 87

Chacarita Cemetery, 95

Chambon-sur-Lignon, 43

Champs Elysées, 206

Charleston, 13, 18, 20, 36, 38-42, 44, 65, 91, 94, 99, 102, 116, 121, 129, 132-135, 141, 152, 161, 177, 188, 192, 194, 211-215, 217-218, 220

Charleston Evening Post, 39

Cheaper By the Dozen (Gilbreth), 41

Chevalier, Maurice, 206

Chile, 27, 38, 216

China, 27, 43, 58, 74

Chitty Chitty Bang Bang, 154

Chopin, Frederic, 60

Christian Science Monitor, 98, 174, 176

Church of the Holy Cross, 110, 128

civil rights, 52, 101, 168

Civilian Defense Force, 22

Clacton-on-Sea, 23

Clockwork Orange, A, 148

Coliseum, 50

College of Charleston, 94, 217

Colombia, 36, 38

Communism, 45, 102, 134

Communist, 9, 29, 58, 98, 102, 134, 141, 148

Community of Peace People, 138

Concejo Deliberante, 157

Conference of American Armies, 71

Confirmado, 151

Connaught Rangers 88th Regiment, 33

Conti, Haroldo, 73

Conti, Martha, 73

Corbetta, Arturo, 90

Cordoba, 45-46, 108, 115, 182, 215

Cordobazo, 45

Cornell University, 136

Coronel, Alberto Ruben, 158

Corrigan, Mairead, 138

Costa Brava, 35

Cox, David, 15, 44, 46, 49, 56, 60, 94, 104, 106, 109, 128, 139, 141-142, 144, 146, 150, 154, 159, 188, 204, 206, 215, 221-222

Cox, Edward John, 22, 24

Cox, Maud Daverio 31-35, 42-43, 49, 51, 54, 57-59, 64, 71-72, 82, 84, 89-90, 93, 95, 98-99, 103-106, 108-109, 114, 116, 124, 126-127, 129, 132-134, 138, 142-143, 147-149, 152-153, 161, 164-165, 176-178, 180-183, 185-190, 198-199, 206-213, 216, 221
    See also Daverio, Matilda "Maud"

Cox, Peter, 60-61, 65-66, 91, 94, 99, 115, 133, 139-140, 142, 146, 159, 181-182, 189-191, 198, 200, 210, 213, 218-220

Cox, Robert Andrew. 95, 133, 142, 207

Cox, Robert J. "Bob," 21-22, 24, 31, 33-35, 42, 50-51, 53, 58, 62, 64, 66, 76-77, 79-80, 82-83, 86, 88-91, 93, 95, 98-99, 102-103, 105-106, 108-109, 111, 126-127, 129-130, 133-135, 145, 152-153, 161, 164-165, 171, 177, 180-181, 183-184, 186-190, 192, 199, 206, 209

Cox, Ruth "Ruthie," 50, 61, 94-95, 99, 133, 135, 159, 182-183, 190, 212

Cox, Victoria, 32, 60, 82, 87, 94, 99, 108, 115, 133, 176, 182-183, 190

Crespi, Eduardo, 163

Cryuff, Johan, 144

Cuba, 25, 38, 45-47, 51, 102

Cutts, Ernest, 135

D

d'Estaing, Valery Giscard, 128

Dachau, 22

Dali, Salvador, 206

Daniel, Clifton, 130

Daniel, Margaret Truman, 58, 130

Daverio, Agustin, 32, 190

Daverio, Matilda "Maud," 34
    See also Cox, Maud Daverio

Daverio, Ruth, 17, 33-34

de Coligny, Gaspard, 69

de la Vega, Diego, 55

de Roman, Carmen Beatriz, 77, 79-80, 84

de Saint-Exupery, Antoine, 148

de Weinstein, Beatriz Rosalia Iparraguirre, 136

death flight, 10-11

Debussy, Claude, 177

Delgado, Julian, 140

Derbyshire, 23, 147

Derian, Patricia, 101, 136, 156, 189

desaparecido, 15-17, 19-20, 67, 103, 110, 128, 136, 138, 162

desarrollo, 38

Di Benedetto, Antonio, 109

Diaz de Solis, Juan, 24

dirty war, 9, 13, 15, 57, 63, 87-88, 91, 96-97, 162, 169, 177, 194, 221

Domon, Sister Alicia, 110

Dordogne, 61

Down and Out in Paris and London, 21

Dreyfus Affair, 108

Dreyfus, Alfred, 108

Drinan, Father Robert, 97

Drinan, Robert F., 197

Duarte, Eva "Evita," 29 59, 115, 206
    See also Peron, Eva "Evita"

Duke University, 34

Duquet, Sister Leonie, 110

E

Ealing Park, 22

East Anglian Daily Times, 23

East Essex Gazette, 23

Edict of Nantes, 41

Eichman, Albert, 186

Eiffel Tower, 206

Einsatzgruppen, 12

Einstein, Albert, 21

el Brujo. 59
    See also Lopez Rega, Jose

El Cronista Comercial, 103

El Olimpo, 161

El Salvador, 80

Elbert, Horacio, 128

Empty Balcony (Saporiti), 28

En Honor de la Verdad (Cox, David), 14

Epelbaum, Renee, 106, 165, 215

Era of the Walrus, 36, 45

Erb, John Delbert, 92

Erb, Patricia Ann, 92

ERP, 47, 63
See also Worker's
Revolutionary Party
ESMA (Escuela Mecanica de la Armada),
10-11, 86, 105, 109, 128, 139, 149, 162,
194, 214
See also Navy Mechanics School
Eva Peron Foundation, 29
Evening Post Publishing Company, 13, 39,
121, 135
Ezeiza International Airport, 55, 123

F

Fagian, Miguel Angel, 213
Falkland Islands War, 148
Fariña family, 160
Fascism, 22, 28, 34, 44
Federal Police Headquarters, 65, 85, 98-99
Fernandez Beiro, Susana, 183
Fernandez Pondal, Rodolfo, 136-137
Festelemps, 61
Field, Michael, 167
Fisher-Price, 53
Fondevilla, Julio, 128
Fontana di Trevi, 49
Fontevecchia, Jorge, 161
forced disappearances, 10, 215
Ford Motor Company, 48
Franco, Francisco, 11, 157
Freeman, Anthony G., 191
French Protestants, 41
Friedman, Townsend B., 191
Frinton-on-Sea, 23-24, 134
Frondizi, Arturo, 25, 31, 34
Fulbright Commission, 81
Fulford, D. W., 196

G

Gabriel, 59, 73
Gainza, Maximo, 191
Gainza, Santiago, 191
Garcia Marquez, Gabriel, 73
Garcia, Alejo, 24

Garzon, Baltasar, 11
Gelman, Juan, 138
Gelman, Marcelo, 138
Germany, 11, 21-22, 28, 73, 90, 129,
147, 186
Gilbreth, Frank B., Jr., 41, 65, 121,
135, 220
Giton, Judith, 41
Goering, Hermann, 143
Golden Gate Bridge, 21
Goncrauski, Irene Birbaum, 141
Goñi, Uki, 126
Goodsell, James Nelson, 174, 176
Goshko, John M., 44
Government House, 34, 70, 77, 79, 83-84,
100, 106, 143, 155, 163, 171
See also Casa Rosada
Graham, Katharine, 42
Graham-Yooll, Andrew, 46, 50, 52, 64-65,
73, 129, 205, 209
Graham-Yooll, Micaela, 92, 209
Graiver, David, 98
Grease, 147
Great Depression, 21
Greene, Graham, 5, 31
grupos de tarea, 12
Guatemala, 52
Guevara Lynch, Ernesto, 46
Guevara, Celia, 46
Guevara, Che, 25, 45-47
Guevara, Juan Martin, 46
Guido, Jose, 25
Guise, Duke of , 69
Gutierrez Ruiz, Hector, 81
Guzzetti, Cesar, 80

H

habeas corpus, 73, 93, 126, 174
Hagelin, Dagmar, 108-109, 138
Harguindeguy, Albano Eduardo, 79
Harris, F. Allen "Tex," 100
Harvard University, 70, 210
Havana, 25
Hearst, Patty, 52

Hidalgo Sola, Hector, 136-137

Highland Park, 17, 43, 57, 94, 105, 110-111, 116, 130, 142-143, 147, 154, 159-161, 174, 187, 190-191, 209, 217

Hill, Robert, 80

Hiroshima, 168

Historic Charleston Foundation, 134

Hitler, Adolf, 21

HMS Mounts Bay, 23

Holland, 140, 144-146

Hollings, Ernest F., 213

Holmberg, Elena, 162, 197

Honorary Consul, The (Greene), 31

House for Mr. Biswas, A (Naipaul), 58

Huguenots, 41-43

Hull Daily Mail, 23

human rights, 51, 80-81, 85-87, 92-93, 97, 100-103, 109, 111, 135-136, 138, 149-150, 152-153, 156, 158, 163, 165, 168, 173, 176-179, 187, 190-191, 193, 196, 213, 219

Human Rights Commission of the Organization of American States, 177

Hunt, Billy Lee, 101

Huntington, Samuel P., 164

I

Illia, Arturo Umberto, 34

Illman, John, 140

imperialist, 9

impunity laws, 12

In Cold Blood (Capote), 51, 130

India, 22, 33, 173

Infamous Decade, 21

Ingham, Harry, 19-20, 53-54, 71, 108, 120, 147, 179-180, 199, 202, 215, 220

Ingrey, Norman, 27, 140

Inter-American Conference for the Maintenance of Peace, 34

Inter-American Press Association, 38, 40, 123, 216

International Herald Tribune, 187, 191

Ipswich, 23

Ireland, 32, 66, 126, 138, 168, 176

Irish Republican Army, 206

Italy, 28, 34, 47, 49

J

James, Barry, 35

Jara, Enrique, 98

Jehovah's Witnesses, 156-157

joggling board, 134

John F. Kennedy International Airport, 130

Jones, Kathleen Milton "Miss Catalina," 32-33

Juan Carlos (king of Spain), 35, 157

junta, 10, 14, 40, 50, 70-73, 76-77, 81, 90, 92-93, 96-97, 101, 110, 129, 136, 138, 143-144, 146-147, 156-158, 161-162, 175, 177, 185, 207, 215

Justo, Agustin Pedro, 21

K

Kahn, Heriberto, 200

Kelly, Father Alfredo, 89

Kempes, Mario, 144

Kennedy, Edward, 138

Kennedy, Jacqueline, 42

Kennedy, John F., 42, 130

King Kong, 206

King, Martin Luther, Jr., 168

Kirkpatrick, Jeanne, 164

Klein, Walter, 53, 70, 86, 99, 147, 180-181, 187

Korean Conflict, 23

L

La Cumparsita, 147

La Opinion(Buenos Aires), 51, 63, 67, 97-98, 100

La Pantera rosa, 70
    See also Pink Panther

La Plata estuary, 24

La Rochelle, 42

La Semana, 161

La Voulte, 42

Laghi, Papal Nuncio Pio, 89

Lancaster Hotel, 31

Lanusse, Alejandro Augustin, 92, 137, 185

Larrabure, Argentino del Valle, 63

Las Abuelas de Plaza de Mayo, 150

Lascaux, caves of , 61

Last Tango in Paris, 148

Laxalt, Paul, 213

Leaning Tower of Pisa, 50

Lebanon, 66

Lent, 17

Little Prince, The, 148

Llamas, Antonio, 163, 169

Lombardo, Betty, 98, 152

London, 16, 18, 21-23, 26, 32, 36, 106, 130, 133, 167, 180, 204-207, 215

London Daily Telegraph, 167

London Zoo, 206

Looking for Mr. Goodbar, 148

Lopez Rega, Jose, 59
    See also el Brujo

Los Angeles Times, 215

Louis XIV (king of France), 41

Louvre, 206

M

Machu Picchu, 32

Mad Mothers of Plaza de Mayo, 105, 107
    See also Mothers of Plaza de Mayo

Madame Tussauds, 206

Maggiore Cemetery, 47

Magnolia Plantation, 214

Manigault, Arthur Middleton, 42

Manigault, Edward, 42

Manigault, Peter, 13, 36, 38, 40, 43-44, 65-66, 91, 99, 121, 132, 141, 152, 188, 211, 218-220

Manigault, Pierre, 42, 218, 220

Manigault, Robert, 42

Mao Tse-tung, 58

Maoists, 9

Mar Dulce, 24

Marconi Men, 22

Marcus, 60-61, 113

Marey, Fred, 64

Maria Moors Cabot Award, 119, 151-153

Marks and Spencer, 206

Martian, 59

Martin Garcia, 24, 29

Martinez de Hoz, Jose, 161

Marxist, 45-47, 96, 129

Mary Poppins, 53

Massera, Emilio, 12, 101, 198

McGee, Hall T., 135

McGee, Peggy, 135

Mendoza, 27, 109

Menendez, Luciano Benjamin, 182, 199

Menotti, Cesar Luis, 147

Mercado, 140

Messina, Elida, 81

Mexico, 80, 102

Meyer, Rabbi Marshall, 152, 162, 177, 189

Miami Herald, 87-88, 98, 152, 211, 215

Michellini, Zelmar, 81

Middleton High School, 146

Mignone, Emilio, 86-87, 152

Mignone, Monica, 86-87

Milan, 32, 47

Ministry of the Economy, 70

Money, Jorge, 63

Monroe, Bill, 174

Montalbano, Bill, 53, 71, 87-88, 91, 99, 152, 215

Montevideo, 25, 71, 82-84, 213

Montoneros, 47, 58, 66, 75, 87, 89, 97-98, 128, 137, 143, 147, 150, 163, 190-192, 210

More Than Human
(Castaño Blanco), 178

Moreno Ocampo, Luis, 215

Mothers of Plaza de Maya, 153-154, 165, 167, 197, 220
    See also Mad Mothers of
    Plaza de Maya

Mr. Banks, 53

Mugica, Carlos, 58

Mullen, Kevin, 75-76, 207

Musich, Arnaldo, 91

Mussolini, Benito, 28

My Fair Lady, 206

N

Naftal, Alejandra, 144
Naipaul, V. S., 57
Nanninga, Dick, 145
National Congress, 35
Navy Mechanics School, 10
   See Also ESMA
Nazar, Juan Ramon, 155
Nazinacionalismo, 12, 100
Nazis, 9, 13, 22, 127
NBC, 165, 174
Neilson, James, 18, 52, 91, 192, 199
Neiman Fellowship, 210-211
New York City, 129-131, 151-152, 154, 189, 210
New York Review of Books, 58
News and Courier (Charleston), 39, 41-42, 44, 102, 116, 133, 152, 212-213
Newsom, David D., 138
Newsweek, 22, 43, 72, 74, 98, 130, 163
Newton, Isaac, 51
Nietzsche, Freidrich, 73
Niño, Gustavo, 127-128
   See also Astiz, Alfredo
Nirgad, Ram, 103, 164
Nixon, Richard M., 44
Nobel Peace Prize, 137
Nobel Prize for Literature, 57
Norte, Darsena, 26
Northern Ireland, 138
Noticias Argentinas, 150
Novitski, Joe, 167
Nunca Mas, 12
Nunciature, 14, 207

O

Oakes, John B., 174
O'Leary, Jeremiah, 174
Oliver!, 206
Onassis, Aristotle, 42
One Generation After (Wiesel), 177

Onganio, Juan Carlos, 35
Order of the British Empire, 120, 140-141
Orfila, Alejandro, 141
Orwell, George, 21
Oxford University, 57

P

Palacios, David Ruiz, 49, 144, 172
Palermo Barrio gang, 160
Palermo Park, 105, 141
Pampas region, 24
Panama, 40, 62
Panama Canal, 40
Passarella, Daniel, 145
Patagonian Rebellion, 45
Penjerik, Norma, 35
Pensione Sitea, 49
People's Revolutionary Army, 47, 71
   See also PRT
Perez Esquivel, Adolfo, 137-138
Perigord, 62
Permanent Assembly of Human Rights, The, 196
Peron, Eva "Evita" 28-30, 33, 47, 58-59, 66, 114, 115, 206
   See also Duarte, Eva "Evita"
Peron, Isabel, 62, 66-68, 85
Peron, Juan Domingo, 12, 24, 25, 27-31, 36, 38, 45, 47, 50-51, 53-56, 58-59, 61-62, 66-68, 85, 114, 127
Peronistas, 25
Perrota, Rafael, 103
Peru, 32, 38-40, 216
Philby, Kim, 184
Philosophiae Naturalis Principia Mathematica, 51
Piaf, Edith, 206
Pink Panther, 70
   See also la Pantera rosa
Pinochet, Augusto, 216
Plaza de Mayo, 30, 77, 84-85, 105, 107, 110-112, 117, 126-127, 148, 150-154, 156, 164-165, 167, 195, 197, 215, 220
Pompidou Museum, 206

Pondal, Marisa Presti, 137
porteños, 27
Portugal, 25, 28, 66
Potts, Caratacus, 154
Potts, Jemima, 154
Potts, Jeremy, 154
Prensa, La (Buenos Aires), 38, 78, 87, 191, 216
Pringle, James, 72
PRT, 47, 71
    See also People's Revolutionary Army

R

Radical Party, 24
Rajneri, Nelida, 216
Ratcliffe, Father Charles, 183-184
Reagan, Ronald, 164
Real Odessa, The – Smuggling The Nazis to Peron's Argentina (Goñi), 127
Recoleta Cemetery, 58
Regimento Uno, 85
Report of the National Commission on the Disappearance of Persons, 156
Reuters news agency, 152
Richards, Father Jose, 88
Richelieu, Cardinal, 42
Richmond Café, 31
Ridley, Nicholas, 205
Rio de Janeiro, 25
Rio de la Plate, 24
River Plate Stadium, 140, 145
Robin Hood, 48, 111
Rodriguez Carmona, Pastor, 210
Roman Catholic Church, 41, 76
Roosevelt, Franklin D., 21, 34
Rosenblum, Mort, 187
Rowland, Toby, 52
Rowsley, 147
Royal Institute of International Affairs (Chatham House), 205
Royal Navy, 23
Rubinstein, Arthur, 33

S

Sabat, Menchi, 64, 215
Sabato, Ernesto, 77
Saint of the Poor, 30
Sajon, Edgardo, 136-137
San Francisco, 21
San Isidro Hospital, 180
San Martin (town), 33
San Martin, Jose, 27
San Patricio's, 32
    See also St. Patrick's
Sandhurst Military College, 33
Santee River, 42
Santos, 25
Saporiti, Piero, 28
Sardinia, 28
Sasebo, 23
Saturday Night Fever, 147
Schroeder, Juan Pablo, 82, 84
Schubert, Franz, 104
Schutzstaffeln, 54
Scilingo, Adolfo, 10, 12
Scotland, 27, 64
Seewee, 135
Serrat, Oscar, 110
Sevilla, Elena, 136
Shakespeare, John, 98, 102
Shrove Tuesday, 17
Smoak, Joseph, 135
soccer, 94, 105, 110, 129, 138-139, 146
socialism, 58
Sofia, Queen (of Spain), 157-158
solicitada, 87, 111
Sosa, Mercedes, 162
Sound of Music, The, 147
Southern Cross, 88, 220
Spain, 10, 12, 25, 28, 31, 78, 80, 157-158
Spanish Supreme Court, 11
Spotty, 15, 60
Squibb, 74
St. Andrew's Scots School, 53
St. Bartholomew's Day massacre, 41
St. Patrick's Catholic Church, 88

St. Patrick's Massacre, 88-89

St. Patrick's, 88
See also San Patricio's

State Intelligence Service (SIDE), 50, 52, 63, 153-154, 191, 208

Suarez Mason, Guillermo, 162

Sullivan's Island, 132

Superintendencia de Seguridad (SS), 10, 12, 143

Sursum Corda Choir, 180

swastika, 12, 54, 100

T

Teatro Colon, 147

terrorism, 9, 12-13, 16, 20, 36, 41, 47, 63-64, 70, 72, 74, 90-91, 96, 109-112, 137, 140, 148, 155-156, 164-166, 168, 175-176, 182, 185, 201-202, 210, 213, 221

The Associated Press, 52, 110, 135, 141

Third World Priest Movement, 47

Thomson, Basil, 23, 26, 65

Tigre Delta, 139

Tilbury, 21, 25, 54, 116, 205

Time, 28, 107

Timerman, Jacobo, 19, 51, 67, 97-98, 100, 104, 108, 149, 162-164, 177-179, 182, 189, 193, 206, 210

Timerman, Jose, 189

Tonbridge, 33

Tragic Week, 45

Trinidad, 57

Triple A, 59

Truman, Harry S., 34, 130

Tucuman Province, 71

U

U.S. National Academy of Sciences Human Rights Committee, 135

Uncle Donald, 49, 61, 205

United Press International, 152

University of Cambridge, 32

University of South Carolina, 217

Uruguay, 36, 38, 82, 96, 195, 213

V

Vance, Cyrus, 98, 110, 136

Vargas Llosa, Mario, 173, 210

Vatican, 13, 75-76, 207

Venezuela, 36, 137, 155

Versailles, 206

Victoria house, 17

Videla, Jorge Rafael, 12, 67, 70-71, 77-79, 81, 89, 93, 98, 100, 111, 128-129, 136-138, 149, 157, 162-163, 182, 185-186, 190, 192-194, 199, 209, 212, 215

Vietnam, 72, 168

Villaflor, Azucena, 127

Villavicencio, 27

Viola, Roberto Eduardo, 149, 182

von Wernich, Christian, 86

W

Wakefield, Ruth, 22

Wales, 129-130

Walsh, Maria Elena, 132

Walsh, Rodolfo, 96-97

Waring, Thomas R., Jr., 102, 135

Warsaw Ghetto, 141

Washington Post, 35-36, 43-44, 72, 76, 98, 141, 151, 167

Washington Star, 174

water-boarding, 101

Watergate. 168

Weimer Republic, 129

Wiesel, Elie, 177

Wilcox, Arthur M. , 135

Willams, Betty, 138

Williams, Guy, 55-57, 116, 198
See also Zorro; Catalano, Armando

Wolter, Karl-Anders, 108

Woodrow Wilson Center for International Studies, 207, 210

Worker's Revolutionary Party, 47
See also ERP

World Cancer Congress , 136

World Cup, 7, 129, 138-140, 142, 144-146

World Press News, 23

World War I, 22

World War II, 22, 26-27, 34, 43, 127, 147, 173, 186

Y

Yrigoyen, Hipolito Solari, 59, 206

Z

Zarate, 74-76
Zorro, 55-57, 116, 198
    See also catalano, Armando;
    Williams, Guy